CAMBRIDGE
UNIVERSITY PRESS

Cambridge Lower Secondary
Computing

LEARNER'S BOOK 9

Evans Chikasa, Victoria Ellis & Sarah Lawrey

Shaftesbury Road, Cambridge CB2 8EA, United Kingdom

One Liberty Plaza, 20th Floor, New York, NY 10006, USA

477 Williamstown Road, Port Melbourne, VIC 3207, Australia

314–321, 3rd Floor, Plot 3, Splendor Forum, Jasola District Centre, New Delhi – 110025, India

103 Penang Road, #05–06/07, Visioncrest Commercial, Singapore 238467

Cambridge University Press & Assessment is a department of the University of Cambridge.

We share the University's mission to contribute to society through the pursuit of education, learning and research at the highest international levels of excellence.

www.cambridge.org
Information on this title: www.cambridge.org/9781009320634

20 19 18 17 16 15 14 13 12 11 10 9 8 7 6 5

Printed in Poland by Opolgraf

A catalogue record for this publication is available from the British Library

ISBN 978-1-009-32063-4 Paperback with Digital Access (1 Year)
ISBN 978-1-009-32062-7 Digital Learner's Book (1 Year)
ISBN 978-1-009-32060-3 eBook

Additional resources for this publication at www.cambridge.org/go

Endorsement statement

2023 CAMBRIDGE DEDICATED TEACHER AWARDS

Teachers play an important part in shaping futures.
Our Dedicated Teacher Awards recognise the hard work that teachers put in every day.

Thank you to everyone who nominated this year; we have been inspired and moved by all of your stories. Well done to all of our nominees for your dedication to learning and for inspiring the next generation of thinkers, leaders and innovators.

CONGRATULATIONS TO OUR INCREDIBLE WINNERS!

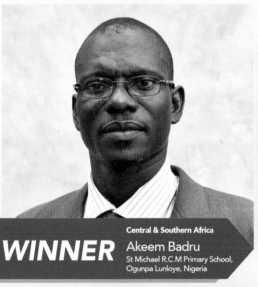

WINNER Central & Southern Africa
Akeem Badru
St Michael R.C.M Primary School,
Ogunpa Lunloye, Nigeria

Regional Winner: East & South Asia
Gaurav Sharma
FirstSteps School, India

Regional Winner: North & South America
Nathalie Roy
Glasgow Middle School, United States

Regional Winner: Australia, New Zealand & South-East Asia
Goh Kok Ming
SJKC Hua Lian 1, Malaysia

Regional Winner: Middle East & North Africa
Uzma Siraj
Future World School, Pakistan

Regional Winner: Europe
Selçuk Yusuf Arslan
Atatürk MTAL, Turkey

For more information about our dedicated teachers and their stories, go to **dedicatedteacher.cambridge.org**

CAMBRIDGE
UNIVERSITY PRESS

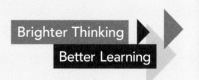

Brighter Thinking
Better Learning

> Introduction

Welcome to Stage 9 of Cambridge Lower Secondary Computing!

Technology plays an instrumental role in our lives and our futures. Learning about how technology works, and how to use it effectively, equips you for an increasingly tech-dependent world.

In this book, you will:

- build your computational skills, including understanding, altering and creating pseudocode

- expand your text-based programming abilities, from developing programs and test plans to programming physical devices to solve problems

- evaluate models and simulations of real-life systems

- learn all about network topologies

- find improvements in the design of products

and so much more!

Throughout this book, you will have lots of opportunities to work with a partner or in a group. Sharing your ideas with other people helps you learn more about how people use computers and technology. You can learn new skills and facts from working with others – just like a computer scientist!

Some of the activities will be done away from a computer. These activities will develop your computing knowledge and understanding, and activities on the computer will develop your computing skills – from presentation skills to Python skills. You will have lots of opportunities to develop your programming skills using physical objects like boxes and paper, which will help you to understand ideas and concepts. There is also a project for you to complete at the end of each unit. These give you the chance to be creative and will help you develop your understanding.

We hope that you are inspired to continue your computing education into IGCSE and beyond. Maybe you will help design the next generation of computers!

Evans Chikasa, Victoria Ellis and Sarah Lawrey

> Contents

Note for teachers: Throughout the resource there is a symbol to indicate where additional digital only content is required. This content can be accessed through the Digital Learner's Book on Cambridge GO. It can be launched either from the Media tab or directly from the page.

The symbol that denotes additional digital content is:

Source files can also be downloaded from the Source files tab on Cambridge GO. In addition, this tab contains a teacher guidance document which supports the delivery of digital activities and programming tasks in this Learner's Book.

> How to use this book

This book contains lots of different features that will help your learning. These are explained below.

This list sets out what you will learn in each topic. You can use these points to identify the important topics for the lesson. ——→

In this topic you will:

- edit algorithms written in pseudocode to change what they do
- edit algorithms written in pseudocode to make them do an additional task
- find errors in algorithms written in pseudocode
- correct errors in algorithms written in pseudocode.

This contains questions or activities to help find out what you know already about this topic. ——→

Getting started

What do you already know?

- Algorithms are a series of steps that solve a problem. They can be represented as flowcharts, pseudocode and in program code.
- You have learned that iteration means to repeat something. Iterative development means repeated development.
- Selection statements use IF, ELSEIF, ELSE to test a condition.

Important words are highlighted in the text when they first appear in the book. You will find an explanation of the meaning of these words in the text. You will also find definitions of all these words in the Glossary at the back of this book. ——→

Key words

efficiency

memory

requirements

robust

You will have the opportunity to practise and develop the new skills and knowledge that you learn in each topic. Activities will involve answering questions or completing tasks by using a computer. Some activities don't require a computer. These are called unplugged activities, and they help you understand important ideas about computing. ——→

Unplugged activity 1.2

You will need: a piece of paper

Work in pairs for this activity.

Write down a series of actions for your partner to do. Make sure these are sensible and safe for where you are, for example standing up, clapping hands or turning around in a circle.

Swap your actions with your partner. Perform your partner's series of actions iteratively (do the sequence repeatedly).

Peer-assessment questions help you evaluate the work of your peers.

> **Peer assessment**
> Discuss with your partner how well they were able to explain their answer. Did they state which was more efficient without any reasons, or were they able to justify their choice?

These tasks help you to practise what you have learnt in a topic.

Programming tasks are in Unit 1

> **Programming task 1.3: Predict, Run, Investigate and Modify**
>
> **You will need:** a pen and paper
>
> The following pseudocode algorithm should:
> - ask the user to input their name and two numbers
> - ask the user to input what the two numbers equal when added together
> - ask the user to input what the two numbers equal when multiplied together
> - output whether each answer input was correct
> - output a message saying how many answers the user got correct in a message.
>
> ```
> OUTPUT "Enter your name"
> INPUT name
> OUTPUT "Enter two numbers"
> INPUT number1
> INPUT number2
> OUTPUT "What is ", number1, " + ", number2,"?"
> INPUT answer
> correct = 0
> IF answer == (number1 * number2) THEN
>     OUTPUT "Correct"
> ```

Practical tasks are in Unit 2

> **Practical task 2.3**
>
> **You will need:** a desktop computer, laptop or tablet with spreadsheet software and Source file **2.2_football_club.xlsx** with Practical tasks 2.1 and 2.2 completed
>
> 1 Open Source file **2.2_football_club.xlsx** and examine the contents.
> 2 In cell I7, write a function to determine the age of the youngest club member.
> 3 In cell I8, place a function to display the age of the oldest club member from the given ages.

Self-assessment questions help you think about your work and how you learn.

> **Self-assessment**
> Think about what you have been able to do with ease on this topic. Did you find any aspect of this topic challenging? How did you work around that challenge?

When you see this icon, you are going to do a digital activity using a Source file or website link. This content can be found on Cambridge GO. Your teacher will help you to get started.

These questions help you to practise what you have just learnt.

Important safety tips to remember when using a computer and going online.

These tell you interesting facts connected to the topic.

This contains questions that ask you to look back at what you have covered and encourages you to think about your learning.

This list summarises the important material that you have learnt in the topic.

These questions look back at some of the content you learnt in each unit. If you can answer these, you are ready to move on to the next unit.

At the end of each unit, there is a project that you might carry out by yourself or with other learners. This will involve using some of the knowledge that you developed during the unit. Your project might involve creating or producing something, or you might solve a problem.

Questions 1.2

1 What does iteration mean?

2 One type of loop in programming is a count-controlled loop. What is the other type of loop?

3 What are the key features of a count-controlled loop?

4 What is the most common count-controlled loop used in programming called?

Stay safe!

When downloading a spreadsheet from the internet, take extra care and avoid opening suspicious links within the spreadsheet, if there are any.

Did you know?

In programming, a sub-routine can be taken out of a program and used elsewhere, for example in another program. If a programmer creates a sub-routine for one program, it will save them

Were you able to follow the instructions independently or did you need help? If you needed help, will you need it next time or do you know what to do now?

Summary checklist

☐ I can program a physical device to solve a problem.
☐ I can develop a prototype.
☐ I can describe iterative development.
☐ I can use iterative development.
☐ I can evaluate how I used iterative development to create a prototype.

Check your progress 1

1 Which of the following is the best description of a programming loop?
   a Every line of code is run once, one after the other.
   b Code inside can run multiple times.
   c A message is output to the screen.
   d More than one item of data is stored in one place.

Project 1: Word guess

Arun and his friends need to choose a project for their computing class. Arun played the game Word Guess in class yesterday and wants to teach his younger brother how to play it. He's decided to create the game for his project and wants to partner with you.

Word Guess is a game where a user has to guess the word a computer stores. The number of letters in a word is output as spaces, for example:

_ _ _ _ _

The user then enters one letter. For example 'H'.

The game outputs the spaces, and if 'H' is in the

Computational thinking and programming

> 1.1 Pseudocode

In this topic you will:

- edit algorithms written in pseudocode to change what they do
- edit algorithms written in pseudocode to make them do an additional task
- find errors in algorithms written in pseudocode
- correct errors in algorithms written in pseudocode.

Key words

algorithm

logic error

Getting started

What do you already know?

- Pseudocode is a tool that is used to design algorithms in the same way that a flowchart is used. Pseudocode means fake code, or not real code.

Continued

- There is no set syntax for pseudocode. Syntax is the specific words and symbols used and the order they appear in. This is why pseudocode is different from program code like Python. However, pseudocode does still have the structure of real code.

  Each statement has the variable on the left (data), an assignment symbol (= or ←) and the data being stored on the right (10).

  Each statement has a command word for input (INPUT or input() or InputData) and a variable where it is stored (data).

- A selection statement is used to test a condition. If the condition is true, then some code is run; if the condition is false, different code can run.

  An ELSEIF is used when a second condition is needed. The ELSEIF condition runs when the first condition is false.

  A selection statement can have many ELSEIF conditions, but it can only ever have a maximum of one ELSE.

Now try this!

Read this pseudocode program with a partner:

```
INPUT numberOfPeople
costPerPerson = INPUT("Enter the cost per person")
IF numberOfPeople > 10 THEN
    costPerPerson = costPerPerson * 0.9
ENDIF
TotalCost ← numberOfPeople * costPerPerson
OUTPUT "The total cost is " & TotalCost
```

Think about how this program would be written in Python (but don't create the program yet.) Work with your partner to identify the differences between this pseudocode program and how the code would be written in Python. For example, are the commands different? Are the symbols different?

Work with your partner to create this program in Python. Did you identify all the differences between the two programs or can you find some more?

Editing pseudocode

An **algorithm** is a series of steps that solve a problem. Algorithms can be represented as flowcharts, pseudocode and in program code. To change an algorithm, you first need to work out what the algorithm does. This uses the same process whether you are using flowcharts, program code or pseudocode.

You might have a description of the algorithm, for example what it currently does. However, you still need to read through the algorithm. You cannot miss this step. Then you need to test the algorithm. You will have previously learnt how to use some data to test the algorithm and find out what happens to the data.

Once you know what the algorithm does, you can start planning how to change it.

Did you know?

An algorithm is a set of rules applied to numbers written in decimal form. The word 'algorithm' is derived from the phonetic pronunciation of the last name of Abu Ja'far Mohammed ibn Musa al-Khowarizmi, who was a Persian mathematician. He invented a set of rules for performing the four basic arithmetic operations (addition, multiplication, subtraction and division) on decimal numbers.

Figure 1.1: Abu Ja'far Mohammed ibn Musa al-Khowarizmi

Programming task 1.1: Predict, Run, Investigate and Modify

You will need: a pen and paper

This pseudocode algorithm should ask the user to enter a number between 1 and 10 and should output whether the data entered is correct or not correct.

Continued

Read this pseudocode algorithm:

```
OUTPUT "Enter a number between 1 and 10"
INPUT number
IF number >= 1 AND number <= 10 THEN
    OUTPUT "That is correct"
ELSE
    OUTPUT "That is incorrect"
ENDIF
```

Predict:

1   What should be output if the user enters the number 1?
2   What should be output if the user enters the number 5?
3   What should be output if the user enters the number 10?
4   What should be output if the user enters the number 11?
5   What should be output if the user enters the number 0?

Run: Work with a partner to use each number from the predict stage and check if your predictions were correct.

Investigate: Discuss with your partner how the algorithm meets the requirements by identifying:

*   how the data is input
*   how the input is compared with the numbers allowed
*   how the output is created.

Modify: The algorithm needs to be changed to allow numbers between 1 and 20 instead of 1 and 10.

Work with your partner to:

1   identify which part of the algorithm needs to be changed
2   identify the change that needs to be made
3   rewrite the algorithm with the change
4   select and use a range of test data to check if your algorithm works.

If your algorithm does not work the first time, that is OK! Repeat the process until it does work.

How did you make sure that your changed algorithm was working correctly? Did you test it once, or did you select a range of test data to make sure it works in lots of different cases? Do you think you should test your program with more data?

Programming task 1.2: Predict, Run, Investigate and Modify

You will need: a pen and paper

A board game uses a pack of cards. Each card has a number or a shape in a different colour:

- The colours are red, green, blue and yellow.
- The card has either a number from 1 to 9 on it or a shape to represent a number:
  - a circle = 10
  - a diamond = 11
  - a square = 12.

This pseudocode algorithm should ask the user for the colour (red, green, blue and yellow) and number (1, 2, 3, 4, 5, 6, 7, 8, 9) or shape (circle, diamond or square) of two playing cards. It will output whether the two cards have the same colour. It will output which card has the highest number.

```
OUTPUT "Enter the first colour"
INPUT colour1
OUTPUT "Enter the first number
or shape"
INPUT number1
IF number1 == "Circle" THEN
    number1 = 10
ELSEIF number1 == "Diamond" THEN
    number1 = 11
ELSEIF number1 == "Square" THEN
    number1 = 12
ENDIF
```

Continued

```
    OUTPUT "Enter the second colour"
    INPUT colour2
    OUTPUT "Enter the second number or shape"
    INPUT number2
    IF number2 == "Circle" THEN
        number2 = 10
    ELSEIF number2 == "Diamond" THEN
        number2 = 11
    ELSEIF number2 == "Square" THEN
        number2 = 12
    ENDIF

    IF colour1 == colour2 AND number1 == number2 THEN
        OUTPUT "They are the same"
    ELSEIF number1 > number2 THEN
        OUTPUT "First number is larger"
    ELSEIF number2 > number1 THEN
        OUTPUT "Second number is larger"
    ENDIF
```

Predict:

1   What should be output if the following inputs are entered?
    Red   9   Red   2

2   What should be output if the following inputs are entered?
    Blue   Circle   Blue   Circle

3   What should be output if the following inputs are entered?
    Yellow   Diamond   Green   2

Run: Work with a partner to use each number from the predict stage and check if your predictions were correct.

Investigate: Discuss with your partner how it meets the requirements by identifying:

•   how the data is input
•   how the card shapes (circle, diamond and square) are converted to numbers
•   how the two cards are compared
•   how matching cards are identified
•   how the largest number is identified.

Continued

Modify 1: The algorithm needs to be changed to output the card number that is largest, for example if the first card is 3 and the second is 9, then 9 should be output.

Work with your partner to edit the algorithm and test it with a range of test data.

Modify 2: The algorithm needs to be changed to output
`"The numbers are the same"` if the colour of each card is different but the numbers are exactly the same.

Work with your partner to edit the algorithm and test it with a range of test data.

Correcting pseudocode

If there is an error in an algorithm in pseudocode then it will not produce the correct, or expected, result. This is called a logic error. You should have learnt how to debug errors in a text-based program previously. The process for text-based programs is the same as for pseudocode.

When you are correcting an algorithm, you first need to find out where the error is. Two ways you can do this are:

1   reading each line of code one by one from the start and making sure each line does what it is supposed to do

2   writing the variable names down and the values stored in them next to each name, then checking whether the values are correct as you follow the algorithm.

Unplugged activity 1.1

You will need: paper and scissors

This pseudocode algorithm should take three numbers as input, multiply the two largest numbers and output the result.

Continued

```
INPUT first
INPUT second
INPUT third
IF first < second AND first < third THEN
    result = second * third
ELSEIF second < third THEN
    result = first * third
ELSE
    result = second * third
ENDIF
PRINT "The result is " + result
```

1   Take a piece of paper and cut it into four separate pieces.
2   On each piece of paper write the name of a variable in the pseudocode algorithm.
3   Follow the algorithm with the inputs: 1   5   10

    Each time data is stored in a variable write it on that piece of paper, crossing out anything that was there before.

4   Repeat with the following sets of input:

    a   5   1   10   b   10   5   1
    c   10   1   5   d   5   5   10
    e   10   10   10

Work with a partner and compare your answers. Which inputs gave the correct result and which didn't?

Work with your partner to identify where the error is in the algorithm.

Change the algorithm to correct the error and then retest it with the same inputs to make sure it works.

Programming task 1.3: Predict, Run, Investigate and Modify

You will need: a pen and paper

The following pseudocode algorithm should:

- ask the user to input their name and two numbers
- ask the user to input what the two numbers equal when added together
- ask the user to input what the two numbers equal when multiplied together
- output whether each answer input was correct
- output a message saying how many answers the user got correct.

```
OUTPUT "Enter your name"
INPUT name
OUTPUT "Enter two numbers"
INPUT number1
INPUT number2
OUTPUT "What is ", number1, " + ", number2,"?"
INPUT answer
correct = 0
IF answer == (number1 * number2) THEN
    OUTPUT "Correct"
    correct = + 1
ELSE
    OUTPUT "Incorrect"
ENDIF
OUTPUT "What is ", number1, " * ", number2, "?"
INPUT answer
IF answer == (number1 * number2) THEN
    OUTPUT "Correct"
    correct = + 1
ELSE
    OUTPUT "Incorrect"
ENDIF
OUTPUT name, " you got ", correct, " correct"
```

Continued

Predict: Write down what you predict the output(s) should be for each set of inputs:

Zara	1	2	3	2
Marcus	5	2	15	10
Sofia	2	4	6	4
Arun	1	10	10	11

Run: Dry run the pseudocode algorithm with each set of inputs. Identify which sets of inputs produced correct outputs and which sets produced incorrect outputs.

Investigate: Work on your own to identify the errors in the program before joining with a partner to compare your answers.

There are three logic errors in this program.

Modify: Work with your partner to change the pseudocode algorithm to remove the logic errors.

Test your new program with the same sets of data to check if your solution is correct.

Peer assessment

Give your partner one thing they did that you found useful and one thing they could improve on. For example, they might be really good at explaining their solution, but they might have taken over and you wanted to do more.

Programming task 1.4: Predict, Run, Investigate and Modify

You will need: a pen and paper

The following pseudocode algorithm should calculate and output the cost of a hotel stay for a customer.

There are two types of room:

- an elite room costs $100 a night
- a basic room costs $50 a night.

Some customers are members. If they are a Gold member, they get a 20% discount. If they are a Silver member, they get a 10% discount. If they are a Bronze member, they get a 5% discount. If the membership level is not recognised, then an error message is output.

Figure 1.2: Checking into a hotel

Continued

```
    OUTPUT "Enter the room type"
    INPUT room
    OUTPUT "Enter the number of nights"
    INPUT nights
    IF room == "elite" AND room == "Elite" THEN
        cost = 100 * nights
    ELSE
        cost = 50 + nights
    ENDIF
    OUTPUT "Are you a member?"
    INPUT member
    IF member == "Yes" OR member == "yes" THEN
    OUTPUT "What level?"
        INPUT level
        IF level == "gold" OR level == "Gold" THEN
            cost = cost * 0.8
        ELSEIF level == "silver" OR level == "Silver" THEN
            cost = cost * 0.9
        ELSE
            cost = cost * 0.95
        ENDIF
    ENDIF
    OUTPUT "Total cost is " * cost
```

Predict: Write down what you predict the output(s) should be for each set of inputs:

elite	3	no	
basic	10	yes	gold
elite	1	yes	bronze
elite	5	yes	steel
basic	7	yes	silver
basic	4	no	

You can use a calculator if you need to.

Run: Dry run the pseudocode algorithm with each set of inputs. Identify which sets of inputs produced correct outputs and which sets produced incorrect outputs.

Continued

Investigate: Work on your own to identify the errors in the program before joining with a partner to compare your answers.

There are four logic errors in this program.

Modify: Work with your partner to change the pseudocode algorithm to remove the logic errors.

Test your new program with the same sets of data to check if your solution is correct.

Self-assessment

Give yourself a rating for your contribution to this programming task. Gold is the top rating, where you worked equally with your partner and you both contributed ideas. Silver is the middle rating, where you helped your partner but provided fewer solutions. Bronze is the third rating, where you supported your partner but allowed them to take the lead in creating the solution.

Activity 1.1

You will need: a desktop computer, laptop or tablet with presentation software

For this activity, you will be working individually. Select one of the pseudocode algorithms that you edited or corrected in this topic so far.

Create a presentation that shows the original code, the errors in the code and your corrections or the changes you made. Make sure you describe what you did and how you checked they were correct.

Questions 1.1

1   What do you need to do before you change an algorithm?
2   How can you find an error in a pseudocode algorithm?
3   What is a logic error?
4   Change this pseudocode algorithm to add three numbers together instead of two:

```
INPUT first
INPUT second
total = first + second
OUTPUT (total)
```

5 Change this pseudocode algorithm to allow numbers between 100 and 200 (inclusive) to be correct inputs.

```
INPUT number
IF number > 100 AND number < 200 THEN
    OUTPUT "Correct"
ELSE
    OUTPUT "Incorrect"
ENDIF
```

6 This pseudocode algorithm should output the smallest number input, but it does not work.

Identify the errors and correct the algorithm.

```
smallest = -99999999
INPUT number1
INPUT number2
INPUT number3
INPUT number4
IF number1 < smallest THEN
    smallest = number1
ENDIF
IF number2 < smallest THEN
    smallest = number1
ENDIF
IF number3 < smallest THEN
    smallest = number1
ENDIF
IF number4 < smallest THEN
    smallest = number1
ENDIF
OUTPUT "The smallest number input was ", smallest
```

7 This pseudocode algorithm should calculate and output the cost of a horse riding lesson. The cost depends on the type of lesson and the level of the rider.

For a half-hour group lesson, a Level 1 rider pays $10, a Level 2 rider pays $15 and a Level 3 rider pays $20.

Riders can select a half-hour lesson or an hour lesson. An hour lesson is twice the cost of a half-hour lesson.

Riders can select a private lesson. A private lesson is twice the cost of a group lesson.

Identify the errors and correct the algorithm.

```
level1 = 10.0
level2 = 10.0
level3 = 20.0

OUTPUT "Choose length 30 or 60 minutes as 30 or 60"
INPUT length
IF length == 30 THEN
    length = 1
ELSE
    length = 2
ENDIF
OUTPUT "Enter rider level as 1, 2 or 3"
INPUT riderLevel
IF riderLevel < 1 THEN
    cost = length * level1
ELSEIF riderLevel == 2 THEN
    cost = length * level2
ELSEIF riderLevel == 3 THEN
    cost = length * level3
ELSE
    OUTPUT "Invalid level, assuming level 3"
    cost = length * level3
ENDIF
OUTPUT "Private or group?"
INPUT type
IF type == "Private" AND type == "private" THEN
    cost = cost + 2
ENDIF
OUTPUT "The total cost is $" & cost
```

Summary checklist

- [ ] I can edit a pseudocode algorithm to do a different task.
- [ ] I can change a pseudocode algorithm to do an additional task.
- [ ] I can find logic errors in a pseudocode algorithm.
- [ ] I can correct logic errors in a pseudocode algorithm.

〉 1.2 Iteration

In this topic you will:

- learn what iteration is in programming
- explore count-controlled loops
- follow flowcharts that use count-controlled loops
- follow pseudocode algorithms that use count-controlled loops
- predict the outcome of an algorithm that uses count-controlled loops.

Key words

condition

condition-controlled loop

count-controlled loop

FOR loop

increment

infinite loop

iteration

loop

Getting started

What do you already know?

- Algorithms are a series of steps that solve a problem. They can be represented as flowcharts, pseudocode and in program code.
- You have learned that iteration means to repeat something. Iterative development means repeated development.
- Selection statements use IF, ELSEIF, ELSE to test a condition.

Continued

Now try this!

Follow this pseudocode algorithm with a partner and work out what its purpose is.

```
count = 0
OUTPUT "Enter a number"
INPUT number
IF number > 10 THEN
    count = count + 1
ENDIF

OUTPUT "Enter another number"
INPUT number
IF number > 10 THEN
    count = count + 1
ENDIF

OUTPUT "Enter another number"
INPUT number
IF number > 10 THEN
    count = count + 1
ENDIF
OUTPUT "There were ", count, "numbers greater
than 10"
```

Iteration and loops

A **loop** in a program is when something happens repeatedly. Code is run, it gets to the end, goes back to the start, the code is run, it gets to the end, goes back to the start in a loop and so on.

Iteration is another word for loop. Think about the word 'iteration.' You might have come across some similar words:

'Reiterate' means to say something again after it has already been said.

'Iterate' means to do something over and over again.

You will need: a piece of paper

Work in pairs for this activity.

Write down a series of actions for your partner to do. Make sure these are sensible and safe for where you are, for example standing up, clapping hands or turning around in a circle.

Swap your actions with your partner. Perform your partner's series of actions iteratively (do the sequence repeatedly).

Stopping a loop

In a program there needs to be a way to stop the loop. If there isn't a way to stop the loop, it will continue forever. This is called an **infinite loop**. An infinite loop will eventually crash the program.

A loop is stopped using a **condition** (a test that gives a true or false result). This is the same as the conditions you use in conditional statements such as IF statements. The loop will also have something to show where it ends. This might be a 'stop loop' or an 'end loop' command. If it's in a language like Python, the code in the loop will be indented.

There are two types of loops in programming:

1   **count-controlled loops**, which run a specific number of times

2   **condition-controlled loops**, which keep running until their condition is true, or while a condition is true.

In this unit, you will only need to use *count-controlled* loops.

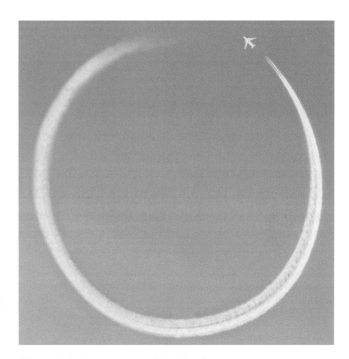

Figure 1.3: An aeroplane flying in a loop

Count-controlled loops

A count-controlled loop runs a specific number of times.

Unplugged activity 1.3

Repeat these four actions two times:

1   stand up
2   clap your hands
3   sit down
4   clap your hands.

In this activity, once you had done all the actions twice, you stopped. If the instruction said:

'repeat these actions five times'

you would have done everything five times and then stopped.

Incrementing

To know how many times a loop has run, a program uses a variable as a counter. Each time the loop finishes, the counter is increased. The value is usually increased by 1, which is also called incrementing. To **increment** something means to increase it by a set amount.

A count-controlled loop can increase by a different number than 1 (for example +2 or +5), but for this unit you only need to use the number 1.

Activity 1.2

You will need: a desktop computer, laptop or tablet with presentation software, animation software or video-editing software and a camera

In a group of four people, create a video or animation showing a count-controlled loop with a physical action. For example, performing a set of actions a set number of times.

You will need to show how the number of loops is counted, for example the number of the loop could be included in the animation, or when a new loop starts, the people being recorded could shout the loop number they are starting.

If you don't have video or animation software or a camera, prepare a presentation and perform it for your class.

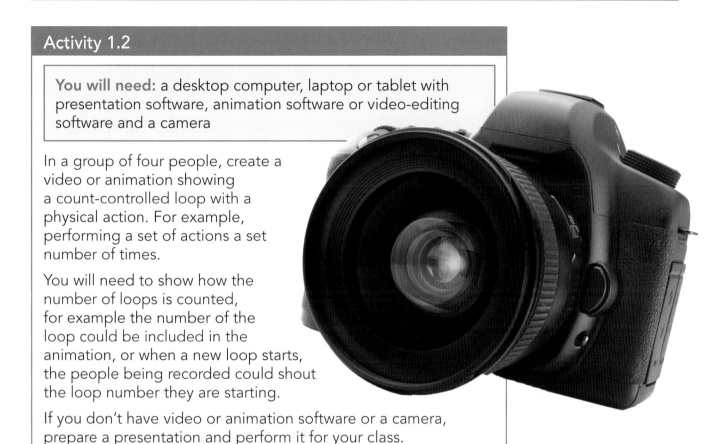

Count-controlled loops in pseudocode

A count-controlled loop has three parts:

1   a variable to store the counter

2   the starting value – the number the variable starts on

3   the end value – when the variable reaches this number, it will run once more and then stop.

FOR loops

In pseudocode and program code, the most common count-controlled loop is a FOR loop, also called a FOR-NEXT loop.

A **FOR loop** has code that repeats a set number of times. The FOR loop statement gives the number that the loop counter starts on and the number that the loop counter stops on. The loop counter increases by 1 each time the loop runs.

Here is an example of pseudocode structure for a FOR loop:

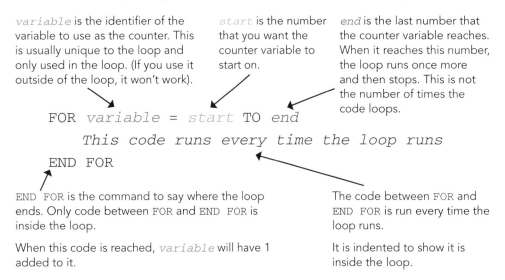

variable is the identifier of the variable to use as the counter. This is usually unique to the loop and only used in the loop. (If you use it outside of the loop, it won't work).

start is the number that you want the counter variable to start on.

end is the last number that the counter variable reaches. When it reaches this number, the loop runs once more and then stops. This is not the number of times the code loops.

```
FOR variable = start TO end
    This code runs every time the loop runs
END FOR
```

END FOR is the command to say where the loop ends. Only code between FOR and END FOR is inside the loop.

When this code is reached, *variable* will have 1 added to it.

The code between FOR and END FOR is run every time the loop runs.

It is indented to show it is inside the loop.

Example 1

Here's an example FOR loop written in pseudocode:

```
FOR count = 0 TO 2
    OUTPUT "Hello"
END FOR
```

Let's trace this algorithm step by step.

The loop will run when count = 0, 1 and 2. This is 'between 0 and 2 inclusive'.

Loop 1:

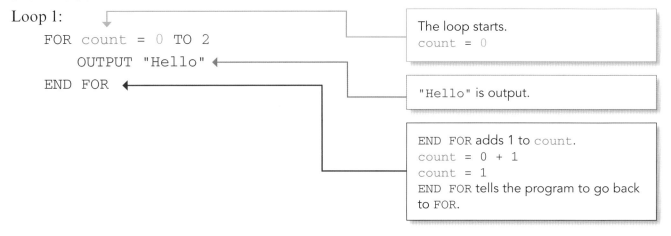

```
FOR count = 0 TO 2
    OUTPUT "Hello"
END FOR
```

The loop starts.
count = 0

"Hello" is output.

END FOR adds 1 to count.
count = 0 + 1
count = 1
END FOR tells the program to go back to FOR.

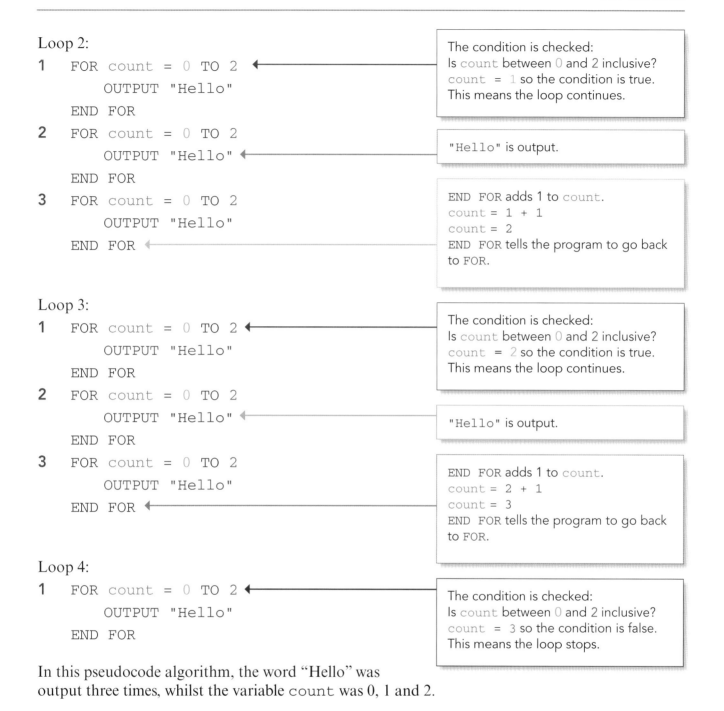

Loop 2:

```
1   FOR count = 0 TO 2
        OUTPUT "Hello"
    END FOR
2   FOR count = 0 TO 2
        OUTPUT "Hello"
    END FOR
3   FOR count = 0 TO 2
        OUTPUT "Hello"
    END FOR
```

The condition is checked:
Is count between 0 and 2 inclusive?
count = 1 so the condition is true.
This means the loop continues.

"Hello" is output.

END FOR adds 1 to count.
count = 1 + 1
count = 2
END FOR tells the program to go back to FOR.

Loop 3:

```
1   FOR count = 0 TO 2
        OUTPUT "Hello"
    END FOR
2   FOR count = 0 TO 2
        OUTPUT "Hello"
    END FOR
3   FOR count = 0 TO 2
        OUTPUT "Hello"
    END FOR
```

The condition is checked:
Is count between 0 and 2 inclusive?
count = 2 so the condition is true.
This means the loop continues.

"Hello" is output.

END FOR adds 1 to count.
count = 2 + 1
count = 3
END FOR tells the program to go back to FOR.

Loop 4:

```
1   FOR count = 0 TO 2
        OUTPUT "Hello"
    END FOR
```

The condition is checked:
Is count between 0 and 2 inclusive?
count = 3 so the condition is false.
This means the loop stops.

In this pseudocode algorithm, the word "Hello" was output three times, whilst the variable count was 0, 1 and 2.

Example 2

Here's another pseudocode algorithm that uses a count-controlled loop. This one includes more code before and after the loop.

```
OUTPUT "Start the loop"
FOR number = 10 TO 15
     OUTPUT number
END FOR
OUTPUT "Loop over"
```

Let's trace the algorithm step by step.

Before the loop starts:

```
OUTPUT "Start the loop"
```

"Start the loop" is output.

Loop 1:

```
FOR number = 10 TO 15
     OUTPUT number
END FOR
```

The loop starts.
number = 10

The data stored in number is output, this is 10.

END FOR adds 1 to number.
number = 10 + 1 = 11
END FOR tells the program to go back to FOR.

Loop 2:

```
FOR number = 10 TO 15
     OUTPUT number
END FOR
```

The condition is checked. Is number between 10 and 15 inclusive? number = 11 so it is true.

The data stored in number is output, this is 11.

END FOR adds 1 to number.
number = 11 + 1 = 12
END FOR tells the program to go back to FOR.

Loop 3:

```
FOR number = 10 TO 15
    OUTPUT number
END FOR
```

The condition is checked.
Is number between 10 and 15
inclusive? number = 12 so it is true.

The data stored in number is output,
this is 12.

END FOR adds 1 to number.
number = 12 + 1 = 13
END FOR tells the program to go back
to FOR.

Loop 4:

```
FOR number = 10 TO 15
    OUTPUT number
END FOR
```

The condition is checked.
Is number between 10 and 15
inclusive? number = 13 so it is true.

The data stored in number is output,
this is 13.

END FOR adds 1 to number.
number = 13 + 1 = 14
END FOR tells the program to go back
to FOR.

Loop 5:

```
FOR number = 10 TO 15
    OUTPUT number
END FOR
```

The condition is checked.
Is number between 10 and 15
inclusive? number = 14 so it is true.

The data stored in number is output,
this is 14.

END FOR adds 1 to number.
number = 14 + 1 = 15
END FOR tells the program to go back
to FOR.

Loop 6:

```
FOR number = 10 TO 15
    OUTPUT number
END FOR
```

The condition is checked. Is `number` between 10 and 15 inclusive? `number = 15` so it is true.

The data stored in `number` is output, this is 15.

`END FOR` adds 1 to `number`.
`number = 15 + 1 = 16`
`END FOR` tells the program to go back to `FOR`.

Loop 7:

```
FOR number = 10 TO 15
    OUTPUT number
END FOR
OUTPUT "Loop over"
```

The condition is checked. Is `number` between 10 and 15 inclusive? `number = 16` so it is false. The loop stops.

`"Loop over"` is output.

This algorithm outputs:

```
Start the loop
10
11
12
13
14
15
Loop over
```

Programming task 1.5: Predict, Run, Investigate and Modify

You will need: a pen and paper

Read this pseudocode algorithm with a partner:

```
FOR counter = 0 TO 9
    value = counter + 1
    OUTPUT value
end for
```

Predict: Work with your partner to identify the numbers that you think will be output before you run the code. Do this by looking at the numbers at the top of the loop and what happens in the loop.

Run: Work with a partner to run the code. Keep track of the values in the variables. You can do this by creating a table and filling in the numbers as they change, for example:

counter	value	Output

Or you can follow it step by step like in Examples 1 and 2.

Investigate: Write the pseudocode algorithm on a piece of paper and highlight the following features:

*   the command word for the loop
*   the identifier of the variable used as a counter
*   the number the variable starts on
*   the number the variable ends on
*   the code that runs each time the loop runs.

Modify 1: Change the algorithm so the counter variable starts on 5 instead of 0.

Run the algorithm and look at how it changes the output.

Modify 2: Change the algorithm so it outputs the numbers 10 to 20. You should only change the loop, not the code inside the loop.

Think about the number you want the loop to start on, and when you want it to end.

Programming task 1.6: Predict, Run and Investigate

You will need: a pen and paper

Read this pseudocode algorithm with a partner:

```
OUTPUT "Enter a number"
INPUT numberInput
FOR count = 1 TO 10
    result = count * numberInput
    OUTPUT result
END FOR
```

Predict: Work with your partner to identify the outputs that the algorithm will produce when the number 10 is input.

Run: Work with a partner to run the code. Keep track of the values in the variables. You can do this by creating a table and filling in the numbers as they change, for example:

numberInput	count	result	output

Or you can follow it step by step like in Examples 1 and 2.

Investigate: Work with a partner to identify:

- the identifier of the counter variable
- the number the counter variable starts on
- the number the counter variable ends on
- what the purpose of the algorithm is.

Self-assessment

Give yourself a rating for how well you could follow and investigate this algorithm.

1 = It was easy. I could follow it without any problems.

2 = I had to think about it, but I could work it out.

3 = I found it quite tricky and need some more practice.

Other formats in pseudocode

You should already understand that pseudocode does not have a set format.
Table 1.1 shows some other examples of how a FOR loop might be shown.
Original:

```
OUTPUT "Before loop"
FOR counter = 0 TO 9
    OUTPUT counter
END FOR
OUTPUT "After loop"
```

Pseudocode algorithm	Description
OUTPUT "Before loop" FOR counter = 0 TO 9: OUTPUT counter OUTPUT "After loop"	There is no END FOR. In this code, the change in the indent shows where the loop ends.
OUTPUT "Before loop" FOR counter = 0 TO 9 OUTPUT counter NEXT counter OUTPUT "After loop"	The END FOR has been replaced with NEXT counter. In this code, NEXT counter is telling the loop to increase the value in counter and works in the same way as the END FOR.
OUTPUT "Before loop" FOR counter IN RANGE(0, 10): OUTPUT counter OUTPUT "After loop"	This is similar to Python FOR loops, which you will look at in Topic 4. In this example, the starting value (0) and end value (10) are inside the brackets. The end value has 1 more added to it. In this code, the loop stops as soon as the second number (10) is reached. When counter is 10 the loop stops and "After loop" is output. The end value is exclusive (which means the final number is not used). For example, if the algorithm runs from 0 to 2 exclusive of the end value, the counter will be 0 then 1, then the loop will stop.

Table 1.1: Other examples of a FOR loop

You might also see arrows in the assignment, for example:

```
OUTPUT "Before loop"
FOR counter ← 0 TO 9
    OUTPUT counter
END FOR
OUTPUT "After loop"
```

Questions 1.2

1   What does iteration mean?

2   One type of loop in programming is a count-controlled loop. What is the other type of loop?

3   What are the key features of a count-controlled loop?

4   What is the most common count-controlled loop used in programming called?

5   Read this pseudocode algorithm:

```
FOR x = 0 TO 9
    OUTPUT x
NEXT x
```

Use these questions to test your knowledge!

   a   What is the identifier of the counter variable?
   b   What is the starting value of the counter variable?
   c   What is the end condition of the loop?
   d   How many times will this loop run?

6   Read this pseudocode algorithm:

```
FOR trace = 10 TO 15
    answer = trace + trace - 1
    OUTPUT answer
END FOR
```

What will this algorithm output?

7   Read this pseudocode algorithm:

```
total = 0
FOR count = 1 TO 100
    INPUT number
    total = total + number
NEXT count
OUTPUT total
```

This algorithm takes 100 numbers as input in a loop, adds them together and then outputs the total when the loop finishes.

   a   Change the algorithm so it takes 10 numbers instead of 100.
   b   Change the algorithm so it takes 55 numbers as input and outputs the average (total divided by quantity) once the loop has finished.

Count-controlled loops in flowcharts

Flowcharts do not have a specific symbol for loops. Instead they use a condition and data flows (arrows) to show where the code loops.

Unplugged activity 1.4

Read this flowchart.

Work with a partner to identify each of the different flowchart shapes and the data flows.

Discuss where this flowchart shows a loop (that is, where the code is repeated).

Try to run the flowchart. Use your finger or a pen to follow the arrows. You will need to keep track of the value of counter and write down the output in each loop.

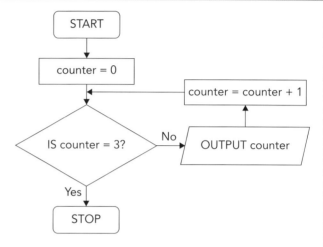

Figure 1.4: An iteration loop in a flowchart

The flowchart in the unplugged activity is a count-controlled loop. It has the three features:

1   A variable to store the counter. This is named `counter`.

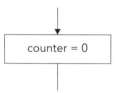

Figure 1.5: A flowchart shape showing a variable storing the counter

2   The starting value: the number the variable starts on.
   `counter` starts at 0

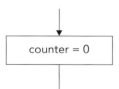

Figure 1.6: Assigning a starting value

3   The end value: when the variable reaches this number, it will run once more and then stop.

When the condition is true (when the counter is 3), the loop stops.

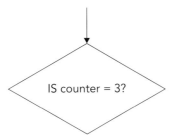

Figure 1.7: Selection statement to provide the end value

The arrows, or data flows, show where the loop is. When `counter` is not equal to 3, the 'No' arrow is followed. The value of `counter` is output, `counter` is incremented and then the arrow rejoins the flowchart before the condition. So, the condition is run again, and if the answer is 'No', the loop continues.

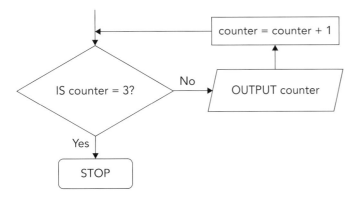

Figure 1.8: The iteration loop in the flowchart

The main difference with writing the algorithm as a flowchart is that you have to change the value of the counter variable yourself. There is an extra process within the loop to increment the value of `counter`.

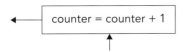

Figure 1.9: Incrementing the value of counter

Example 1: This is the pseudocode algorithm that we walked through earlier and the matching flowchart.

```
FOR count = 0 TO 2
    OUTPUT "Hello"
END FOR
```

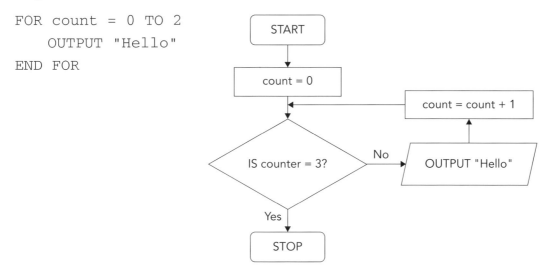

Figure 1.10: Pseudocode and flowchart

The variable counter is named `count` in both algorithms.

Both set `count` to start at 0.

Both check if `count` reaches the end value:

- The pseudocode reads `FOR count = 0 TO 2`
- The flowchart reads `IS counter = 3?` This could also be written as `IS counter > 2?`

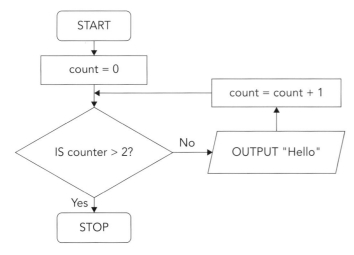

Figure 1.11: Another way of checking the counter

Both algorithms increase `count` by 1 each time. The pseudocode algorithm does it by using the FOR loop, the flowchart uses the process `count = count + 1`.

Programming task 1.7: Predict, Run and Investigate

You will need: a pen and paper

Read this flowchart with a partner:

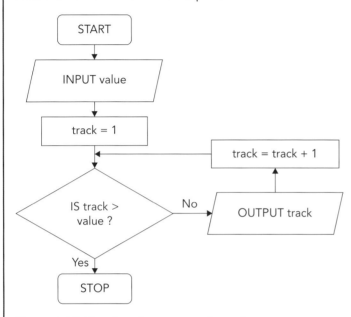

Figure 1.12: Flowchart for programming task

Predict: Work with your partner to identify the numbers that you think will be output when the number 5 is input before you follow the flowchart step by step.

Run: Work with your partner to test the flowchart. Keep track of the values in the variables. You can do this by creating a table and filling in the numbers as they change, for example:

value	track	output

Investigate: Write the pseudocode algorithm on a piece of paper and highlight the following features:

- the identifier of the variable that counts the number of loops
- the number the variable counter starts at
- the condition when the counter stops
- the process where the counter is incremented.

Programming task 1.8: Predict, Run, Investigate and Modify

You will need: a pen and paper

Read this flowchart with a partner.

Predict: Work with your partner to identify what you think will be output when the number 10 is input.

Run: Work with your partner to test the flowchart. Keep track of the values in the variables. You can do this by creating a table and filling in the numbers as they change, for example:

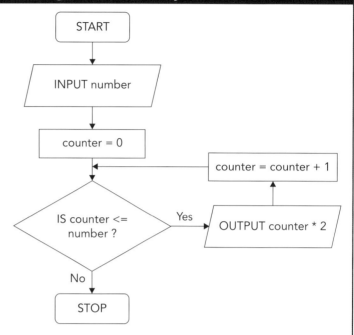

Figure 1.13: Flowchart for programming task

number	counter	output

Investigate: Discuss these with your partner:

1   What would happen if `counter` started at 10 instead of 0?
2   What would happen if a negative number (for example −10) is input?
3   What would happen if the arrow from `counter = counter + 1` joined above `counter = 0` instead of below?

Modify 1: Change the condition in the selection box, and the 'Yes' and 'No' arrows (if needed) so the flowchart still gives the same output but uses a different condition.

Modify 2: Change the flowchart so it only loops ten times if the number 10 is input.

How did you work out how to change the flowchart? Did you test a few options first and then decide which one worked? How did you test that it worked? Do you think you tested it methodically and thoroughly?

Questions 1.3

1 Read this flowchart.

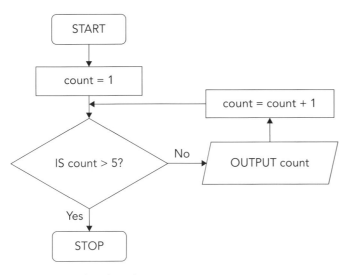

Figure 1.14: Flowchart for questions

a What is the identifier of the counter variable?

b What is the starting value of the counter variable?

c What is the end condition of the loop?

d How many times will this loop run?

2   Read this flowchart.

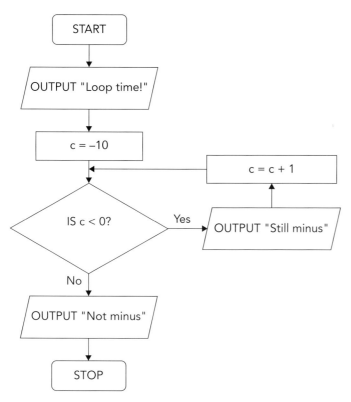

Figure 1.15: An iteration loop in a flowchart

Write down the output that this flowchart will create.

Summary checklist

☐   I can describe what iteration is in programming.
☐   I can describe the purpose of a count-controlled loop.
☐   I can describe the parts of a count-controlled loop.
☐   I can follow a count-controlled loop in pseudocode.
☐   I can change a count-controlled loop in pseudocode.
☐   I can follow a count-controlled loop in a flowchart.
☐   I can change a count-controlled loop in a flowchart.

> 1.3 Creating algorithms

In this topic you will:

- create algorithms using flowcharts and pseudocode
- create a flowchart that uses sequence, selection and iteration
- create an algorithm in pseudocode to solve a problem
- use sequence, selection and iteration to create an algorithm using pseudocode
- use predefined sub-routines in flowcharts and pseudocode.

Key words

call

key word

predefined
sub-routine

sub-routine

Getting started

What do you already know?

- Sequence statements are where one line of code runs after the other, in the order they are written.
- Selection statements include a condition. If the condition is true, the statements inside the selection statement are run.

  Flowcharts use the diamond shape for a condition and data flows that are labelled 'True' and 'False' (or 'Yes' and 'No').

  In pseudocode, selection statements use IF statements.

Continued

- Iteration statements are loops. Code is repeated multiple times. A count-controlled loop runs a set number of times.

  In a flowchart, the loop is controlled by a decision statement in a diamond shape.

  You should have already created selection statements in a text-based programming language like Python.

Now try this!

Create a flowchart that takes three numbers as input from a user. It should add together the three numbers and output the result. It should then multiply the numbers and output the result.

Test your flowchart with the inputs 1, 2 and 3. Before you test the flowchart, calculate what you expect the answer to be, and then check if the flowchart gives the same result.

Creating an algorithm with selection

You will have previously learnt to follow algorithms in flowcharts and pseudocode that use selection statements. In this topic, you are going to write your own algorithms.

When you create a flowchart of a pseudocode algorithm with selection, you follow the same steps as when you create a text-based program with selection. Selection is where a condition is tested. If the condition is true, some code will run. If the condition is false, other code might run.

Follow these steps:

1 Identify the condition that can be true or false.
2 Identify the code that will run when the condition is true.
3 Identify the code that will run when the condition is false.

Selection in a flowchart

When creating a flowchart:

- The condition goes in a diamond-shaped box as a question, usually with a question mark (?).
- Two data flows (arrows) come from the diamond. One is labelled 'True' (or 'Yes') and the other is labelled 'False' (or 'No').

When you are writing code that uses selection, you need to remember these steps.

- The data flow labelled 'True' or 'Yes' goes to the code that runs when the condition is true.
- The data flow labelled 'False' or 'No' goes to the code that runs when the condition is false.

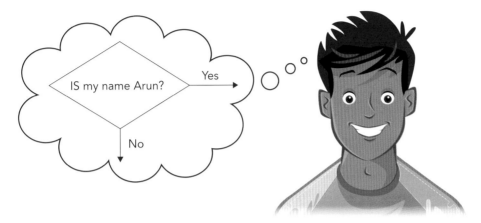

A flowchart asks a user to input a number. A message is output if the number is 10, and a different message if it is not 10.

1   Identify the condition that can be true or false:
    The number input = 10
2   Identify the code that will run when the condition is true:
    OUTPUT "You entered 10"
3   Identify the code that will run when the condition is false:
    OUTPUT "You did not enter 10"

This is how we write the decision in the flowchart:

1   The condition is placed in a diamond.
2   Two data flows come from the diamond – one labelled 'True' and one labelled 'False'.
3   Insert the code that runs when the condition is true and when it is false.

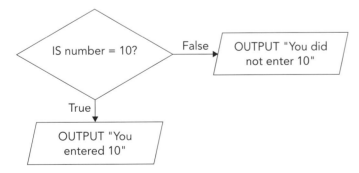

Figure 1.16: Decision in the flowchart

Then finish the flowchart with the sequences that run before and after the selection statement and join the data flows together. Make sure you have a start box and an end box, and that all boxes join to another box.

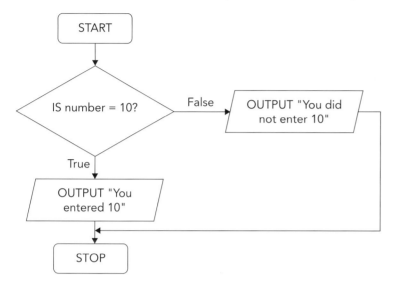

Figure 1.17: The final flowchart

Unplugged activity 1.5

You will need: a partner and a piece of paper

Work together to write down the conditions for each of these problems:

1 Input the cost of an item and the quantity of items bought. Output a message if the total cost is over $100.

2 Input two numbers and output the smallest number.

3 Input three numbers and output a message if the average is more than 5.

4 Input a number and subtract it from 100. Output a message that says whether the result is positive or negative.

Programming task 1.9: Predict, Run, Investigate, Modify and Make

You will need: a pen and paper

This flowchart should output a message if the user enters the correct answer to 3 * 3, and a message if they enter an incorrect answer.

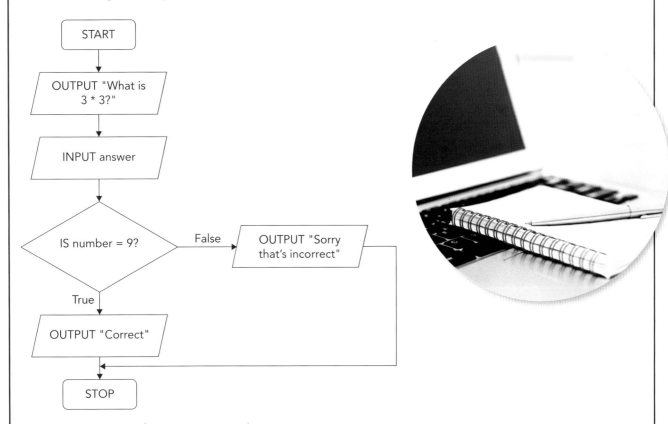

Figure 1.18: Flowchart for programming task

Predict: Write down the value, or values, that will result in the output "Correct" and the value, or values, that will result in the output "Sorry that's incorrect". If there are lots of possible values, only write down five.

Run: Follow the flowchart with each item of data you identified. Put a tick next to each one that you correctly predicted and a cross next to those you incorrectly predicted.

Continued

Investigate: Work with a partner to identify the following features of the flowchart (this could be by pointing them out, highlighting them or circling them):

- the condition
- the code that always runs
- the code that only runs when the condition is true
- the code that only runs when the condition is false.

Modify: Work with your partner to change the flowchart to ask the user what 10 * 2 is and output a message if they get it correct or incorrect.

Make: Create a flowchart that outputs the definition of a computer science term (for example, 'binary'). Ask the user what the definition is describing and output a message if the answer is correct, and a different message if the answer is incorrect.

Multiple conditions, such as ELSEIF statements in pseudocode, have multiple selection boxes. The second selection runs when the first is false. A third runs when the first and second are false.

Programming task 1.10: Predict, Run, Investigate, Modify and Make

You will need: a pen and paper

This flowchart should output a message if the user answers the question correctly ('orange'), and a different message if they enter 'brown', 'purple' or any other answer.

Continued

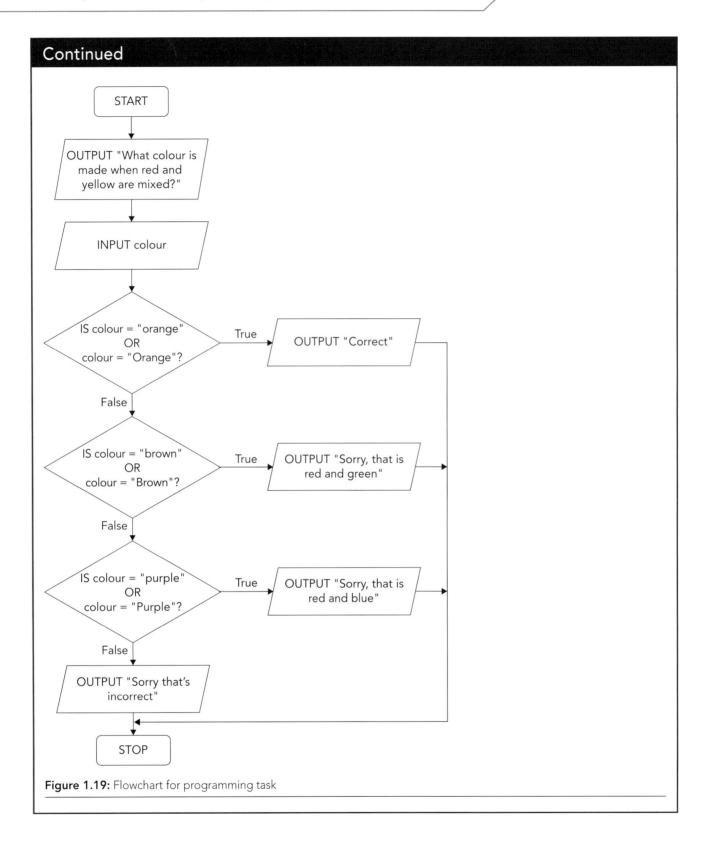

Figure 1.19: Flowchart for programming task

Continued

Predict: Write down what will be output when the following data is input:

1 ORANGE
2 Blue
3 Purple
4 Orange
5 Red
6 Brown
7 purple

Run: Follow the flowchart with each item of data input. Put a tick next to each output that you correctly predicted and a cross next to those you incorrectly predicted.

Investigate: Identify the different conditions used in the flowchart. Highlight the output that happens when all of the conditions are false.

Modify: Change the flowchart to include a suitable output if the user inputs the colour pink, white or black.

Make: Create a flowchart that asks the user what mathematical function the operator + is. Check and output "Correct" if the user's input is 'add' or 'addition'. Output a different message if the user enters 'multiplication' or 'multiply', 'division' or 'divide', or 'minus' or 'subtract'.

Selection in pseudocode

Selection in pseudocode uses IF statements.

An ELSE statement includes the code that runs when the condition is false. In this example, "Negative" is output when the condition is true, and "Positive" is output when the condition is false:

```
IF value < 0 THEN
    OUTPUT "Negative"
ELSE
    OUTPUT "Positive"
ENDIF
```

The same three stages are used to plan the selection statement as we've seen in flowcharts:
1 the condition that can be true or false
2 the code that will run when the condition is true
3 the code that will run when the condition is false.

A pseudocode algorithm is needed that takes the cost of two items as input and outputs a message saying the total is $20 or more, or it is less than $20.

1 Identify the condition that can be true or false:

The number input >= 20

2 Identify the code that will run when the condition is true:

OUTPUT "It is 20 or more"

3 Identify the code that will run when the condition is false:

OUTPUT "It is less than 20"

The condition is written in an IF statement:

```
IF numberInput >= 20 THEN
ENDIF
```

The code that runs when the condition is true is added:

```
IF numberInput >= 20 THEN
    OUTPUT "It is 20 or more"
ENDIF
```

The code that runs when the condition is false is added in an ELSE statement:

```
IF numberInput >= 20 THEN
    OUTPUT "It is 20 or more"
ELSE
    OUTPUT "It is less than 20"
ENDIF
```

Include the code that happens before and/or after the selection statement:

```
OUTPUT "Input a number"
INPUT numberInput
IF numberInput >= 20 THEN
    OUTPUT "It is 20 or more"
ELSE
    OUTPUT "It is less than 20"
ENDIF
```

Programming task 1.11: Predict, Run, Investigate, Modify and Make

You will need: a pen and paper

This pseudocode algorithm asks a user to enter the x-coordinate and y-coordinate of a character in a game. The character is off the screen if either value is less than 0 or more than 1024.

```
OUTPUT "Enter the x-coordinate"
INPUT xCoord
OUTPUT "Enter the y-coordinate"
INPUT yCoord
IF xCoord < 0 OR yCoord < 0 OR
xCoord > 1024 OR yCoord > 1024
THEN
    OUTPUT "Your character is
    off the screen"
ELSE
    OUTPUT "Your character is
    still on screen"
ENDIF
```

Predict: Complete the table to identify five different sets of values for the two variables and the output they will result in. An example has been filled out for you. You must have at least one set of values for each output.

xCoord	yCoord	Output
−5	100	Your character is off the screen

Continued

Run: Follow the pseudocode algorithm with each set of your test data and check whether your predictions were correct.

Investigate: Identify the smallest number that can be stored in each variable for the character to still be on screen.

Identify the largest number that can be stored in each variable for the character to still be on screen.

Modify: Change the pseudocode algorithm so that the x-coordinate 0 is off screen, and the y-coordinate 0 is off screen.

Make: Create a pseudocode algorithm that checks the x-coordinate and y-coordinate of a character.

If either coordinate is less than 0, the value is changed to store 0.

If either coordinate is greater than 1024, the value is changed to store 1024.

For example:

- The x-coordinate is −10 and the y-coordinate is 20. The x-coordinate is changed to store 0 instead of −10.
- The x-coordinate is 1050 and the y-coordinate is −3. The x-coordinate is changed to store 1024. The y-coordinate is changed to store 0.

Multiple conditions are written using ELSEIF statements. Each ELSEIF is run only when the previous statement or statements are false.
An ELSEIF can only have one ELSE statement at the end, for example:

```
IF condition 1 THEN
    Runs if condition 1 is true
ELSEIF condition 2 THEN
    Runs if condition 1 is false, condition 2 is true
ELSEIF condition 3 THEN
    Runs if condition 1 and 2 are false, condition 3 is true
ELSE
    Runs if conditions 1, 2 and 3 are false
ENDIF
```

Programming task 1.12: Predict, Run, Investigate, Modify and Make

You will need: a pen and paper

This pseudocode algorithm checks if a game user is able to purchase the Shield of Strength in a computer game. They can purchase the item if they already have the Emerald Stone, they have at least $100 and are on or above Level 3.

```
OUTPUT "How much money do you have?"
INPUT money
OUTPUT "Do you have the Emerald Stone?"
INPUT stone
OUTPUT "What level are you on?"
INPUT level
IF level < 3 THEN
    OUTPUT "Your level is not high enough yet"
ELSEIF stone = "no" OR stone = "NO" OR stone = "No" THEN
    OUTPUT "You need to find the Emerald Stone"
ELSEIF money < 100 THEN
    OUTPUT "You don't have enough money yet"
ELSE
    OUTPUT "Congratulations, here is the Shield of Strength"
ENDIF
```

Figure 1.20: The Shield of Strength

Predict: Complete the table to identify the output when each set of values is input:

Input 1	Input 2	Input 3	Output
100	Yes	5	
110	No	3	
50	YES	4	
10	yes	2	
99	no	10	
300	Yes	6	

Continued

Run: Follow the pseudocode algorithm with each set of your test data and check whether your predictions were correct.

Investigate:

- Identify the different conditions used in the algorithm.
- Identify when condition 2 will run.
- Identify when condition 3 will run.
- Identify the code that will output when all of the conditions are false.

Figure 1.21: The Emerald Stone

Modify: Change the pseudocode algorithm so that the user also has to enter their age.

Change the algorithm so they can only get the Shield of Strength if they are also over the age of 14.

Make: A game allows a character to purchase the Bow of Truth. To purchase the bow the character needs:

- to own the Shield of Strength
- to be on level 5 or above
- to have at least $1000
- to have the Knowledge of Wisdom.

Write a pseudocode algorithm to take the required data as input, and then output a message either telling the character they can purchase the Bow of Truth or telling them why they are not allowed to purchase the Bow of Truth.

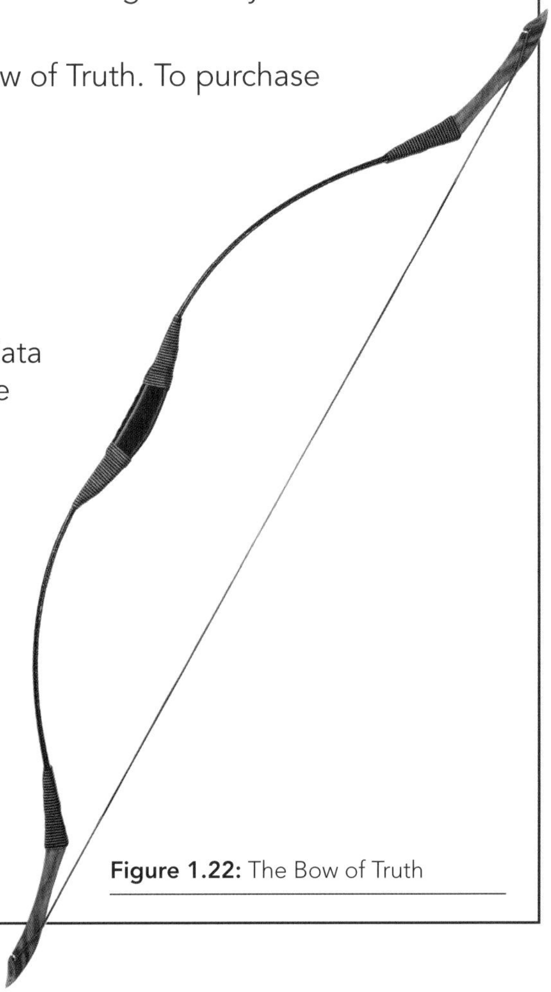

Figure 1.22: The Bow of Truth

Creating an algorithm with count-controlled loops

In Topic 1.2, we looked at what count-controlled loops are and how they work. We are now going create an algorithm using a count-controlled loop. Each count-controlled loop has:

1   a counter variable
2   a starting value for the counter variable
3   an end value for the counter variable
4   a way to increase the counter variable.

A count-controlled loop runs a specific number of times.

Count-controlled loops in a flowchart

To create a count-controlled loop in a flowchart:

1   Set a counter variable to the starting value in a process box (rectangle). In this example, the variable is named `counter` and it starts at 0.

2   Use a decision box (diamond) to check if the counter is at the end value. In this example, the loop stops when the counter is 10.

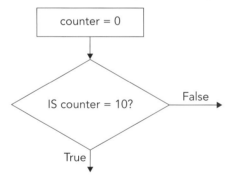

Figure 1.23: Count-controlled loop flowchart 1

3   Inside the loop, change the counter variable by adding 1 to it, and join it to the original data flow before the decision.

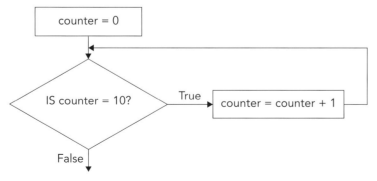

Figure 1.24: Changing the variable

4 Insert any processes inside the loop. These processes include inputs and outputs, for example outputting the counter variable:

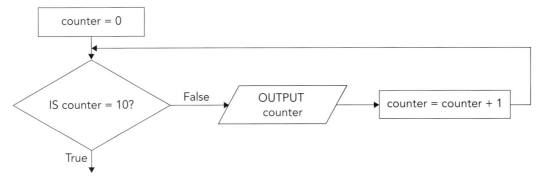

Figure 1.25: Outputting the counter variable

5 Insert the rest of the actions before and after the loop, for example:

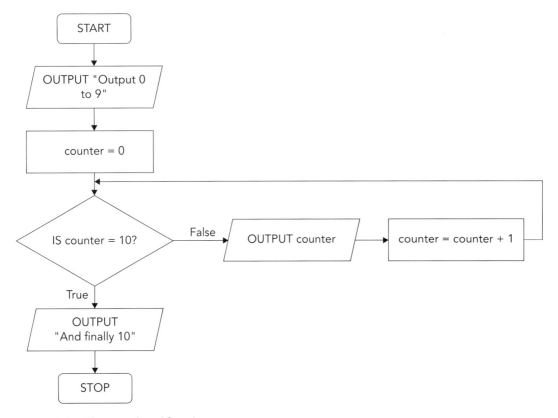

Figure 1.26: The completed flowchart

Unplugged activity 1.6

You will need: a pen and paper

A flowchart has been created that outputs the numbers 1 to 10 and whether they are odd or even. The boxes have been mixed up and need to be put back together, and the data flows need to be added.

Work with a partner to identify the order of the flowchart boxes. Then redraw the flowchart with the data flows.

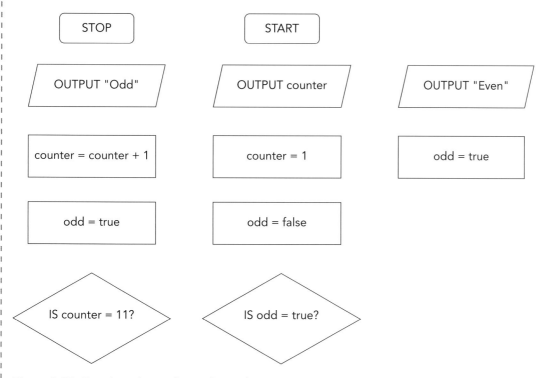

Figure 1.27: Flowchart shapes for unplugged activity

Note: We know the first number is going to be 1 and 1 is equal to odd.
What will the next number be?

Programming task 1.13: Predict, Run, Investigate, Modify and Make

You will need: a pen and paper

This flowchart adds together all the numbers from 1 to the number the user inputs.

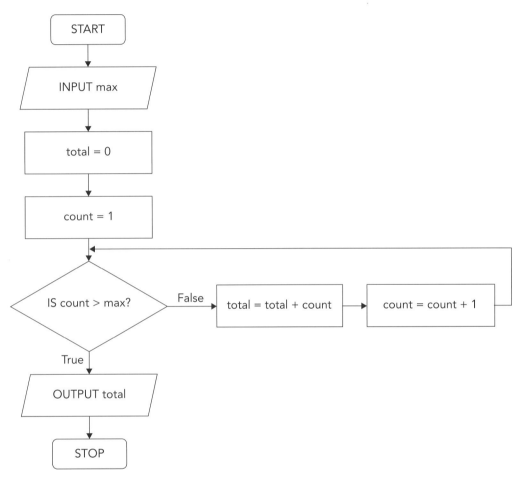

Figure 1.28: Flowchart for programming task

Predict: What will be output when the following values are input:

- 2
- 5
- 8
- 10

Continued

Run: Follow the flowchart with each of the inputs and check whether your predictions were correct.

Investigate:

- Identify the counter variable used in the flowchart.
- Identify the instruction that increases the counter variable.
- Identify the instructions that run before the loop.

Make: Create a flowchart that:

- takes the loop start value as input from the user
- takes the loop end value as input from the user
- adds together and totals all of the numbers from the start value to the end value (including the start and end values).

For example, if the user inputs 10 and 13, the flowchart adds 10 + 11 + 12 + 13 and outputs 46.

Modify: Change the flowchart you have created so the loop will only run when the end value input is larger than the start value input.

For example, if the user inputs the start value of 10 and the end value of 5, the loop will not run.

Programming task 1.14: Predict, Run, Investigate, Modify and Make

You will need: a pen and paper

This flowchart takes ten numbers as input and totals how many were positive (0 or more).

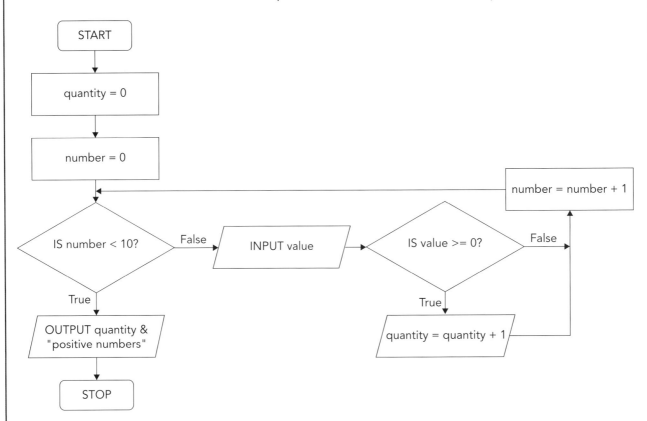

Figure 1.29: Flowchart for programming task

Predict: What will be output when the following sets of numbers are input?

- 10   −1   3   −55   0   0   2   −99   10   80
- −1   −2   −3   −4   0   1   2   3   4   5
- 100   99   98   97   96   95   94   93   92   91
- −10   −9   −8   −7   −6   −5   −4   −3   −2   −1

Run: Follow the flowchart with each of the inputs and check whether your predictions were correct.

Continued

Investigate: Identify the conditions that are used in the flowchart.

Identify which condition is inside the loop.

Modify 1: Change the flowchart so that it outputs how many numbers are greater than 0.

Modify 2: Change the flowchart to allow the user to enter the quantity of numbers they want to input, for example they might want to input 20 numbers instead of 10.

Make: Create a flowchart that:

- takes as input the quantity of numbers the user wants to enter
- totals the number of negative numbers entered (numbers that are less than 0)
- totals the number of numbers greater than 0
- calculates the percentage of numbers that were:
    - less than 0
    - equal to 0
    - greater than 0.

Count-controlled loops in pseudocode

In pseudocode, a count-controlled loop is a FOR loop.
The FOR loop has:

- a counter variable
- a start value for the counter variable
- an end value for the counter variable.

For example, a count-controlled loop that runs 10 times:

```
FOR counter = 0 TO 9
    code that will run in the loop
NEXT counter
```

This pseudocode has the statement `next counter`, which is used to show where the loop ends and that the variable increases.

However, statements that show where the loop ends might not always appear in pseudocode. This algorithm will also run 10 times:

```
FOR counter = 0 TO 9
    code that will run in the loop
```

The important part in a FOR loop is the indentation. If you remember, indentation is where code has extra spaces before it starts on the line. The code inside the loop is indented (it is moved to the right). This shows that the indented code is inside the loop. Code that is not indented is outside the loop, for example:

```
FOR counter = 0 TO 9
    code that will run in the loop
code that is outside the loop
```

To create a count-controlled loop in pseudocode:

1   Write the FOR command with the counter variable and its start value:

```
FOR counter = 1
```

2   Include the end value (this value will run, the loop will stop after it has run):

```
FOR counter = 1 TO 10
```

3   Include the end statement to finish the FOR loop (when used):

```
FOR counter = 1 TO 10


NEXT counter
```

4   Insert the code that will run every time the loop runs:

```
FOR counter = 1 TO 10
    OUTPUT (counter * 2)
NEXT counter
```

Programming task 1.15: Predict, Run, Investigate, Modify and Make

You will need: a pen and paper

This pseudocode algorithm outputs the times table for the number the user inputs:

```
OUTPUT "Enter a number"
INPUT number
FOR counter = 1 TO 10
    answer = number * counter
    OUTPUT answer
NEXT counter
```

Continued

Predict: Identify what you think the output will be when the following numbers are input:

- 1
- 2
- 4
- 5
- 10

Run: Follow the pseudocode with each of the inputs and check whether your predictions were correct.

Investigate: Identify the following features of the algorithm:

- the identifier (name) of the counting variable
- the starting value of the counting variable
- the end value of the counting variable.

Modify: Change the pseudocode algorithm so that it outputs numbers up to 20 times the number the user inputs.

Make: Create a pseudocode algorithm that takes as input a number, then outputs the number multiplied by each number from 100 to 200. For example, if the user enters 2, it first outputs 200 (2 * 100), then 202 (2 * 101), 204 (2 * 102) and so on.

Programming task 1.16: Predict, Run, Investigate, Modify and Make

You will need: a pen and paper

This pseudocode algorithm asks the user to enter the cost of five items. It adds together the values and outputs the total.

```
total = 0
FOR count = 0 TO 4
    OUTPUT "Enter the cost of an item"
    INPUT cost
    total = total + cost
NEXT count
OUTPUT "The total cost is $" & cost
```

Figure 1.30: Receipts show the cost of items

Continued

Predict: Predict what you think the output will be when the following numbers are input:

- 1   2   3   4   5
- 10   10.50   25   15.60   22.89
- 0   0.5   0.75   1   1.5

Run: Follow the pseudocode with each of the inputs and check whether your predictions were correct.

Investigate: Identify the following features of the algorithm:

- the identifier (name) of the counting variable
- the starting value of the counting variable
- the end value of the counting variable.

Modify 1: Change the pseudocode algorithm so that the counting variable starts at 1 but still takes five numbers as input.

Modify 2: Change the pseudocode algorithm so that the user can enter the quantity of numbers they want to enter.

Modify 3: Change the pseudocode algorithm so that the algorithm also calculates and outputs the average cost of the items.

Make: Create a pseudocode algorithm that allows the user to enter the different costs of four items and the quantity of each item. The algorithm calculates and outputs the total cost. For example:

> 10 of item 1 at cost $2
>
> 3 of item 2 at cost $1.50
>
> 1 of item 3 at cost $20
>
> 2 of item 4 at cost $15
>
> The total is (10 * 2) + (3 * 1.50) + (1 * 20) + (2 * 15) = 74.50

Modify 4: Change your pseudocode algorithm to allow the user to enter how many different items they want to enter the quantity and cost of.

In this task, the user was asked to input five items, but the end value of the original code was 4. This is because there are five digits from 0 to 4: 0, 1, 2, 3, 4. There are also five digits from 1 to 5: 1, 2, 3, 4, 5.

When writing count-controlled loops that have a start value of 0, you always need to subtract 1 from the number of times you want the loop to run for the end value. If you don't, your loop will run too many times. For example:

- to run 5 times, start value = 0, end value = 4
- to run 10 times, start value = 0, end value = 9.

Activity 1.3

You will need: a desktop computer, laptop or tablet with word-processing or desktop-publishing software

Work with a partner to create an A4 document that explains the difference between selection and iteration in algorithms.
The document must include an example of a selection algorithm and an iteration algorithm in both flowchart and pseudocode form.

How did you and your partner approach this task? Did you plan it together or did you rely on one of you to make the plans? What was your contribution to the planning?

Did you create new algorithms, or use ones you had already created? Was this the best choice or would you do it a different way next time?

Using sub-routines

You have previously learnt about sub-routines and how to use these in flowcharts.

A **sub-routine** is a self-contained algorithm. It has an identifier (name) and can be **called** from another algorithm using this identifier. Calling a sub-routine means that:

1   the original algorithm stops running its own code
2   the sub-routine runs
3   when the algorithm in the sub-routine finishes, the sub-routine stops and control returns to the algorithm that called it – this algorithm continues from where it called the sub-routine.

Using a sub-routine in a flowchart

A sub-routine in a flowchart starts with the symbol:

Figure 1.31: Sub-routine symbol for flowcharts

The name is written inside, usually with (), for example:

Figure 1.32: Calling a sub-routine (identifiers in the flowchart cannot contain a hyphen (-), so 'sub-routine' will need to be spelt as 'subroutine' in the flowchart)

These brackets show that it is a sub-routine and not a different component. Here is an example sub-routine:

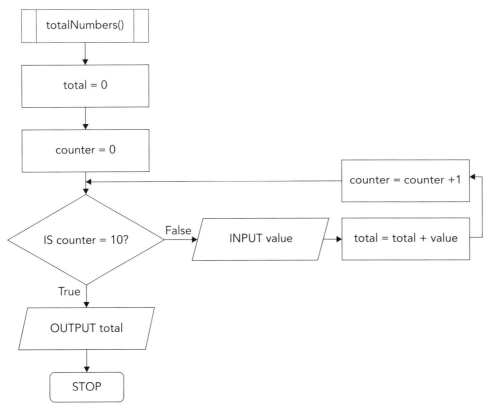

Figure 1.33: Flowchart of a sub-routine

This sub-routine has the identifier `totalNumbers()`. To call `totalNumbers()` in a flowchart, use the same symbol that is used when declaring the sub-routine.

This flowchart calls the sub-routine `totalNumbers()` at the start, and then a second time if the user enters 'yes'.

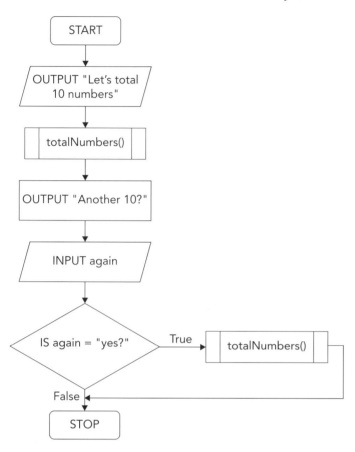

Figure 1.34: Flowchart with a sub-routine included

Programming task 1.17: Predict, Run, Investigate, Modify and Make

You will need: a pen and paper

The sub-routine `correct()` adds 1 to the variable `totalCorrect` and then outputs "Congratulations, that is correct".

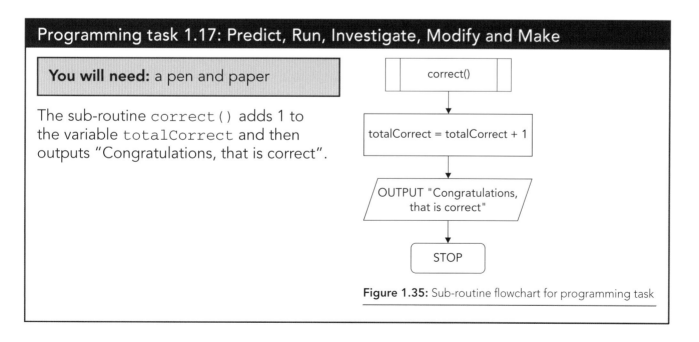

Figure 1.35: Sub-routine flowchart for programming task

Continued

The following flowchart uses the sub-routine `correct()` when the user gets an answer in a quiz correct.

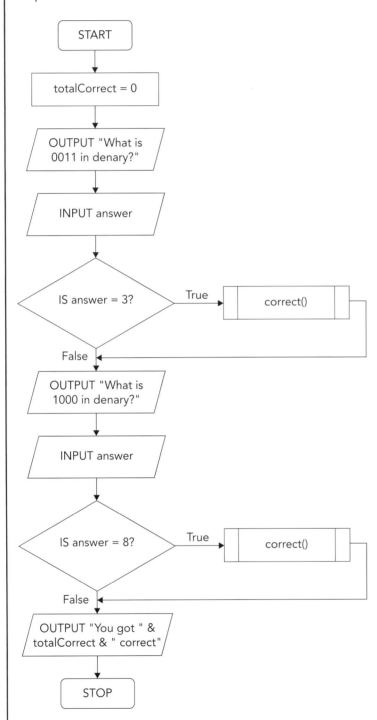

Figure 1.36: Flowchart for programming task

Continued

Predict: Identify what you think the output will be when the following numbers are input:

- 3 8
- 4 8
- 3 6
- 2 5

Run: Follow the flowchart with each of the inputs and check whether your predictions were correct.

Investigate: Identify where the sub-routine is called and the purpose of the sub-routine in this flowchart.

Modify 1: Change the flowchart so that there is a third question and the sub-routine `correct()` is called if the answer is correct.

Modify 2: A second sub-routine is named `incorrect()`. The flowchart for this sub-routine is shown in Figure 1.37.

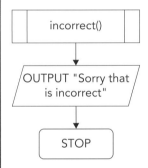

Figure 1.37: Second sub-routine flowchart for programming task

Change your flowchart to call `incorrect()` each time an answer is incorrect.

Make: The sub-routine `colour()` stores a colour.

The sub-routine `shape()` stores a shape.

The sub-routine `mammal()` stores a type of mammal.

The sub-routine `bird()` stores a type of bird.

Continued

The flowcharts for the sub-routines are shown.

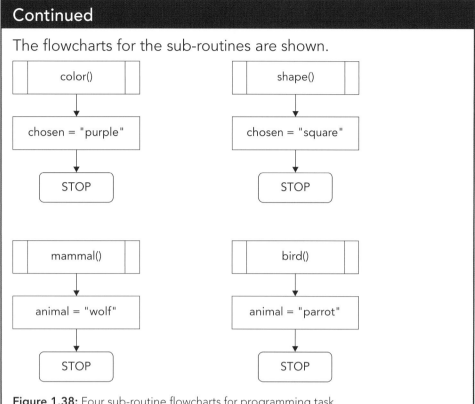

Figure 1.38: Four sub-routine flowcharts for programming task

Create a flowchart that uses the sub-routines to ask the user if they want a shape or a colour, then a mammal or a bird, then outputs the chosen items, for example "purple parrot".

Did you know?

In programming, a sub-routine can be taken out of a program and used elsewhere, for example in another program. If a programmer creates a sub-routine for one program, it will save them rewriting the entire sub-routine again for another program.

Using a sub-routine in pseudocode

In pseudocode, a **key word** is used to identify that a sub-routine is being used. A key word is a word that has a particular meaning in a programming language and cannot be used as an identifier, for example IF, SUB-ROUTINE, FOR.

In this section, we will use the key word SUB-ROUTINE. For example, this pseudocode declares a sub-routine with the identifier mySub:

```
SUB-ROUTINE mySub()
```

The sub-routine will often have an end key word to show where the sub-routine will end. In this section, we will use the key word END SUB.

All pseudocode between SUB-ROUTINE and END SUB is within the sub-routine.

This sub-routine:

- has the identifier adding
- takes two numbers as input

- adds together the two inputs and outputs the total.

```
SUB-ROUTINE adding()
    INPUT number1
    INPUT number2
    total = number1 + number2
    OUTPUT(number1 & "+" & number2 & "=" & total)
END SUB
```

To call a sub-routine from the main code, you use the identifier and the brackets. The word SUB-ROUTINE is not used. For example adding() will call the sub-routine adding.

This pseudocode algorithm calls adding three times.

```
FOR count = 0 TO 2
    adding()
NEXT count
```

Main code (FOR loop)

Calling sub-routine

Main code (FOR loop)

There are different key words for sub-routines. Here are some other ways the sub-routine adding might be written in pseudocode:

1   In this example, the key word SUB-ROUTINE has been replaced with the word PROCEDURE.

```
PROCEDURE adding()
    INPUT number1
    INPUT number2
    total = number1 + number2
    OUTPUT(number1 & "+" & number2 & "=" total)
ENDPROCEDURE
```

2   In this example, sub-routine has been replaced with the word DEF. There is no end key word, so the indentation is used to show where the sub-routine ends.

```
DEF adding():
    INPUT number1
    INPUT number2
    total = number1 + number2
    OUTPUT(number1 & "+" & number2 & "=" total)
```

Did you know?

Some languages have different types of sub-routine called procedures and functions. Some languages just have one type of sub-routine, which they usually call functions. Python only has functions, and it uses the key word def to define each function.

Programming task 1.18: Predict, Run, Investigate, Modify and Make

You will need: a pen and paper

A computer game character has an x position (xCoord) and a y position (yCoord) on the screen. Each position must be between 0 and 1024 (inclusive).

The following pseudocode sub-routine moveRight() adds 1 to the character's x position. If the x position is greater than 1024 it is replaced with 1024.

```
SUB-ROUTINE moveRight()
    xCoord = xCoord + 1
    IF xCoord > 1024 THEN
        xCoord = 1024
    ENDIF
END SUB
```

The following pseudocode algorithm uses the sub-routine moveRight() if the user wants to move to the right.

```
xCoord = 500
yCoord = 450
OUTPUT "Do you want to move right?"
INPUT choice
IF choice = "YES" OR choice = "yes" OR choice = "Yes" THEN
    moveRight()
ENDIF
OUTPUT "New position is x=" & xCoord & " y= " & yCoord
```

Predict: Identify what you think the output will be when 'yes' is entered and when 'no' is entered.

Run: Follow the pseudocode with each of the inputs and check whether your predictions were correct.

Investigate: Identify where the sub-routine is called in the pseudocode algorithm.

Identify the code that runs each time the sub-routine is called.

Continued

Modify 1: The following pseudocode sub-routine subtracts 1 from the character's x position. If the new value is less than 0 it is replaced with 0. The sub-routine is called `moveLeft()`:

```
SUB-ROUTINE moveLeft()
    xCoord = xCoord - 1
    IF xCoord < 0 THEN
        xCoord = 0
    ENDIF
END SUB
```

Change the pseudocode algorithm to ask the user if they want to move left or right, and then call the most appropriate sub-routine.

Modify 2: Change your modified pseudocode algorithm to repeatedly ask the user if they want to move left or right ten times.

Make: The sub-routines `moveUp()` and `moveDown()` change the character's y-coordinate.

The pseudocode for the sub-routines are shown.

```
SUB-ROUTINE moveDown()
    yCoord = yCoord - 1
    IF yCoord < 0 THEN
        yCoord = 0
    ENDIF
END SUB
SUB-ROUTINE moveUp()
    yCoord = yCoord + 1
    IF yCoord > 1024 THEN
        yCoord = 1024
    ENDIF
END SUB
```

Create a pseudocode algorithm that asks the user if they want to move up or down, and then calls the appropriate sub-routine.

Modify 3: Combine your pseudocode algorithms to ask the user 100 times if they want to move up, down, left or right and call the appropriate sub-routine.

Continued

Self-assessment

Give yourself a rating for your problem-solving in this programming task. Number 1 is the highest and means you worked through any errors or problems independently before asking for any help. Number 5 is the lowest and means you asked for help before you tried to solve any problems yourself.

Using a predefined sub-routine

You can either write your own sub-routine, use a **predefined sub-routine** from a program library that you have imported, or use a predefined sub-routine that someone else has written and given to you to copy into your program.

A predefined sub-routine is one that has already been written and tested for you. You already learnt about calling sub-routines and functions from program libraries in Python. To use a predefined sub-routine, you call it in the same way you would if you were using a sub-routine that you had written.

Remember, if you are using a predefined sub-routine from a library, you need to import the library into your code.

Questions 1.4

1   What is a sub-routine?

2   What is the difference between selection and iteration?

3   Create a flowchart that asks a user how many friends they have. It then asks the user to enter the height of each of their friends in centimetres. The flowchart outputs the name of the friend who is the tallest.

    (Think about what inputs you will need.)

4   Create a pseudocode algorithm that asks the user to enter 20 numbers. After each input, the algorithm outputs whether that number is higher than, lower than or equal to the previous one. The first number is compared to the number 0.

5   The sub-routine `wordLength()` calculates the number of
    letters in the string `myWord` and stores this number in the
    variable `myWordLength`.

    (You do not need to create the flowchart `wordLength()`.
    Just assume it exists and call it from your main flowchart.)

    a   Create a flowchart that asks the user to enter 100 words.
        It adds together the number of letters in all the words.
        It then outputs the total and the average number of letters
        in each word.

    b   Create a pseudocode algorithm that asks the user to enter
        100 words. It should calculate and output the word with
        the most letters and the word with the fewest letters.

Summary checklist

- [ ] I can create a count-controlled loop using a flowchart.
- [ ] I can create a count-controlled loop in pseudocode.
- [ ] I can identify the features of a sub-routine in a flowchart.
- [ ] I can identify the features of a sub-routine in pseudocode.
- [ ] I can create a flowchart that calls a sub-routine.
- [ ] I can create a pseudocode algorithm that calls a sub-routine.

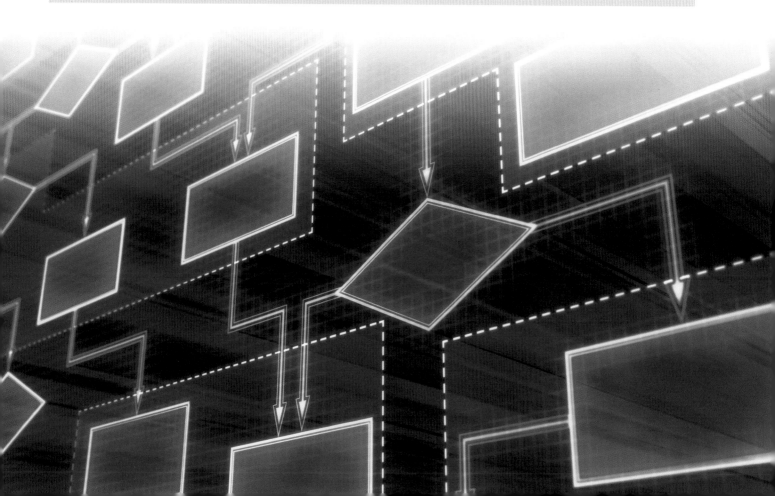

> 1.4 Loops in text-based programming

In this topic you will:

- explore how count-controlled loops are written in Python
- follow algorithms that use count-controlled loops in Python
- change algorithms that use count-controlled loops in Python
- create programs that use count-controlled loops in Python.

Getting started

What do you already know?

- Python is a text-based programming language that you can use to write computer programs.
- Selection statements in Python use the command if. An if statement can have many elif statements and a maximum of one else statement, for example:

```
if(number1 == number2 and number2 == number3):
    print("All numbers are the same")
elif(number1 >= number2 and number1 >= number3):
    print(number1, "is the largest")
elif(number2 >= number3):
    print(number2, "is the largest")
else:
    print(number3, "is the largest")
```

```
@app.route("/")
def home():
    check_db()
    all_books = db.session.query(Book).
    return render_template("index.html",

@app.route("/edit", methods=["GET","POST"])
def edit():

    if request.method == 'POST':
        book_id = request.form["id"]
        book_to_update = Book.query
        book_to_update.rating =
        db.session.commit()
```

Continued

- Indenting is important in Python. The code inside the IF statement is indented. This tells Python which code is inside the IF statement and which is outside.

Now try this!

Copy this Python program into the editor you use, for example IDLE:

```python
value1 = int(input("Enter a number "))
value2 = int(input("Enter a second number "))
choice = input("Enter + or - ")
if choice == "+":
    print(value1, "+", value2, "=", (value1 + value2))
elif choice == "-":
    print(value1, "-", value2, "=", (value1 - value2))
else:
    print("That was not one of the options")
```

Test the program to see what the output is with the following inputs:

3	2	+
10	5	–

Extend the program to also allow the user to select multiplication.

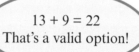

13 + 9 = 22
That's a valid option!

FOR loops in Python

The count-controlled loops in Python are FOR loops. Count-controlled loops use the key word `for`.

There are two different ways that the start and end value can be given in Python.

The FOR IN RANGE loop (type 1)

The first example is the **FOR IN RANGE loop**. Here's an example of the format:

```python
for variable in range(number of loops):
```

If the number of loops is 10, then the variable will start at 0, and run up to and including 9.

This program will output the numbers 0 to 9:

```
for count in range(10):
    print(count)
```

(Note the colon at the end of the first line.)

This program will run and print '0', then go back to the beginning and add 1 to the variable count. Then it will run again, and print '1', and so on until it has run 10 times.

The FOR IN RANGE loop is a specific type of FOR loop in Python where either:

1   the start value and end value are given in brackets after the in-range statement, and the end value is 1 more than the stopping value

or:

2   the number of iterations is given in the brackets after the in-range statement.

This type of loop is useful when you know how many times the loop has to run, and you do not need to set the counter variable as a specific number (for example, to loop between 100 and 200). This is because you cannot control what number the counter variable starts at – it will always start at 0.

Programming task 1.19: Predict, Run, Investigate, Modify and Make

You will need: a pen and paper, a desktop computer, laptop or tablet with an IDE for Python

Read this Python program:

```
for counter in range(20):
    print(counter)
```

Predict: Work with a partner to identify the numbers that you think will be output when this code is run.

Run: Enter the code into a Python IDE and run the code.

Was your prediction correct?

Investigate: What is the name of the counter variable in the program?

If you change this to variable in the first line of code, where else will you need to change it?

Modify 1: Change the algorithm so that it outputs the numbers 0 to 100 (including 100).

Modify 2: Change the algorithm so it outputs the phrase "snap, bang" five times.

Continued

Make: Create a program that will output the numbers 0 to 50, each multiplied by itself. For example:

- 0 * 0 = 0.
- 1 * 1 = 1,

up to:

- 49 * 49 = 2401
- 50 * 50 = 2500.

Self-assessment

Give your first FOR loop program a rating: gold, silver or bronze.

Gold means it worked first time, or you were able to solve your own errors independently.

Silver means it didn't work first time and you needed some hints or support to solve the errors.

Bronze means you needed some help writing the FOR loop and to solve any problems.

Programming task 1.20: Predict, Run, Investigate, Modify and Make

You will need: a pen and paper, a desktop computer, laptop or tablet with an IDE for Python

Read this Python program:

```python
quantity = int(input("How many numbers do you want to output?"))
for count in range(quantity):
    print(count + 1)
```

Predict: Work with a partner to identify the numbers that you think will be output when the number 5 is input.

Run: Enter the code into a Python IDE and run the code.

Was your prediction correct?

Investigate: How does this program change the counter variable so that it does not start by outputting the number 0?

How is the end value of the counter variable set in this program?

Continued

Modify: Change the algorithm so that it outputs the number the user entered multiplied by 10.

For example: if the user enters 5 it will output 1*10 = 10, 2 * 10 = 20, 3 * 10 = 30, 4 * 10 = 40, 5 * 10 = 50.

Make: Create a program that will ask the user to input the quantity of numbers they want to add together.

The program then needs to take this quantity of numbers as input and add them all together.

For example: the user inputs that they want to enter five numbers.

The user then inputs 1 3 6 4 3.

The program adds these numbers together.

Unplugged activity 1.7

Write down a FOR loop for your partner to follow. This must be in the format of Python, but the code inside the FOR loop can make your partner perform actions, for example:

```
for count in range(3):
    shout out the value in count
```

In this example, they will need to shout out 0, then 1, then 2.

You need to check if your partner's actions are correct.

The FOR IN RANGE loop (type 2)

This is a second format that a **FOR IN RANGE** loop can be in:

```
for variable in range(startnumber, endnumber):
```

- start_number is the initial value given to the counter variable.
- end_number is 1 more than the last loop. If the end number is 10, the loop will run when the counter is 9 but not when it is 10.

This program will output the numbers 0 to 9:

```
for count in range(0, 10):
    print(count)
```

This type of loop is useful when you want to set the start and the end value. This might be because you need to use the counter variable inside the loop. For example, you might want the loop to start counting at a number that is not 0, such as 100, and loop until it gets to 200.

Programming task 1.21: Predict, Run, Investigate, Modify and Make

You will need: a pen and paper, a desktop computer, laptop or tablet with an IDE for Python

This Python program should count how many numbers are between the two numbers the user enters (including the two numbers entered).

```python
start = int(input("Enter the start value"))
end = int(input("Enter the end value"))
quantity = 0
for counter in range(start, end + 1):
    quantity = quantity + 1
print("There were", quantity, "numbers")
```

Predict: Work with a partner to identify the output when each of the following sets of inputs are entered:

Input set 1:   1   10

Input set 2:   18   27

Run: Enter the code into a Python IDE and run the code.

Was your prediction correct?

Investigate: Why does the loop end value have a +1 included?

What would happen if the quantity started with the number 0?

Modify: Change the algorithm so that it does not include either of the numbers the user entered.

Make: Create a program that adds together all the numbers between the two numbers a user enters.

In the code in this programming task, the code that was run during the FOR loop was indented. Once the FOR loop had stopped, the program went to the next line, which was:

```python
print("There were", quantity, "numbers")
```

Always be aware of the indentation in Python. Indentation tells the program what is inside a statement or a loop (this bit is indented), and what is the main code (this bit is not indented).

Programming task 1.22: Predict, Run, Investigate, Modify, Make

You will need: a pen and paper, a desktop computer, laptop or tablet with an IDE for Python

This Python program should calculate and output the learner who got the highest score in a test:

```
numberLearners = int(input("How many learners
    are in the class?"))
highestScore = 0
highestLearner = 0
for learner in range(0, numberLearners):
    score = int(input("Enter their score"))
    if score > highestScore:
        highestScore = score
        highestLearner = learner + 1
print("Learner", highestLearner "got the
    highest score of", highestScore)
```

Predict: Work with a partner to identify the output when each of the following data items is input:

5   3   20   9   15   88

Run: Enter the code into a Python IDE and run the code.

Was your prediction correct?

Investigate: Why does the loop counter start with the value 0?

If this was changed to 1, what other changes would need to be made for the program to still work?

Why is 1 added to the content of the variable `learner` when it is assigned to `highestLearner`?

Modify: Change the algorithm so that it also finds and outputs the learner with the highest score and the learner with the lowest score.

Make: Create a program that asks the user to enter the number of different items that they have purchased.

For each item they need to enter the quantity purchased and the cost per item.

The program needs to calculate the total cost of all the items and then output the cost of the item they purchased the most of.

Activity 1.4

> **You will need:** a desktop computer, laptop or tablet with word-processing software

Work with a partner to design and create an A5 help sheet about the different FOR loops in Python. This must include at least one example of each type of FOR loop and show the different outputs produced. This must be concise and printable as an A5 document that you and your partner can use to help you when you are writing FOR loops in the future.

Questions 1.5

1   What is the key word for starting a count-controlled loop in Python?

2   How many times will this loop run?

```
for count in range(10):
```

3   What value will the counter variable start at in this loop?

```
for count in range(35):
```

4   How many times will this loop run?

```
for counter in range(1, 15):
```

5   When will this loop stop running?

```
for count in range(0, 3):
```

6   What will this program output?

```
for counter in range(1, 10):
    print(counter * 2)
```

7   Change the is algorithm to loop 25 times.

```
for count in range(15):
    print(count)
```

8   Change this algorithm to output the total of the values the user inputs within the loop.

```
for quantity in range(0, 5):
    number = int(input("Enter a number"))
```

9   Create a Python program to take 20 numbers as input from the user and output the average, the smallest number and the largest number input.

Common errors

You might have already had some errors when writing your programs, or you might not have had any yet. It is OK for programs to have errors. Even the best programmers make errors all the time.

How you find and correct the errors is how you learn to program.

Each line of code in Table 1.2 has an error.

Code	Error	Correction
`for counter = 0 to 10:`	Python needs the command words 'in range'.	`for counter `**`in range`**`(0, 10):`
`FOR counter in range(10):`	The command word must be in lowercase.	**`for`**` counter in range(10):`
`for counter in range(10, 0):`	The numbers in the brackets are in the wrong order, the start value comes first.	`for counter in range`**`(0, 10):`**
`for count in range(1, 10):`	This was intended to loop 10 times. It will not loop when `count` is 10.	`for count in range(1, `**`11):`**
`for count in range(10):` `print(count)`	The output line in the loop is not indented.	`for count in range(10):` **`print`**`(count)`

`for count in range(10)`
    `print(count)`
	The colon was missed out at the end of the `for in range` line.	`for count in range`**`(10):`**
		    `print(count)`

Table 1.2: Errors in code

Summary checklist

☐ I can describe how count-controlled loops are written in Python.
☐ I can follow algorithms that use count-controlled loops in Python.
☐ I can change algorithms that use count-controlled loops in Python.
☐ I can create programs that use count-controlled loops in Python.

> 1.5 Programming with data

In this topic you will:

- learn about the character data type
- explore string functions
- learn about the purpose of arrays
- learn how arrays are used to store multiple data items
- explore how lists can be used as arrays in a text-based programming language
- access data from a one-dimensional list.

Key words

append()
array
Boolean
casting
character
data structure
index
integer
len()
list
lower()
nesting
real
string
upper()

Getting started

What do you already know?

- A variable is a space in memory, with an identifier (name) where you can store a value. You can access that value, change it and delete it.

  When you assign data to a variable, you use an assignment statement, for example:

  ```
  newVariable = 10
  ```

  This variable has the identifier newVariable, it is assigned the number 10.

  Variables can be used in sequence statements, for example to access the data or change it.

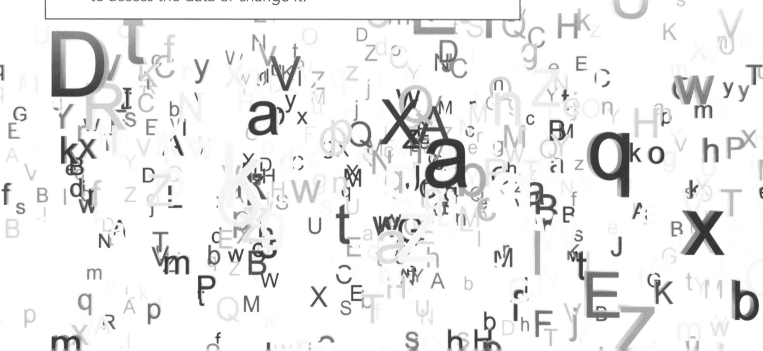

Continued

- Programming constructs are the main tools used in writing programs. The three main constructs are: sequence, selection and iteration.

- In programming, the selection construct is an IF statement: A condition is tested and if it is true the code within the IF statement runs. If it is false there could be an ELSEIF statement to check another condition. There can be many ELSEIFs but only a maximum of one ELSE at the end.

- Iteration is another construct. Iteration is a loop where code will run multiple times. A count-controlled loop uses a counter variable to count how many times the loop has run. The code inside the loop runs until the counter variable reaches the end condition.

- When you store data in a computer you often need to identify what type of data it is.

Now try this!

Open a program that you have written in Python, or an algorithm you have written in pseudocode.

Identify any data that is being stored in the program or algorithm. Discuss with a partner what type of data each of these data items is.

Data type

A computer needs to know the type of data that is being used, for example if it is a number or a word. You have already been introduced to the data types integer, real, string and Boolean.

Use Table 1.3 to remind yourself about these data types.

Data type	Description	Example
integer	a whole number	0, 22, 34, 998
real	a number with a decimal	0.0, 1.25, 33.598
string	one or more letters, numbers and symbols	"hello", "001", "22.1!!"
Boolean	either True or False	True, False, TRUE, FALSE

Table 1.3: Data types

Character data type

You should already know that a **string** is one or more characters. These characters can be:

- letters, for example H or h
- numbers, for example 1 2 or 0
- symbols, for example # . or ?

The character data type stores only one character, no more.

Any data stored as the **character** data type needs to be in quotation marks. Some programming languages prefer character data to use single quotation marks, for example 'h' instead of "h". This shows that it is different from a string. However, in many of these languages, "h" with double quotation marks will still work.

Unplugged activity 1.8

You will need: a pen and paper

Work individually to group these items of data in the table into integers, real, string, Boolean and character data types. Select the most appropriate data type for each item of data – some items could be stored as multiple data types.

22	13.52	'p'	false
FALSE	"purple"	True	1.1
'!'	TRUE	'1'	"pop"
"hello"	888	"no"	999985
13.0	"1 2 3"	true	"YES"

When you have finished, compare your answer with a partner. Did you decide on the same data type for each item of data? Are there any that could be more than one type of data?

Characters in Python

Python does not have a character data type. Python only uses strings. If you want to convert data to a character, you convert it to a string data type.

In Python, it is best practice to use the single quotation mark (') for any single character. Double quotation marks (") are usually only used for more than one character in a string. However, this is not compulsory.

Converting data types

You will have previously learnt about **casting**. These are some examples of data types you can convert:

> Remember, casting converts data from one data type to another!

Integer:

To convert a value to an integer, we use the command `int()`.

Converting a string to an integer:

In this example, we will start with "123" as a string. This means it is the character 1, the character 2 and the character 3 combined into one string. It is not the number 123 (one hundred and twenty-three).

```
myInteger = int("123")
```

The double quotation marks in this example identify "123" as a string.

However, when the program runs, it will store the integer 123 (one hundred and twenty-three) in the variable `myInteger`.

Converting a real number to an integer:

The number 123.1 is a real number because it has a decimal.

```
myInteger = int(123.1)
```

When the program runs it will store the integer 123 in the variable `myInteger`. The decimal is removed to turn it into an integer.

(Note that Python removes the decimal rather than rounding up or rounding down, so:

- 123.1 will become 123
- 123.9 will also become 123. It will not become 124.)

Real:

To convert a value to a real number, we use the command `float()`.

Converting a string to a real number:

The double quotation marks in this example show that 123.255 is a string. It is made up of the characters for each digit.

```
myReal = float("123.255")
```

When the program runs it will store the real number 123.255 in the variable `myReal`.

Converting an integer to a real number:

The number 123 is an integer because it does not have a decimal point.

```
myReal = float(123)
```

When the program runs it will store the real number 123.0 in the variable `myReal`. The integer is given a decimal point and the number 0 after the decimal point because there is no decimal value.

Boolean:

To convert a value to a Boolean, we use the command `bool()`.

Converting a string to a Boolean:

The string "True" has double quotation marks because it is a string, and each character value is stored: first the character 'T', then 'r', then 'u', then 'e'.

```
myBoolean = bool("True")
```

When the program runs, it will store Boolean value True in the variable `myBoolean`.

All strings apart from "False" will be converted to True.

Converting an integer to a Boolean:

```
myBoolean = bool(1)
```

The integer 1 is converted into Boolean True.

If the number was a 0 it would be converted into Boolean False.

All numbers apart from 0 will be converted to True.

String:

To convert a value to a string, the command `str()` is used:

Converting a real number to a string:

The number 256.58 is a real number because it has a decimal.

```
myString = str(256.58)
```

When the program runs, 256.58 is converted to a string.
The characters "256.58" will be stored in `myString`.
This means the characters '2', '5', '6', '.', '5' and '8' are combined into one string.

Converting an integer to a string:

The number 123 is an integer because it is a whole number without a decimal.

```
myString = str(123)
```

When the program runs, 123 is converted to a string.
The characters "123" will be stored in `myString`.

To convert to	Command	Examples
integer	int()	myInteger = int("123") myInteger = int(123.1)
real	float()	myReal = float("123.255") myReal = float(123)
Boolean	bool()	myBoolean = bool("True") myBoolean = bool(1)
string	str()	myString = str(256.58) myString = str(123)

Table 1.4: Commands to convert data types

Strings

You have already learnt how strings are used to store one or more characters. There are lots of ways that you access and change strings. These are commonly known as string manipulation functions.

In this topic, you will learn how to access specific characters in a string, how to find the length of a string and how to convert a string between lowercase and uppercase.

Accessing one character in a string

In Python, you might need to access one character from a string.

The first character in a string is in position 0. The second character in a string is in position 1.

Consider this string: "Education"

Position	0	1	2	3	4	5	6	7	8
Character	E	d	u	c	a	t	i	o	n

Table 1.5: The word 'Education' and the position of its letters

The character in position 0 is 'E'. The character in position 1 is 'd'.

To access a character, first you need to make sure the data is a string, for example "123" and not the integer 123. You do this by casting the data.

    myString = str(256.58)

This will give you the string "256.58".

The first character in a string is in position 0. The second character in a string is in position 1.

Position	0	1	2	3	4	5
Character	2	5	6	.	5	8

Table 1.6: String containing '256.58'

The character in position 0 is '2'. The character in position 1 is '5', and so on.

To access the first character from a string, use the command `[0]` after the identifier. For example, `myString[0]` will access the first character in the string stored in `myString`. It is important that these are square brackets, and the number 0 is included (not the letter o). For example, see how it works for these two numbers:

- 256.58, which is a real number
- 123, which is an integer.

```
myString = str(256.58)
```

> The real number 256.58 is cast as a string and stored in the variable `myString`.

```
myString = myString[0]
```

> The first character stored in the string "256.58" is accessed and stored in `myString`. `[0]` accesses the first character, so "2" is stored in `myString`.

```
mySecondCharacter = str(123)
```

> The integer 123 is cast as a string and stored in `mySecondCharacter`.

```
mySecondCharacter = mySecondCharacter[1]
```

> The second character in the string "123" is accessed and stored in `mySecondCharacter`. `[1]` accesses the second character, so "2" is stored in `mySecondCharacter`.

Programming task 1.23: Predict, Run, Investigate, Modify and Make

You will need: a pen and paper, a desktop computer, laptop or tablet with an IDE for Python

Read this Python program:

```
data1 = 123
data2 = "12.34"
data3 = 123.4
data4 = True
print(data1, "is an integer")
print(data2, "is a string")
print(data3, "is a real number")
print(data4, "is a Boolean")
```

Predict: Work with a partner to identify the output from this program.

Run: Enter the code into a Python IDE and run the code.

Was your prediction correct?

Investigate: Identify the identifier of each variable in the program and the data type of the data in each variable.

Modify 1: Change the algorithm to:

- convert data1 to a string, then output that this data is a string
- convert the string in data1 to a character (accessing the first character), then output that character.

Modify 2: Continuing Modify 1, change the algorithm to convert data2, data3 and data4 to characters and output their first characters in a suitable message.

Make: Create a program that asks the user to enter a word.

Convert their word to a character and output the character.

You can access other characters in the same way. You just need to change the number in the brackets.

Table 1.7 shows a string and the numeric position of each character.

0	1	2	3	4	5	6	7	8	9	10	11
H	e	l	l	o		w	o	r	l	d	!

Table 1.7: String containing 'Hello world!'

Unplugged activity 1.9

You will need: a pen and paper

You will need to work individually and then with a partner for this activity.

The string "Twinkle twinkle little star how I wonder what you are" is stored in a variable.

Write down the character that will be accessed in each of these positions:

0   1   5   7   10   11   24   42   53

Work with a partner to compare your answers. If you have any differences, work out which answer is correct.

In Python, the character number is placed in square brackets after the string, or the variable containing the string. For example, this statement will output the first character in the variable `word`:

```python
print(word[0])
```

This statement will output the second character in the string "Hello":

```python
print("Hello"[1])
```

Programming task 1.24: Predict, Run, Investigate, Modify and Make

You will need: a pen and paper, a desktop computer, laptop or tablet with an IDE for Python

Read this Python program:

```python
firstName = input("What is your first name?")
colour = input("What is your favourite colour?")
newName = firstName[0] + firstName[1] + firstName[2] +
    colour[0] + colour[1] + colour[2]
print("Your new name is", newName)
```

Predict: Write down what the output will be when you enter your first name and your favourite colour.

Run: Enter the code into a Python IDE and run the code.

Was your prediction correct?

My favourite colour is purple. That makes my new name Arupur!

Continued

Investigate: What is the identifier of the variable where your name is stored?

How many characters are accessed from your first name?

Which character is first accessed from the colour input?

Modify: Change the algorithm to only generate the new name when both the first name and colour are three or more letters long.

Make: Create a program that generates a username for a user.

The username is the first two characters from the user's first name, followed by the first three characters from their second name and lastly followed by their year of birth.

Length

A string can have any number of characters from 0 upwards. If your program asks a user to enter a string, you don't know how many characters they will enter. You might need to know this for your program. Some reasons you might need to know this include:

- you might need to access the first 10 characters
- you might need to stop them entering an invalid option
- you might need to make sure they have actually entered something.

Programming languages have a built-in length function that calculates and returns the length of a string.

In Python, this function is `len()`.

The string you are finding the length of goes inside the brackets.
For example:

```
len("Hello")
```

This will return 5 because there are five characters in "Hello".

It is important to remember that a space is also a character.
For example:

```
len("Hello world")
```

This will return 11. "Hello" has 5 characters, "world" has 5 characters and the space is 1 character. So that means that the total characters = 11.

A variable can also be sent to the function `len()`.

This program stores a string in a variable, then uses `len()` to identify the number of characters in the string and output this value.

```
word1 = "my string"
```

> The characters "my string" are stored in the variable `word1`.

```
length = len(word1)
```

> The variable `word1` is sent to the function `len()`.
> `len()` returns the number of characters in "my string", which is 9.
> This number, 9, is now stored in the variable `length`.

```
print(length)
```

> The data stored in the variable `length` is output. This is 9.

Unplugged activity 1.10

You will need to work individually for this task and then with a partner.

Individually, identify the value that will be returned by the function call `len()` for each of these strings:

```
"hi!"
"I am a computer"
"Purple is a great colour"
"Cockatiels are cute birds"
"Sleep sleep time :)"
```

Now, find a partner and compare your answers.

Did you know?

There are limits to the data you can store in programs, but some of these limits are so large that it is very unlikely you will ever store that much data in one variable.

In Python, you can store approximately 2 billion characters in a string variable!

On average a book has around 55,000 words. If each word is on average 6 letters long, that is 330,000 characters. Each word has a space after it, which is a character, so that's another 55,000 = 385,000. There are other characters and numbers in a book, but even with these that is not even nearly 2 billion! So, one string variable can store an entire book.

Figure 1.39: There are about 400,000 characters in an average book

Programming task 1.25: Predict, Run, Investigate, Modify and Make

You will need: a pen and paper, a desktop computer, laptop or tablet with an IDE for Python

Read this Python program:

```python
message = input("Enter a message ")
numberChars = len(message)
print("You entered", numberChars, "characters")
```

Predict: Work with a partner to identify the output from this program when "today is a day" is input.

Run: Enter the code into a Python IDE and run the code.

Was your prediction correct?

Investigate: Identify the function that calculates the length of the string.

Identify the identifier of the variable that stores the string.

Identify the identifier of the variable that stores the number of characters in the string.

Modify: Change the algorithm to output a message if the input is more than ten characters, and a different message if the input is ten characters or less.

Make: Create a program that asks the user to enter six characters. Output:

- a message if they entered a word with six characters
- a message telling them there were not enough if they entered less than six
- a message telling them they entered too many characters if they entered more than six.

Programming task 1.26: Predict, Run, Investigate, Modify and Make

You will need: a pen and paper, a desktop computer, laptop or tablet with an IDE for Python

Read this Python program:

```python
message = input("Enter a message")
for count in range(0, len(message)):
    print(message[count])
```

Predict: What will be output when the input "Sunday" is entered?

Run: Enter the code into a Python IDE and run the code.

Was your prediction correct?

Investigate: What is the starting value of the loop counter?

What sets the end value of the loop counter?

What is the purpose of this algorithm?

Modify: Change the algorithm to check each character one at a time and count how many are lowercase vowels (a, e, i, o or u).

Hint: Characters can be compared in the same way that strings can be compared. For example:

```python
letter1 = "p"
if letter1 == "p":
    print("Yes it is p")
else:
    print("No it is not p")
```

Make: Create a program that asks the user to enter a password. Count how many of the characters are numbers and output an error message if none of the characters are numbers.

Uppercase and lowercase

You have previously learnt that in programming languages, uppercase and lowercase letters have different values. This means that 'H' does not equal 'h'. This can cause a problem when you don't know how the user will input a word, for example 'yes' or 'Yes' or 'YES'. A common way of solving this is to convert the input to uppercase, or to lowercase.

In Python, the function `.upper()` converts the string before the full stop to uppercase.

In this example, the code will return "YES" and store this in the variable `word`:

```
word = "Yes".upper()
```

In this example, the code will return "NO" and store this in the variable `answer`:

```
answer = "No".upper()
```

As with the function len(), you can also use a variable with upper(). In this example the code will return the contents of the variable `word` ("hello") in uppercase ("HELLO") and store this in the variable `answer`:

```
word = "hello"
answer = word.upper()
```

In Python, the function `.lower()` converts the string before the full stop to lowercase.

In this example, the code will return "yes" and store this in the variable `wordLower`:

```
wordLower = "YES".lower()
```

In this example, the code will return "no" and store this in the variable `answerLower`:

```
answerLower = "No".lower()
```

In this example, the code will return the contents of the variable `word` ("Hello") in lowercase ("hello") and store this in the variable `answer`:

```
word = "Hello"
answer = word.lower()
```

Both `lower()` and `upper()` only change letters, they will not change numbers or symbols.

Unplugged activity 1.11

You will need: a pen and paper

You will need to work with a partner for this activity.

Work with your partner to discuss and then write down the value that will be returned from each of these function calls.

```
"hello".lower()          "hello".upper()
"Goodbye".lower()        "Goodbye".upper()
"GOODNIGHT".lower()      "GOODNIGHT".upper()
```

Programming task 1.27: Predict, Run, Investigate, Modify and Make

You will need: a pen and paper, a desktop computer, laptop or tablet with an IDE for Python

Read this Python program:

```python
answer = input("Which animal neighs?")
answer = answer.lower()
if answer == "horse":
    print("Correct")
else:
    print("No, it's a horse")
```

Predict: What will be output when each of these inputs are entered:

Horse

horse

HORSE

bird

BIRD

Run: Enter the code into a Python IDE and run the code.

Was your prediction correct?

Continued

Investigate: Identify the function that changes the case of the string.

What is the purpose of changing the case of the string in this program?

Modify: Ponies can also neigh. Change the algorithm to also accept 'pony' as a correct answer.

Make: A player has an x-coordinate and a y-coordinate on a grid.

Create a program that asks the user which direction they would like to move: up, down, left or right.

If they enter 'up' increase the y-coordinate by 1.

If they enter 'down' decrease the y-coordinate by 1.

If they enter 'right' increase the x-coordinate by 1.

If they enter 'left' decrease the x-coordinate by 1.

The user must be able to enter the direction in any case, for example 'LEFT' or 'left' or 'LeFt'.

Activity 1.5

You will need: a desktop computer, laptop or tablet with internet access and word-processing software

Working individually, create an electronic document that shows how to use the different string manipulation functions. You should include: `len()`, `upper()`, `lower()` and accessing a single character using `[]`.

Use a web browser to search for one more Python string manipulation function. Investigate how to use it and include it in your document.

Questions 1.6

1   What is the most suitable data type for each item of data in the table?

Data	Data type
22	
13.8	
True	
*	
"Hi"	

2   Why is "green" not a character data type?

3   Why can "$" be stored as a character and a string data type?

4   What does the function `len()` return in Python?

5   What will be stored in `newVariable` after this Python code runs?

```
newVariable = len("Flower")
```

6   What will be stored in `second` after this Python code runs?

```
second = "no".upper()
```

7   What will be stored in `second` after this Python code runs?

```
second = "Let's go!"
second = second.lower()
```

Arrays

A variable has one identifier and can store one item of data.
For example:

- one integer value: 1, 10 or 5203
- one real number: 1.2, 3.14, 123.456
- or one string: "a", "hello" or "the sun has got his hat on".

In some programs, there might be a lot of different items of data to store. If each of these needed to be stored, they would each need their own variable, each with its own unique identifier. Then every time you wanted to access the data, you would need to know which identifier to use. This could end up with you having thousands of identifiers to remember in a program, which could get very complicated.

This is where an **array** is used. An array is a **data structure** that can store multiple items of data, all with the same identifier.

You can think of an array as a row of boxes. Each box stores a different data item. The array in Table 1.8 has the identifier `myArray`.

10	11	5	3	8	66	999	125

Table 1.8: An array

An array can only store data of the same type. If it stores integers, it can only store integers – you cannot store "Hello" in one of the boxes.

An array has an **index**. This is a number that represents the data item you are accessing. The first box, or element, in the array is index 0. The second element is index 1. This is the same as when you access a character in a string.

In this book we will always start at index 0. Many programming languages start with 0 as the first number. Some languages might start with 1 as the first number and some languages let you choose which you want to start with. When you start learning a different text-based language, make sure you check whether it starts counting at 0 or at 1.

Table 1.10 shows the same array, `myArray`, as before. This time the index is above each element.

Index	0	1	2	3	4	5	6	7
Data	10	11	5	3	8	66	999	125

Table 1.10: An array with an index

Unplugged activity 1.12

1   Work with a partner to find the following index numbers from `myArray` in Table 1.10 and identify the data that each one holds:

index 0

index 3

index 7

2   Work with your partner to identify the result when the data in each given index is added together. The first one is done for you.

Example: index 2 + index 7 = 5 + 125 = 130

a   index 0 + index 1

b   index 5 + index 2

c   index 7 + index 6

Using arrays in Python

An array is only one type of data structure. Python does not have a built-in array data structure. It has a different data structure called a **list** that can be used instead.

A list has similarities to and differences from an array.

Similarities	Differences
They can both store many data items with one identifier.	When you create an array, you need to state how many items it can store.
	When you create a list you do not need to state how many items it can store.
They both store data in an index starting with 0.	The size of an array is fixed, if it has ten elements then it always has ten elements.
	The size of a list can change. It can start with 0 items then you can add or remove an item and the size will change.
They both have brackets after the identifier to put the index in that you want to access.	
They can both have data accessed from them using an index.	
Data can be stored in both of them using an index.	

Table 1.11: Similarities and differences between a list and an array

In this unit, we will be using lists in Python to represent an array. However, we will keep the array rules, such as the rule that the list can only store data of one data type. (Python will not produce an error, though, if you try to use data of different types.)

Accessing data in an array

Each index in an array is identified using brackets. Some languages use round brackets ( ) and some languages use square brackets [ ]. In this section, we will use [ ] because this is what you will use in Python.

Here's an example:

```
myArray[0]
```

This will access the data in the array `myArray` in index 0. If you look at Table 1.10, this is the data value 10.

This statement can be used like a variable. For example, you can output it:

```
print(myArray[0])
```

You can store it in another variable, for example:

```
theData = myArray[0]
```

Unplugged activity 1.13

You will need: ten small pieces of paper

Work with a partner for this activity.

Write an index (0 to 9) on one side of each piece of paper and then write an action (for example, jump, or sit down, or sing a song) on the other side.

Place the pieces of paper so the index is facing up and they are in order with 0 on the left all the way to 9 on the right.

Give your set of paper pieces a name, for example myActions. This is your array of actions.

Give your partner instructions to access specific elements in the array. For example, you could say:

myActions index 1.

Then your partner will find index 1, turn the paper over and perform the action before turning the paper back over. Take it in turns.

Swap your array with another pair without seeing what their actions are. Repeat the same activity by giving your partner instructions to access elements in the new array. Take it in turns.

Storing data in an array

You do not need to store data in an array or a list at this stage. However, you will see this code in some Python programs so it is good practice to recognise the code even though you will not need to write it yourself.

In Python, a list first needs to be declared as a list. This is an assignment statement. You should already know that an assignment statement has:

*   the destination on the left (the identifier),
*   followed by an assignment symbol (= or ← in pseudocode)
*   the data to be stored on the right.

In this case, the data to be stored is an empty list, which is written as `[]`
For example, this code declares a new list named `array1`:

```
array1 = []
```

This creates an empty list.

An array can be created with multiple data items already within it. For example, this statement creates an array (list) with five elements:

*   index 0 stores 1
*   index 1 stores 2
*   and so on.

```
array1 = [1,2,3,4,5]
```

Data can also be stored to an individual element, for example this code will store the number 10 in index 0:

```
array1[0] = 10
```

It is important that you make sure that a specific index is created before you try to use it. In a list, you can only store data in a specific index if that index already exists in the list. For example, you can only store data in index 5 if index 5 exists.

Example

Marcus has a list that stores five numbers: 3, 1, 4, 1, 5

Index	0	1	2	3	4
Data	3	1	4	1	5

Table 1.12: An array with five numbers

However, he now wants the list to store six numbers: 3, 1, 4, 1, 5, 9

He can't do this because there is no index 5 for him to store the number 9 in.

This is important because, in Python, a list can be created with 0 elements. (If an array is created in a different programming language, it is created with a set number of elements.)

For example, in this program an error will be produced:

```
myListArray = []
myListArray[0] = 100
```

The second line is trying to store the number 100 in index 0. However, this list is empty and so there is no index 0 to store anything in. Instead in Python the `.append()` function can be used. Append means to add onto the end. In this program the number 100 is added onto the end of the list:

```
myListArray = []
myListArray.append(100)
```

`myListArray = []`	This line creates a list with 0 elements.
`myListArray.append(100)`	This line adds the number 100 onto the end of the list. This means that one more element is created, and the number 100 is added to it.

Table 1.13: Creating a list and adding to the list

The array now has 1 element, index 0, which stores 100.

We can put some more appends in:

```
myListArray = []
myListArray.append(100)
myListArray.append(3)
myListArray.append(2)
```

So I could write `myListArray.append(9)` and I would have 3, 1, 4, 1, 5, 9

Thinking of the list as a row of boxes, it will now look like Table 1.14.

Index	0	1	2
Data	100	3	2

Table 1.14: Updated `myListArray`

Unplugged activity 1.14

You will need: ten small pieces of paper

Work with a partner for this activity.

Write an index (0 to 9) on one side of each piece of paper and the number 0 on the other side of each piece of paper.

Take it in turns to tell each other an index number and a data item to store an integer within, for example 'store 10 in index 1'. The piece of paper for that index needs to be turned over, the current data crossed out and the new data written in its place.

This is an array, so remember that the data must be of the same type. You cannot insert a string into an array of integers.

Programming task 1.28: Predict, Run, Investigate, Modify and Make

You will need: a pen and paper, a desktop computer, laptop or tablet with an IDE for Python

Read this Python program:

```python
myArray = [1,2,3,4]
print(myArray[0])
print(myArray[1])
print(myArray[2])
print(myArray[3])
```

Predict: What will be output from this program?

Run: Enter the code into a Python IDE and run the code.

Was your prediction correct?

Investigate: What is the identifier of the list?

Which line stores data into the list?

Which index is output in each statement?

Modify: Change the algorithm to add together the four numbers within the list and output the total.

Make: Create a program to output the colours of the rainbow in order. For this program, use this order: red, orange, yellow, green, blue, indigo, violet.

Use this statement as the first line of your program to declare the array with the string values for each colour:

```python
stringArray = ["Indigo", "Yellow", "Orange", "Green", "Blue",
    "Red", "Violet"]
```

Looping through an array

One useful feature of an array is that it has one identifier that can be used to access lots of different values. These values are accessed by the index, which is a number that increases by 1 for each element.

The `for variable in range` loop

In a count-controlled loop, a counter variable is increased by 1 each time through the loop. This counter variable can be used to access the index.

Let's look at an example:

```
myData = [10, 20, 30, 40]
for count in range(0, 4):
    print(myData[count])
```

In this Python program, there is a list with four items:

```
myData = [10, 20, 30, 40]
```

The first item is index 0 (10), then 1 (20), then 2 (30) and finally index 3 (40).

The loop starts with 0 and then ends with 3:

```
for count in range(0, 4):
```

> **Note:** Remember in Python the second number (4) is always 1 larger than the last loop counter.

The first time through the loop `count` is 0, then 1, then 2, then finally 3. This matches the array's index.

The code inside the loop outputs the data at the variable counter index.

On the first loop `count` is 0, so the data in index 0 is output.

Then `count` is 1, so the data in index 1 is output.

Then `count` is 2, so the data in index 2 is output.

Then `count` is 3, so the data in index 3 is output.

Then `count` is 4 and it stops.

The `for variable in array` loop

Python has a second type of count-controlled loop that is useful when using arrays. Instead of writing how many times the loop should run, you can tell it to run for every element in the array. This is what the code looks like:

```
for variable in array:
```

The *array* slot is where the identifier of your array goes, and *variable* is where the data from each element in turn will be stored. Here's an example to walk through:

```
myData = [10, 5, 3]
for item in myData:
    print(item)
```

The array has the identifier `myData`:

```
myData = [10, 5, 3]
```

The `for` loop uses the variable `item`:

```
for item in myData:
```

The first time through the loop, `item` stores the data in index 0. This is the number 10.

The second time through the loop, `item` stores the data in index 1. This is the number 5.

The third time through the loop, `item` stores the data in index 2. This is the number 3.

The program outputs the data in the variable `item`. So this program outputs 10, then 5, then 3.

```
print(item)
```

Both loops are correct and either can be used. Sometimes it depends on what you need. If every item needs to be looked at or used, then looping through each item might be easier. If you need to start part way through an array, for example miss a few elements, then it might be easier to use the `in range()` version.

In the next programming tasks, there is an IF statement inside a FOR statement. Putting one programming construct inside another is called **nesting**.

A nested statement is a programming construct, for example a loop or selection statement, that starts and ends inside another programming construct. In this case, there is an IF statement inside a FOR loop. One statement is nested inside the other statement. This means that there are two instances of indentation:

```
for count in range(0, 10):              } FOR statement
    if dataCheck[count] < smallest:     }
        smallest = dataCheck[count]     } } IF statement
    print("The smallest number is", smallest)
```

The statements will run the usual way.

Programming task 1.29: Predict, Run, Investigate, Modify and Make

You will need: a pen and paper, a desktop computer, laptop or tablet with an IDE for Python

Read this Python program:

```
numberArray = [10, 5, 1, 8, 6, 3, 5, 10]
total = 0
for counter in range(0, 8):
    total = total + numberArray[counter]
print("The total is", total)
```

Predict: What will be output from this program?

Run: Enter the code into a Python IDE and run the code.

Was your prediction correct?

Investigate: How many elements are in the array?

What is the index of the last item in the array?

What number does the counter variable start at?

Why does the counter variable end at 8?

How is the counter variable used within the loop?

Modify 1: Change the algorithm to multiply all of the numbers together and output the result.

Modify 2: Change the algorithm to use the alternative FOR loop structure instead of in range().

Make: Use this statement to declare the array theData with the following data:

```
theData = [22.0, 15.2, 99.5, 12.3, -11.1, 2.05, -1.5, 888.9]
```

Create a program that uses a loop to access each array element and adds together all the positive numbers (0 or greater).

Programming task 1.30: Predict, Run, Investigate, Modify and Make

You will need: a pen and paper, a desktop computer, laptop or tablet with an IDE for Python

Read this Python program:

```
dataCheck = [8, 9, 10, 55, 62, 41, 5, 36, 98, 7]
smallest = 9999
for count in range(0, 10):
    if dataCheck[count] < smallest:
        smallest = dataCheck[count]
print("The smallest number is", smallest)
```

Predict: What will be output from this program?

Run: Enter the code into a Python IDE and run the code.

Was your prediction correct?

Investigate: How many elements are in the array `dataCheck`?

What is the identifier of the counter variable in the loop?

How many times will the loop run?

Which line of code accesses the data in the array?

Modify: Change the algorithm to also find the largest number in the array and output this value at the end of the program.

Make: Use this statement to declare the array `myIntegers` with the following data:

```
myIntegers = [9, 5, 8, 4, 2, 3, 7, 5, 6, 1, 3, 8]
```

Create a program that first calculates the average (mean) value in the array, then counts and outputs how many data items are above the average and how many are below the average.

You will need two loops for this program, the first to find the average and the second to count the values.

How did you approach writing the programs in this topic? Did you revisit past programs or those provided in the text to help you? How can you use past programs to help you write programs in the future?

Questions 1.7

1   What is an array?

2   What is an array index?

3   Which index is the first element in an array?

4   Why can't this data all be stored in the same array?
    "hello"   20   "no"   True

5   What will this program output?

```
myArray = ["plants", "like", "I", "growing"]
print(myArray[2], myArray[1], myArray[3], myArray[0])
```

6   What will this program output?

```
theData = [1, 2, 3, 4, 5, 6, 7, 8]
total = 0
for counter in range(0, 5):
    total = total + theData[counter]
print(total)
```

Common errors

You might have already had some errors when writing your programs, or you might not have had any yet. It is OK for programs to have errors – even the best programmers make errors all the time. How you find and correct the errors is how you learn to program.

Each line of code in Table 1.15 has an error.

Code	Error	Correction
`"Hello".len()`	The string needs to be inside the brackets.	`len("Hello")`
`length("No")`	The function is `len()` instead of `length()`.	`len("No")`
`upper("hello")`	The string comes before the function call.	`"hello".upper()`
`"hello".uppercase()`	The function is called `upper()` instead of `uppercase()`.	`"hello".upper()`
`lower("heLLo")`	The string comes before the function call.	`"heLLo".lower()`
`"HELLO".lowercase()`	The function is called `lower()` instead of `lowercase()`.	`"HELLO".lower()`
`myArray(0)`	An array element is accessed with square brackets [].	`myArray[0]`

`theData = [1, 2, 3]`
 	
`for counter in range(0, 4):`
 	
`    print(theData[counter])`
	The array only has three elements (0, 1 and 2), so the loop counter needs to end on 3, not 4.	`theData = [1, 2, 3]`
		
		`for counter in range(0, 3):`
		
		`    print(theData[counter])`

Table 1.15: Common errors

Summary checklist

- ☐ I can describe the character data type.
- ☐ I can use the string functions `upper()`, `lower()` and `len()`.
- ☐ I can describe the purpose of arrays.
- ☐ I can explain how arrays are used to store multiple data items.
- ☐ I can explain how lists can be used as arrays in a text-based programming language.
- ☐ I can write program code to access data from a one-dimensional list.

> 1.6 Comparing algorithms

In this topic you will:

- identify features of algorithms that can be compared
- compare algorithms against requirements
- compare algorithms for efficiency.

Key words

efficiency

memory

requirements

robust

Getting started

What do you already know?

There are lots of ways of solving a problem and writing computer programs to solve a problem.

You and your friend will have written a program in entirely different ways. Your focus when writing a program should be on solving the problem.

Now try this!

Work individually to write a program in Python to meet these requirements:

- ask the user to input a number
- multiply the number by itself and output the result
- repeat the previous step until the result is over 100,000.

When you are finished, work with a partner and test each other's programs to see if they meet the requirements. If you find any errors, work together to solve them and then retest the program.

Comparing algorithms

A problem can be solved in many ways. Some solutions might be better than others. Therefore, there are different criteria that can be used to compare two algorithms that are intended to perform the same task.

In this topic, you will be comparing algorithms based on the **requirements** that they fulfil. Requirements are the set tasks that a program needs to do.

Then you will start to look at the **efficiency** of algorithms. Efficiency is how much effort it takes to complete something – the less the effort the more the efficiency.

Efficiency is important in programming because some programs are very large. They can have millions of lines of code, and an inefficient program might take twice as long to run as a more efficient program. Imagine you are playing a computer game and there are two versions. One version responds twice as fast as the other version. Which version will you want to play?

Comparing against requirements

The first way you can compare two algorithms is to look at the original requirements. Do both algorithms do what they are supposed to do? Does one of them do anything extra that makes it a better solution to the problem?

Let's look at an example:

A program is needed that will ask for the year a user was born and will output how old they are. Arun and Zara have each written a solution:

Arun's program:

```
year = int(input("Enter your year of birth "))
age = 2022 - year
print("In 2022 you were", age, "years old")
```

I am 13 years old

Zara's program:

```
year = int(input("Enter your year of birth "))
if year < 1900:
    print("That is not a realistic year of birth,
        try again")
elif year > 2020:
    print("That is not a realistic year of birth,
        try again")
else:
    age = 2022 - year
    age2 = age - 1
    print("You are either", age, "or", age2,
        "years old")
```

Let's check if they meet the requirements. As a reminder, the requirements were:

1   Ask the user for the year they were born.
2   Output how old the user is.

Arun's program:

```
year = int(input("Enter your year of birth "))
age = 2022 - year
print("You are probably", age, "years old")
```

This line takes the year the user was born as input (requirement 1).

This line calculates their age.

This line outputs their age (requirement 2).

Both requirements are met.

Zara's program:

```
year = int(input("Enter your year of birth "))
    if year < 1900:
    print("That is not a realistic year of birth,
        try again")
elif year > 2020:
    print("That is not a realistic year of birth,
        try again")
else:
    age = 2022 - year
    age2 = age - 1
    print("You are either", age, "or", age2,
        "years old")
```

This line takes the year the user was born as input (requirement 1).

This line calculates their age.

This line outputs their age (requirement 2).

Both requirements are met.

There is some extra code at the start:

```
if year < 1900:
    print("That is not a realistic year of birth,
        try again")
elif year > 2020:
    print("That is not a realistic year of birth,
        try again")
else:
```

This code checks if the year the user entered is reasonable. It is very unlikely that the year of birth of the user is before 1900 or after 2020, so an error message is output.

There is also some extra code at the end:

```
age = 2022 - year
age2 = age - 1
print("You are either", age, "or", age2,
    "years old")
```

This code states how old the user is. If the user has had their birthday, they will be the age stored in `age`. If the user has not had their birthday this year, they will be the age stored in `age2`.

This extra code makes the program more **robust**. Robust means that something is reliable, or that a program is less likely to produce an error or crash. Crashes and errors are less likely because the program tries to make sure data is appropriate before it is used. This stops an invalid result being given.

Unplugged activity 1.15

You will need: a pen and paper

A program is needed to read ten numbers from the user, calculate the mean (average) and output this value.

Arun and Zara have each written a program to meet these requirements.

Arun's program:

```
total = 0
for count in range (0, 10):
    total = total + int(input("Enter a number"))
average = total / 10
print(average)
```

Zara's program:

```
total = 0
for count = 0 to 9:
    total = total + input("Enter a number")
average = total / 10
print(average)
```

Continued

Work with a partner to compare these two programs based on the requirements.

Write down whose program is more efficient on a piece of paper and list the reasons for your choice.

Now, get together with another pair and compare your answers.

Did you come to the same decision? Did you have the same reasons for your decision?

Peer assessment

Discuss with your partner how well they were able to explain their answer. Did they state which was more efficient without any reasons, or were they able to justify their choice?

Comparing for efficiency

The second way to compare algorithms is for efficiency. This is a comparison of how much effort is taken to do something. In computer programs, efficiency is measured in lots of ways, for example how much memory they use.

In this section, we will be looking at how much memory the program uses.

Computers have **memory** where data is stored. The more memory a computer has, the more data can be stored in it.

When a program is written, data might need to be stored. You have used data structures such as variables, constants and arrays to store data. Each time you create a data structure, it takes up a space in memory. The more data structures you have, the more memory is used.

Did you know?

There are specific calculations that can be used to measure the efficiency of a program. This is called Big O complexity and can be used to measure how much memory the program will use and how fast it will run.

Did you know?

There are different types of data structure that allow programmers more control over how much memory is used. For example, a local variable will not be created until the sub-routine it is within starts running. As soon as the sub-routine finishes, the variable is no longer needed and this memory is no longer used. Programmers can use this to increase the efficiency of their programs in terms of memory usage.

In the programs you are writing, using an extra variable won't make much difference to the memory usage. However, some programs have millions and millions of lines of code. Think about a computer game and how many items of data need to be stored and updated every second.

The fewer data structures you use, the more efficient your program might be.

Let's look at an example.

A program is needed that will ask the user to enter three numbers and add them together.

Marcus and Sofia have each written a different solution. Here is my program!

Marcus's program:

```
firstNumber = int(input("Enter a number"))
secondNumber = int(input("Enter a number"))
thirdNumber = int(input("Enter a number"))
total = firstNumber + secondNumber + thirdNumber
print(total)
```

Sofia's program: And here's mine!

```
total = int(input("Enter a number"))
total = total + int(input("Enter a number"))
total = total + int(input("Enter a number"))
print(total)
```

Marcus's program:

```
firstNumber = int(input("Enter a number"))
secondNumber = int(input("Enter a number"))
thirdNumber = int(input("Enter a number"))
total = firstNumber + secondNumber + thirdNumber
print(total)
```

The first variable is named firstNumber.

The second variable is named secondNumber.

The third variable is named thirdNumber.

The fourth variable is named total.

Marcus's program has four variables.

Sofia's program:

```
total = int(input("Enter a number"))
total = total + int(input("Enter a number"))
total = total + int(input("Enter a number"))
print(total)
```

> The first variable is named total.

Sofia's program has one variable.

Both programs meet the requirements. Marcus's uses three more variables. This uses more memory. Sofia's program is more efficient.

The efficiency of a program should only be checked when both programs meet requirements. This is why this is the second method of comparing algorithms. If one program does not meet the requirements, the program does not meet the requirements, so its efficiency is not important because the program does not work.

Unplugged activity 1.16

You will need: a pen and paper

A program is needed to find the largest number out of six numbers the user enters.

Marcus and Sofia have each written a program to meet these requirements.

Marcus's program:

```
largest = 99999
for count in range(0, 6):
    number = int(input("Enter a number"))
    if number > largest
```

Sofia's program:

```
total = 0
for count = 0 to 9:
    total = total + input("Enter a number")
average = total / 10
print(average)
```

Work with a partner to compare these two programs based on the requirements.

Write down whose program is more efficient on a piece of paper and list the reasons for your choice.

Then, work with another pair and compare your answers.

Did you come to the same decision? Did you have the same reasons for your decision?

Activity 1.6

You will need: a desktop computer, laptop or tablet with word-processing software and an IDE for Python or access to the MakeCode website

You will need to work in a group of four for this activity.

Decide as a group which of these problems to write a program to solve:

1   Take as input the name, cost and quantity of items purchased on a shopping trip. Output the total cost, the item you purchased most of and the most expensive item.

2   Output an action for a user to perform with a device (for example, shake it). Calculate and output the number of times the user does this action in one minute.

3   Ask the user to enter a maths calculation that they want the answer to (for example, 10 + 3). Calculate and output the answer.

4   A device outputs symbols to represent the temperature and light level in a room. This should change every ten seconds.

Split into pairs and work with your partner to write a program to solve the problem.

Rejoin the group and compare your programs. Write down the result of your comparison using word-processing software.

You might decide that one program is better overall, or that one is better for efficiency, but the other is better for meeting requirements. Make sure you explain your reasons for whichever you choose.

Consider what you have learnt about efficiency. Do you think you have been writing efficient programs, or could you go back and make them more efficient? How will you make sure future programs you write are efficient?

Questions 1.8

1   What are two ways of comparing algorithms?

2   Describe how to compare the memory use of two programs.

3   When can you compare the efficiency of two programs?

4   These two programs should:

   •   take four numbers as input

   •   output the largest number.

Program 1:

```
first = int(input("Enter number 1"))
second = int(input("Enter number 2"))
third = int(input("Enter number 3"))
fourth = int(input("Enter number 4"))
if first > second:
    if first > third:
        if first > fourth:
            print(first, "is the largest")
    else:
        if third > fourth:
            print(third, "is the largest")
        else:
            print(fourth, "is the largest")
else:
    if second > third:
        if second > fourth:
            print(second, "is the largest")
        else:
            print(fourth, "is the largest")
    else:
        if third > fourth:
            print(third, "is the largest")
        else:
            print(fourth, "is the largest")
```

Program 2:

```
largest = 99999
for count in range(0, 4):
    number = int(input("Enter a number"))
    if number > largest:
        largest = number
print(largest, "is the largest")
```

Compare the efficiency of program 1 and program 2.

Summary checklist

- [ ] I can compare two algorithms against the requirements.
- [ ] I can compare the efficiency of two algorithms.
- [ ] I can decide which algorithm is the best and justify my choice.

> 1.7 Searching algorithms

In this topic you will:

- learn the steps in a binary search
- use a binary search to find data in a set of data.

Getting started

What do you already know?

- Searching algorithms are used in programs where an item needs to be found in a set of data. There are lots of different searching algorithms, some of these are better in some programs than others. It depends on the data being searched.

- A linear search checks each item in turn, starting with the first item. It checks each item until it finds the item, or it runs out of items.

Now try this!

Take a piece of paper and cut it into nine pieces. Write words (or numbers) on the back of the pieces of paper. Mix them up and place them in a line face down.

Use a linear search to look for a specific card, word or number.

Do this on your own first, and then work with a partner. With your partner, give them instructions on what to do, for example 'turn over the first card'.

Binary search

A **binary search** is a different searching algorithm that uses a sorted list. This search still looks for an item in a set of data, but it does it in a different way to a linear search.

Before a binary search can start, the data must be in order. The order can be **ascending** (going up, for example 1 to 10 or A to Z) or **descending** (going down, for example 10 to 1 or Z to A).

For now, we are just going to use ascending order because this is how lists are usually sorted.

The order can be alphabetical or numerical, but it must be based on what you are searching for. If you are searching for the number 5, then the data must be in numerical order. If you are searching for the word 'red', then the data must be in alphabetical order.

Figure 1.40: Ascending means going up

Unplugged activity 1.17

Work with a partner for this activity.

1   Put this list of colours into ascending alphabetical order:

    red   orange   blue   green   grey

2   Put this list of numbers into ascending numerical order:

    12   10   5   99   102   3

3   Put this list of numbers into ascending numerical order:

    0.5   0.6   0.51   0.59   0.48   0.43

The word 'binary' in 'binary search' has the same meaning as in 'binary numbers'. There are two options. In a binary search, the set of data is split into two halves.

The centre item is checked first. If there is not a centre item (because there is an equal number of data items in each half), either the one to the left or right of the centre is selected. It doesn't matter which one, as long as you always choose the same.

- If the centre item is what you are searching for, then congratulations! You have found it.

- If this centre item is *greater* than the one you are looking for, you only need to search through the data items that are less than the centre. This means you can get rid of all the data on the right-hand side. Because you put everything into ascending order, every data item on the right of the centre will be greater than the item you are looking for.

- If the centre item is *less* than the one you are looking for, you only use the data items that are greater than the centre. This means you can get rid of all the data on the left-hand side as every data item to the left of the centre will be less than the item you are looking for.

Then you repeat with your new (smaller) set of data.

Example 1: Look for the number 7 in this data:

    1   2   3   4   5   6   7

The smallest is on the left, the largest on the right.

1   Select the centre value. 4 is in the centre.

        1   2   3   **4**   5   6   7

2   4 is less than 7. 4 < 7. Discard all the data to the left (and the centre). You are left with:

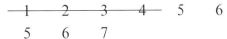

        5   6   7

3   Repeat. Select the centre value. 6 is in the centre.

        5   **6**   7

4   6 is less than 7. 6 < 7. Discard all the data to the left (and the centre). You are left with:

        ~~5   6~~   7

        7

5   Repeat. There is only value left. We still need to check it before the binary search is complete. 7 = 7, you have found it!

Unplugged activity 1.18

You want to look for the number 2.
Use a binary search on the same set of data:

    1   2   3   4   5   6   7

Circle each number that you are comparing to the number 2. Cross out the numbers you discard.

Example 2: Here is a set of data, it is text and in alphabetical order:

eight   five   four   one   seven   six   three   two

Do not be tricked by what the words say. They are words so we are looking at alphabetical order.

Let's look for the item 'five'.

1   Select the centre value. There are eight items. This is an even number so there is no centre. Choose left or right. Let's go right.

eight   five   four   one   **seven**   six   three   two

2   'Five' is less than 'seven' (f comes before s). Discard the right-hand set of data.

eight   five   four   one

3   Repeat. Select the centre value. There are four items, so no centre value. We went right before, so we will do the same again.

eight   five   **four**   one

4   'Five' is less than 'four' (fi in 'five' < fo in 'four'). Discard the right half.

eight   five

5   Repeat. Select the centre value. There are two items, no centre value. Select the right half.

eight   **five**

6   'five' = 'ive'. We found it!

Unplugged activity 1.19

You will need: a pen and paper

You want to look for the text 'eight'. Use a binary search on the same set of data:

eight   five   four   one   seven   six   three   two

Circle each item that you are comparing to 'eight'. Cross out the numbers you discard.

Example 3: In this example, we will look at what happens when the data is not in the list.

Here is the data, already in order.

black   blue   green   orange   purple   yellow

Let's use a binary search to find the data 'pink'.

1   Select the centre value. There is no centre value because there is an even number. So we will go left, and always go left half.

    black   blue   **green**   orange   purple   yellow

2   Compare 'green' to 'pink'. '**pink**' is > '**gr**een'. So discard the left half.

    orange   purple   yellow

3   Repeat. Select the centre value. There is one this time.

    orange   **purple**   yellow

4   Compare 'purple' to 'pink'. '**pi**nk' is < '**pu**rple'. So discard the right half.

    orange

5   There is one item left. 'pink' does not equal 'orange'. Item not found.

Unplugged activity 1.20

You will need: a pen and paper

You want to look for the text 'brown'. Use a binary search on the same set of data:

    black   blue   green   orange   purple   yellow

Circle each item that you are comparing to 'brown'. Cross out the colours you discard.

Unplugged activity 1.21

You will need: a set of cards, or pieces of paper that are all the same size with a number written on one side of each piece of paper

You can do this task on your own or with a partner.

Put the cards into ascending order: numerical order if you are going to search for a number, or alphabetical order if you are going to search for a word.

Decide which value you are going to search for.

Continued

Search for the card using a binary search, following these steps:

1 Find the centre value.
2 Compare the value you are searching for to this centre value.
3 If the value you are searching for is less than the centre value, discard the right-hand set of values and the centre value.
4 If the value you are searching for is more than the centre value, discard the left-hand set of values and the centre value.
5 Repeat from step 1 until either you have found the item or there are no items left to check.

Were you able to follow the instructions independently or did you need help?

If you needed help, will you need it next time or do you know what to do now?

Activity 1.7

You will need: a desktop computer, laptop or tablet with animation software or video-editing software and a camera

You will need to work in a group of up to four people for this activity. Your group will be creating a video tutorial on how to use a binary search.

This can be a video of you doing a binary search, or a series of images of different stages with a voiceover that plays like a video. Alternatively, you can create an animation.

Your video must explain:

- the fact that the data needs to be in order first
- how to find the centre value
- how to compare the search criteria to the elements in the data set
- how to discard data
- what happens when the data value is not found.

The videos can then be played for the rest of your class.

> **Continued**
>
> **Self-assessment**
>
> Give yourself and your group a rating out of 5 (1 is the lowest, 5 the highest) for:
>
> * how many of the requirements your video met
> * how well your team worked together and divided the tasks
> * how clearly your video shows the steps in a binary search
> * your contribution to the group work.

Questions 1.9

1 What form does the data need to be in for a binary search to work?

2 Which data item is checked first in a binary search?

3 What are the steps in a binary search?

4 When do you stop repeating the binary search?

5 Why is a binary search called a binary search?

6 How will a binary search look for the number 10 in this set of data?

       1   3   5   7   10   20   21

7 How will a binary search look for the word 'tree' in this set of data?

   flower   grass   hedge   rose   tree

8 How will a binary search look for the number 2 in this set of data?

       1   3   5   7   9   11   13

9 Why will a binary search not work on this set of data?

   T-shirt   skirt   jumper   trousers   socks

Summary checklist

- [ ] I can describe a binary search.
- [ ] I can use a binary search to look for a value in a set of data.

> 1.8 Testing

In this topic you will:

- identify normal, extreme and invalid test data for a program
- create a test plan that includes normal, extreme and invalid data
- identify syntax, logic and run-time errors in programs
- use a trace table to find an error in a program.

Key words

extreme test data

run-time error

syntax error

trace table

validation

Getting started

What do you already know?

- There are different types of data that can be used to test a program:

    - Normal data is accepted by the program, it is within any bounds.
    - Invalid data is not accepted by the program, it is outside any bounds.
    - Boundary data is right next to the boundary between normal and invalid. It might be on the normal side of the boundary and be accepted, or it might be on the invalid side of the boundary and be rejected.

Continued

- Not all programs can be tested with all types of test data. For example, a program on a micro:bit where the user can press buttons might not have boundary data because there are no boundaries! This program also might not have any invalid data because the button is either pressed or not pressed – there is no invalid choice.

- Test plans are used to identify all of the data you are going to use to test a program. The test plan includes the data and what the output should be. Table 1.16 shows one example of how this can be structured.

Test data type	Description	Input	Expected output

Table 1.16: Example structure of a test plan

For a program that asks the user to enter the quantity of books bought at a shop, the test table could look like Table 1.17.

Test data type	Description	Input	Expected output
Normal	Input is 0 or more and less than 100	1	Accepted
Normal	Input is 0 or more and less than 100	20	Accepted
Invalid	Input is less than 0	−1	Error output stating this is not accepted
Invalid	Input is greater than 99	110	Error output stating this is not accepted
Boundary	Input is 0 (just within lower bound)	0	Accepted
Boundary	Input is −1 (just outside lower bound)	−1	Error output stating this is not accepted
Boundary	Input is 99 (just within upper bound)	99	Accepted
Boundary	Input is 100 (just outside upper bound)	100	Error output stating this is not accepted

Table 1.17: Test table for program that asks the user to enter the quantity of books

Continued

Now try this!

This pseudocode algorithm should take a number between 1 and 12 from the user, and then output the times table from 1 to 10 for the number input.

```
INPUT number
IF number < 1 OR number > 12 THEN
    OUTPUT "Invalid number"
ELSE
    FOR count = 0 TO 10
        OUTPUT number * count
    NEXT count
ENDIF
```

Create a test plan for this program by identifying normal, invalid and boundary test data for this program.

If the program does not produce the output you expect, identify the error(s) in the algorithm.

Test data and test plans

It is important to test programs with lots of different types of data to make sure the program works. It also checks that the program cannot be broken, for example by entering something that the program cannot use.

There are four types of test data:

* normal
* invalid
* boundary
* extreme.

You should be familiar with the first three from previous learning, but extreme data is new.

Extreme test data is accepted, it is valid. However, it is right on the edge of what is accepted. It is the last possible value that can be accepted, because the next one will be rejected.

For example, a program takes a user's age as input. They need to be between 10 and 18 inclusive.

- 10 is the smallest possible number that can be accepted because 9 needs to be rejected.
- 18 is the largest possible number that can be accepted because 19 needs to be rejected.

The extreme data for this program is 10 and 18.

This is similar to boundary test data. The difference is that boundary data also includes the first value that is rejected.

For the same program, the boundary data would be 9 and 10 (either side of the lowest boundary), as well as 18 and 19 (either side of the highest boundary). In this topic, we will use extreme test data and not boundary test data.

Some data can be multiple types of test data! In the program above, the input of 10 is normal data, extreme data and boundary data.

Unplugged activity 1.22

You will need: a pen and paper

Work with a partner for this activity.

Individually write down a description of data that needs to be entered within bounds, for example a number between 100 and 200 inclusive, or a year of birth between 1900 and 2010.

Swap descriptions with your partner. For your partner's description, write down examples of:

- normal test data
- invalid test data
- extreme test data.

Discuss your test data with your partner and decide if you identified appropriate data for each type.

When you create a test plan, you need to include extreme data when appropriate. Remember, not every program will have every type of test data.

Example

A program allows a user to enter the number of nights they want to stay in a hotel. The minimum number of nights is 1, the maximum in one booking is 6 nights.

Normal data is any that is accepted, for example: 1, 2, 3, 4, 5 and 6.

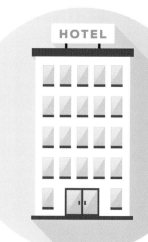

Test data type	Description	Input	Expected output
Normal	Number between 1 and 6 inclusive	1	Accepted
Normal	Number between 1 and 6 inclusive	2	Accepted
Normal	Number between 1 and 6 inclusive	3	Accepted
Normal	Number between 1 and 6 inclusive	4	Accepted
Normal	Number between 1 and 6 inclusive	5	Accepted
Normal	Number between 1 and 6 inclusive	6	Accepted

Table 1.18: Test table for example program

Invalid data is any data that is rejected, for example: 0, −1, 7 and 8.

Not every invalid input will need to be tested. In this program, this would be every number that isn't 1 to 6. There are too many. It is usual to pick a small number of examples either side of the data range. See Table 1.19, for example.

Test data type	Description	Input	Expected output
Invalid	Number below 1	0	Rejected
Invalid	Number below 1	−1	Rejected
Invalid	Number more than 6	7	Rejected
Invalid	Number more than 6	8	Rejected

Table 1.19: Test table with invalid test data

Extreme is the limit of what is accepted: 1 and 6.

Test data type	Description	Input	Expected output
Extreme	Smallest acceptable value	1	Accepted
Extreme	Largest acceptable value	6	Accepted

Table 1.20: Test table with extreme test data

Activity 1.8

You will need: a pen and paper, a desktop computer, laptop or tablet with an IDE for Python

Create this program in Python.

```
nights = int(input("How many nights would you like to stay?"))
if nights >= 1 and nights <= 6:
    cost = nights * 100
    print("That will cost $", cost)
else:
    print("The number of nights must be between 1 and 6")
```

Create the test plans with an extra column for the actual output.

Test the program using the test data to identify if the program works.

Activity 1.9

You will need: a pen and paper, a desktop computer, laptop or tablet with an IDE for Python

A person can go on a fairground ride if they are more than 100 cm tall.

The following Python program takes a user's height in cm and outputs whether they can go on the ride.

```
height = int(input("Enter your height in cm"))
if height > 100:
    print("You can go on the ride")
else:
    print("You cannot go on the ride")
```

Create a test plan for this program including normal, invalid and extreme data.

Copy the program into Python and complete your test plan by testing your program.

Types of error

At some point, you will have written a program that doesn't work. This will have been because there was an error in the program.

You have previously learnt about **syntax errors** and logic errors.

A syntax error occurs when the code does not follow the rules of the language. It could be that the incorrect word is used, for example `pint` instead of `print`. A bracket might be missing, for example `print("hello"` instead of `print("hello")`.

A syntax error will stop the program from running. When the statement that contains the syntax error is reached, the program will stop and report the error.

Activity 1.10

You will need: a pen and paper, desktop computer, laptop or tablet with an IDE for Python

The following program is written in Python.

```
choice = input(Enter A to purchase cake,
enter B to purchase bread")
if choice == "A":
    choice2 = input("Enter A to purchase a
    baguette, enter B to purchase a loaf"
    if choice2 == "A":
        price = 2.20
```

Continued

```
      elseif choice2 == "B":
          price = 1.90
  elif choice == "B":
      price = 4.00
  quantity = int(input("How many?"))
  total = quantity * price
  print("Total cost = $" total)
```

Write the program in a Python IDE. There are *five* syntax errors in the program.

Identify and correct each error.

A logic error is when the program runs but it does not do what it is supposed to do. It might produce an output, do calculations, take input, and so on, but something will be wrong. For example, it could be that a calculation is incorrect, or it could add instead of subtract. The program could have the wrong comparison in a selection statement, for example: < instead of <=.

To find a logic error, you will need to know the requirements of the program and then read the code, trace the code and work out where the program goes wrong or does not meet the requirements.

Activity 1.11

You will need: a pen and paper, a desktop computer, laptop or tablet with an IDE for Python

A program is needed to take as input whether the user wants to buy a hardback or a paperback book. A hardback book costs $12.00 and a paperback book costs $5.00.

The program is written in Python.

```
choice = input("Would you like to buy
a book?")
bookPrice = 0
if choice == "yes":
    choice2 = input("Hardback or paperback?")
```

Continued

```
      if choice2 == "Hardback":
          bookPrice = 10.0
      elif choice2 == "paperback":
          bookPrice = 5.00
   print("Cost is", bookPrice)
```

The test table (Table 1.21) shows the data that should be input with each input.

Test data type	Description	Input	Expected output
Normal	Hardback cost	yes Hardback	Cost is 12.00
Normal	Hardback in different case	yes hardback	Cost is 12.00
Normal	Yes in different case	Yes Hardback	Cost is 12.00
Normal	Paperback cost	yes Paperback	Cost is 5.00
Normal	Paperback in different case	yes paperback	Cost is 5.00
Invalid	Neither hardback nor paperback entered	Book	Invalid choice
Normal	User does not want to buy a book	No	No output

Table 1.21: Test table for Activity 1.11

Copy the program into a Python IDE. The program has several logic errors.

Use the test table to identify which tests do not give the required output.

Identify the logic errors and correct them.

Run-time error

A third type of error is a **run-time error**. This is an error that happens when the program is running. Run-time errors make the program crash. For an error to be a run-time error, the syntax must be correct (that is, it isn't a syntax error). With a run-time error, the program might not crash every time the program runs.

A run-time error could happen when an invalid input is entered. For example, if the word 'one' instead of the number '1' is input and then the program tries to add a number to 'one', which it cannot do.

The most common example is division by 0. Nothing can be divided by 0 and if a program tries to do this, it will report an error.

Did you know?

Has your computer ever crashed? Did it stop working or give you a black or blue screen so you could not do anything? This might have been because of a run-time error. Something happened that the program did not predict and the software did not know what to do, so it stopped.

Validation

Not all run-time errors are predictable, but one way of catching them is using **validation**. Validation is a way of testing that data is reasonable and follows the rules. For example, a person's age must be between 0 and 120. Validation stops inappropriate data being used. Before the data is used, use a selection statement to make sure it is appropriate.

In this example, the user needs to enter two numbers. The first number will be divided by the second.

```
first = int(input("Enter the first number "))
second = int(input("Enter the second number "))
print("What is", first, "/", second,"? ")
answer = float(input())
if answer == first / second:
    print("Correct")
else:
    answer = first / second
    print("Incorrect, the answer is", answer)
```

At present, the user could enter 0 for either number.

Activity 1.12

You will need: a pen and paper, desktop computer, laptop or tablet with an IDE for Python

Copy the program code above into a Python IDE and test it with the following data:

Test 1:   10   2

Test 2:   10   0

Test 3:   0   10

Test 4:   0   0

What happened in Tests 2, 3 and 4? Why did this happen?

The program can use selection to stop the calculation if a 0 is entered. In this amended code, there is a selection statement. If either number is (or both numbers are) 0, the ELSE statement runs and "0 cannot be entered as one of the numbers" is output.

```python
first = int(input("Enter the first number "))
second = int(input("Enter the second number "))
if first != 0 and second != 0:
    print("What is", first, "/", second,"? ")
    answer = float(input())
    if answer == first / second:
        print("Correct")
    else:
        answer = first / second
        print("Incorrect, the answer is", answer)
else:
    print("0 cannot be entered as one of the numbers")
```

Activity 1.13

You will need: a pen and paper, a desktop computer, laptop or tablet with an IDE for Python

Update your program from Activity 1.12 with the selection statement. Test your program again with the four sets of test data.

Identify the differences in the outputs.

Another example of a common run-time error is accessing an element in an array that does not exist.

For example: you have an array with five elements:

```
myArray = [5, 10, 5, 66, 34]
```

If you try to access `myArray[0]`, the number 5 will be accessed. If you try to access `myArray[4]`, the number 34 will be accessed. If you try to access `myArray[5]`, an error will occur because there is no data in `myArray[5]` – it doesn't exist.

Here's an example Python program that will produce a run-time error:

```python
myArray = [0,0,0,0]
for index in range(0, 6):
    myArray[index] = int(input("Enter a number "))
```

Activity 1.14

> **You will need:** a pen and paper, a desktop computer, laptop or tablet with an IDE for Python

Enter the code for the example program that produces a run-time error into a Python IDE.

Amend the program so that six numbers can be entered and stored in the array.

Trace tables

A **trace table** is a table where you write down the values stored in each variable, or data structure, in a program. You can walk through the program one statement at a time, you manually do what each statement instructs, and you write the change in values in the table.

A trace table can be used to find errors in a program. By updating the values after each statement, you can find out where the program has an error. A value might change incorrectly because the wrong arithmetic operator has been used. When you follow the values, you can see where the error happens and change it.

A trace table has one column for each variable and one column for any output. Here's an example pseudocode program with line numbers to help you follow it:

```
01    first = 1
02    last = 4
```

```
03     FOR count = first TO last
04         OUTPUT count
05     NEXT count
06     OUTPUT "Finished"
```

This program needs four columns, one for the output and one for each of the three variables in this program: first, last and count. Each of the identifiers is a column heading. Output is the final column heading.

first	last	count	Output

Table 1.22: Example trace table

Follow the program one line at a time. Write any changes in the trace table. Some people like to write each change on a completely new line, whilst other people prefer to write each change on the next line in each column. There is no set way to do this – try different ways to see which you prefer. The only rule is that every change must be written in the table and in a new box. Do not cross out a value and replace it.

Let's run this program and fill in the trace table one line of code at a time.

1 01   first = 1

This line stores 1 in the variable first, so write 1 in the first column.

first	last	count	Output
1			

Table 1.23: Storing 1 in the variable first

2 02   last = 4

This stores 4 in last.

first	last	count	Output
1	4		

Table 1.24: Storing 4 in the variable last

3 03   `FOR count = first TO last`

`count` is the variable counter and it starts at number 1.

first	last	count	Output
1	4	1	

Table 1.25: count starting at number 1

4 04   `OUTPUT count`

The content of `count` is output. Look at the column `count` and use the last value you wrote in it.

first	last	count	Output
1	4	1	1

Table 1.26: Outputting the content of count

5 05   `NEXT count`

The command `NEXT` adds 1 to the value in the counter. `count` currently stores 1, adding 1 to it changes this to 2.

first	last	count	Output
1	4	1	1
		2	

Table 1.27: Adding 1 to count

6 At the end of a FOR loop it goes back to check the condition.

  03   `FOR count = first TO last`

The value in `count` (2) is not more than the value in `last` (4). There is no change to the trace table as no values change, but the code within the trace table continues.

7 04   `OUTPUT count`

first	last	count	Output
1	4	1	1
		2	2

Table 1.28: Outputting the content of count

8 05   NEXT count

first	last	count	Output
1	4	1	1
		2	2
		3	

Table 1.29: Adding 1 to count

9 Back to the top of the loop again.

03   FOR count = first TO last

The value in count (3) is not more than the value in last (4). There is no change to the trace table as no values change, but the code within the trace table continues.

10 04   OUTPUT count

first	last	count	Output
1	4	1	1
		2	2
		3	3

Table 1.30: Outputting the content of count

11 05   NEXT count

first	last	count	Output
1	4	1	1
		2	2
		3	3
		4	

Table 1.31: Adding 1 to count

12 Back to the top of the loop again.

    03   `FOR count = first TO last`

The value in `count` (4) is not more than the value in `last` (4). There is no change to the trace table as no values change, but the code within the trace table continues.

    04   `OUTPUT count`

first	last	count	Output
1	4	1	1
		2	2
		3	3
		4	4

Table 1.32: Outputting the content of count

13 05   `NEXT count`

first	last	count	Output
1	4	1	1
		2	2
		3	3
		4	4
		5	

Table 1.33: Adding 1 to count

14 Back to the top of the loop again.

    03   `FOR count = first TO last`

The value in `count` (5) is more than the value in `last` (4). This stops the loop and the code beneath the loop now runs.

15   `06`   `OUTPUT "Finished"`

The text "Finished" is output. Make sure you write this output exactly in the trace table, checking the use of upper- and lowercase letters and punctuation.

first	last	count	Output
1	4	1	1
		2	2
		3	3
		4	4
		5	Finished

Table 1.34: Outputting "Finished"

Unplugged activity 1.23

You will need: a pen and paper

The following program is written in Python.

```
01    number1 = int(input("Enter a number"))
02    number2 = int(input("Enter another number"))
03    if number1 > number2:
04        print(number1, "is the largest")
05    elif number2 > number1:
06        print(number2, "is the largest")
07    else:
08        print("The numbers are the same")
```

1   Create a trace table for this program. There are two variables used in the program.

2   Use your trace table to trace the program for each of the following sets of data:

   a   10   2

   b   1   15

   c   20   20

3   Use your trace table to identify the purpose of this program.

Unplugged activity 1.24

You will need: a pen and paper

The following program in Python is supposed to add together the cost of five items that a user has purchased. The program does not currently work.

```
01      total = 1
02      for counter in range(1, 4):
03          print("Enter cost of item", counter)
04          cost = float(input())
05          total = total + cost
06      print("Total cost = $", counter)
```

1   Create a trace table for this program. There are three variables used in the program.

2   Use your trace table to trace the program for each of the following sets of data:

   a   1.5   13.0   2.75   15.0   22.5

   b   22.0   1.6   15.8   19.6   30

> **Note:** If you find yourself looking ahead or missing lines, put a ruler or piece of paper over the program. Move the item down to reveal one line at a time. Do the action this line states and then reveal the next line. This will help you focus on the program and not try to guess what is coming next. If you look away, you will also know exactly where you were before.

3   Use your trace table to identify the error(s) and correct the program.

Self-assessment

Give yourself a grade from 1 to 3 for how accurately you completed the trace table.

1   You followed the program one line at a time without error, you didn't look ahead or try to guess what was going to happen.

2   You might have made an error and had to change something, or you tried to guess what was happening and fill the table in without following one line at a time.

3   You might have made a few errors when tracing, you didn't always follow the program one line at a time and tried to jump ahead.

How will the methods you learnt in this unit help you write programs in the future? Which method of testing and finding errors did you find the most useful? How will you use this in a future program?

Questions 1.10

1   What is extreme test data?

2   How is a test table used in programming?

3   What is the difference between boundary and extreme data?

4   A program allows a user to enter the number of people who are in a group of Scouts. The minimum number of people in a group is 2, and the maximum number of people in a group is 50.

  Identify normal, invalid and extreme test data for this program.

5   What is an example of a run-time error?

6   What is the difference between a logic error, a syntax error and a run-time error?

7   What is a trace table used for?

8   Describe the structure of a trace table.

9   The following program should:

  •   take five numbers as input
  •   output a message if any of the numbers is less than 1 or greater than 20
  •   identify the largest number input
  •   identify the smallest number input
  •   add together all the valid numbers
  •   output a message if zero valid numbers (between 1 and 20) were entered
  •   if at least one valid number was entered, output the smallest number, largest number and total.

```
one = 0
two = -2
total = 0
invalid = 0
```

```
for count in range(0, 4):
    number = int(input("Enter a number
    between 1 and 20 inclusive "))
    if number < 1 or number > 20:
        if number > one:
            one = number
        if number < two:
            two = number
        total = total + number
    else:
        print("Invalid number")
        invalid = invalid + 1
if invalid == 0:
    print("You entered 0 valid numbers")
else:
    print("Smallest is", one)
    print("Largest is", two)
    print("Total is", number)
```

There is at least one error in the program.

Create and complete a trace table for the program. Trace the algorithm with the following sets of data:

Data 1:   1   2   3   4   5

Data 2:   -1   0   50   20   1

Identify and correct the errors in the program.

Summary checklist

- [ ] I can identify normal, extreme and invalid test data for a program.
- [ ] I can develop a test table that includes normal, extreme and invalid data.
- [ ] I can identify logic errors, syntax errors and run-time errors in a program.
- [ ] I can describe what is meant by a run-time error.
- [ ] I can create a trace table.
- [ ] I can use a trace table to follow a program.
- [ ] I can use a trace table to find an error in a program.

> 1.9 Physical computing

In this topic you will:

- program a physical device to use data to solve a problem
- develop a prototype using iterative development
- evaluate the processes you took when developing a program.

Key words

evaluation

iterative development

prototype

Getting started

What do you already know?

A BBC micro:bit is a small computer that you can program to take inputs, process data and produce outputs. The micro:bit is programmed using the MakeCode website where you combine blocks. You then download the programs to a computer where you transfer them to a micro:bit.

Figure 1.41 shows the layout of the MakeCode website.

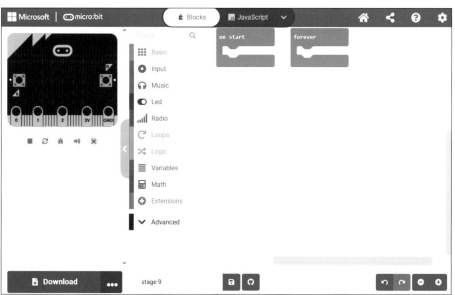

Figure 1.41: MakeCode website

Continued

You access the blocks from the menu and drag them to the screen on the right. There is a virtual micro:bit on the left that you can use to test your programs.

Micro:bits can also transmit data to another micro:bit using radio waves. For a micro:bit to receive a message, you must set the receiving micro:bit to the same group number as the micro:bit that is sending the message.

Now try this!

Work with a partner to program two micro:bits to send a message to each other. This could be a direction, a symbol to show a button has been pressed or anything else you can think of.

You will need to decide which group number you are going to use and make sure it is different from the number anyone else is using to send messages nearby.

Both micro:bits will need programming to send a message and will need blocks to tell them what to do when they receive a message.

Prototypes and iterative development

A prototype is an early version of a program that is made during development. It can be used to test the program or to find out how the program will work in practice. The prototype might only be for one part of a program, for example the first options that appear. It might be just the interface, so you can see what it looks like but nothing actually works.

The prototype can then be amended, added to and adapted in a continual process that adds more and more to the program until a final program is developed.

Prototypes can also be used in iterative development. This is where the program is created one part at a time. The program is then extended, tested, evaluated and then another part added or changed.

The program is tested again, evaluated and then another element added. This continues until there is a final program.

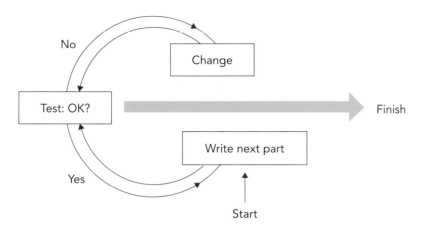

Figure 1.42: Iterative development of a computer program

In this topic, you will be creating a program by building a prototype using iterative development. To do this you will:

1 identify the requirements of the program (what does the program need to do?)

2 decide which part to create first as a prototype

3 create the prototype

4 test the prototype

5 decide what to do next

    a change the prototype if it needs to do something different

    b correct the prototype if it doesn't work

    c add to the prototype

6 write the program to change the prototype

7 test the program

8 repeat from step 5 until finished.

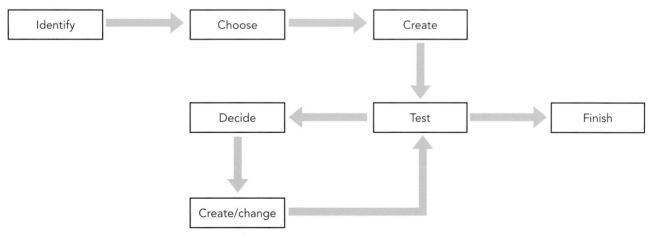

Figure 1.43: Building a prototype using iterative development

Evaluating the development process

An **evaluation** is a review of something that involves reflecting on what has happened and giving positive and negative points about it. In this topic, you will be evaluating the development of a program, specifically a prototype.

To evaluate the development, you need to identify the positive points. For example, what went well? You then identify the negative points. For example, what problems did you find?

These points could be related to:

* the final product
* the way you created the product
* how you worked with other people.

Marcus and Sofia both worked together on a project. Here is part of Marcus's evaluation:

Sofia and I created a program to play noughts and crosses using two micro:bits. We made a prototype that output the image of the board. This did not work the first time because we used the wrong LED numbers. We then changed this and fixed it. It worked the next time.

We then added a way for someone to choose which square to use. We decided to use the buttons and then transmit the choice to the other micro:bit. We did not know how to transmit the data so had to plan how to do that, but we got it working the first time we tried.

Here is part of Sofia's evaluation:

Marcus and I wrote down the requirements for the project. These included:

1 display the board

2 user selects which space to play

3 display the choice on the board

4 check if there are 3 in a row.

We made a prototype for requirement number 1 and kept changing it until it worked. Then we started on requirement 2. We got requirement 2 working and were going to start number 3 but ran out of time. We worked well together and our program met two of the requirements. We liked just doing one small part of the program at a time, but we did have a few errors, like the board not displaying properly at first.

Unplugged activity 1.25

You will need to work with a partner for this activity.

Look back at the evaluations from Marcus and Sofia. Identify the positive points they make about their programs and the negative points they make about their programs. Identify:

1 whether each evaluation covers the final product

2 the way they created the product

3 how well they worked together.

Identify which areas Marcus could add to his evaluation and which areas Sofia could add to her evaluation.

Programming task 1.31: Make

You will need: two or more micro:bits and a desktop computer, laptop or tablet with access to the MakeCode for micro:bit website

You will be working in a group for this task. You will need multiple micro:bits to test the final system.

A prototype needs developing to create a fireworks display using multiple micro:bits. One micro:bit will control the fireworks display by sending signals to other micro:bits. These micro:bits will then light up in different ways depending on the signals they receive.

You can design your own display, but a few ideas are given here to help get you started:

- The micro:bits together create one display. LEDs move from one micro:bit to the next, spreading out in turn.

- Each micro:bit has its own firework, or explosion, by lighting its LEDs. Each one could have multiple patterns that light up depending on the signal it receives. The micro:bits all have their own displays that combine together to create a larger display.

1 Work in your group to plan your fireworks display. Decide what each micro:bit will display and when it will display it. These are your requirements.

2 Decide which micro:bit you are going to program first as your prototype.

Continued

3   Create your prototype using the MakeCode website.

4   Test your prototype using the MakeCode website and a micro:bit.

5   Does your program need altering or does it work?
- If it needs to be altered, work together to identify what change is needed and go to step 3.
- If it works, go to step 6.

6   Have you finished your program? Do you have more micro:bits to program?
- If you have finished, go to step 8.

7   If you have more micro:bits to program, work together to identify which you are going to program next and how it will work. Then go back to step 3.

8   You have finished!

Unplugged activity 1.26

You will need: a pen and paper

Work with your group to discuss these questions about the program you created for Programming task 1.31.

1   Does your prototype meet your original requirements?

2   Did you have to change your requirements or do something differently? Why was this?

3   How did you use iterative development? Which parts of the process did you repeat?

4   If you had not used iterative development, how would you have created the prototype?

Now work individually. Using the answers you and your group have given, write an evaluation of the processes you followed when carrying out Programming task 1.31.

Programming task 1.32: Make

You will need: two or more micro:bits and a desktop computer, laptop or tablet with access to the MakeCode for micro:bit website

You will need to work in pairs for this task and you will need one micro:bit each.

A prototype needs developing to create a two-player game called Speed Action.

One player will send an instruction from their device to the other person's device with an action to perform. Instructions could be to tip the micro:bit upside down or shake the micro:bit.

You will need to work out how to transmit data from one micro:bit to another and how to give that instruction. For example, will you use a symbol or a number to mean a specific action?

The player will get a score for the number of seconds it took them to perform the correct task. The lower the score the better.

Work with your partner to identify the requirements for your program. Create a prototype for your program using iterative development: plan, create, test and evaluate one part of the program and then repeat by adding a new part in each iteration.

Activity 1.15

You will need: a desktop computer, laptop or tablet with presentation software

Work individually to create a presentation about the prototype you built for Programming task 1.32. Include slides that show or describe:

- how you planned the program
- the different stages of the prototype
- how you used iterative development to create your prototype
- how well your prototype meets the requirements.

Continued

Self-assessment

Give your presentation a rating from 1 to 10. A score of 10 means it covered all requirements and you have expanded each of your points to explain how you used iterative development. A score of 1 means you have covered at least one of the requirements.

Questions 1.11

1   What is a prototype?
2   How are prototypes used when developing a program?
3   What is the iterative development process?
4   What should you do to evaluate the processes involved in the development of a program?

Summary checklist

☐   I can program a physical device to solve a problem.
☐   I can develop a prototype.
☐   I can describe iterative development.
☐   I can use iterative development.
☐   I can evaluate how I used iterative development to create a prototype.

Project 1: Word guess

Arun and his friends need to choose a project for their computing class. Arun played the game Word Guess in class yesterday and wants to teach his younger brother how to play it. He's decided to create the game for his project and wants to partner with you.

Word Guess is a game where a user has to guess the word a computer stores. The number of letters in a word is output as spaces, for example:

_ _ _ _ _

The user then enters one letter. For example 'H'.

The game outputs the spaces, and if 'H' is in the word, this is output. For example:

H _ _ _ _

Figure 1.44: Guess the word!

The game continues until the user has guessed all of the letters in the word, or they run out of lives.

The user starts with 10 lives. One life is lost each time they guess a letter that is not in the word. If the user reaches 0 lives, the game is over.

You will need to work in pairs to:

- design and program a prototype for the game
- design a test plan for the program
- follow an iterative development process to create the program
- test the program using your test plan
- evaluate the development process you followed.

Outcomes

You need to produce:

- a design for the program
- a test plan
- a program that allows a user to play the game
- a completed test plan
- an evaluation of the iterative development process.

Challenge

Store three words of different lengths: an easy, medium and hard word. Ask the user which word they want to play and then allow them to play the game for the word chosen.

Project 2: Flowchart → Pseudocode → Program code

Zara and Sofia have decided to create an interactive education system to show how to create a flowchart, convert it to pseudocode and then convert that into program code. They want you to join their group.

You will work in groups to decide how you will create your system. This needs to be interactive so that the user can choose what they want to see or which part they want to follow. The system must also include a range of media such as text, images, sound, video and/or animation.

The system must show the different data structures you can use (variables, constants, arrays) as well as the constructs you can use (sequence, selection, iteration).

Outcomes

You need to produce:

- a plan for the content and structure of your system
- the system that contains examples and descriptions of flowcharts, pseudocode and program code.

Challenge

Include a range of programs that have different types of error for the user to find and correct.

Check your progress 1

1   Which of the following is the best description of a programming loop?

   a   Every line of code is run once, one after the other.

   b   Code inside can run multiple times.

   c   A message is output to the screen.

   d   More than one item of data is stored in one place.   [1]

2   What is the identifier of the counter used in this pseudocode algorithm?

```
INPUT num
FOR counter = 1 TO num
    PRINT(counter)
NEXT counter
```
      [1]

3   How many times will this pseudocode loop run?

```
FOR count = 1 TO 9
    PRINT(count)
NEXT count
```
      [1]

4   What does a searching algorithm do?   [1]

5   How does a binary search work?   [4]

6   Show how a binary search would look for the number 10 in the following list of data:

   1   2   3   5   7   9   10   11   [6]

7   Which of the following is the definition of a sub-routine?

   a   code that runs multiple times using a condition

   b   an operator that divides one number by another

   c   independent code with an identifier that can be called from other parts of the program

   d   a part of a flowchart that runs when a condition is true   [1]

8   This Python program should output the numbers 20 to 30. Complete the program.

```
for count in range(20, ..........................):
    print(.........................)
```
      [2]

9   What is the difference between the string and character data types?   [2]

10 What is the Python function that:

    a   calculates the length of a string?

    b   converts a character to uppercase?

    c   converts a character to lowercase? **[3]**

11 A program asks the user to enter their mark in a test. The lowest mark is 0, the highest mark is 50.
Identify normal, invalid and extreme test data for this program. **[4]**

12 Write a Python program to take 100 numbers as input from the user, add them together and output the total. **[6]**

13 Change the following Python program to count how many numbers in the array are between 10 and 20 inclusive.

```
theArray = [10, 2, 13, 36, 99, 12, 16, 25, 36, 31, 12, 0, 19]
quantity = 0
for item in theArray:
    if item == 10:
        quantity = quantity + 1
print(quantity)
```
[3]

14 Identify the three syntax errors in the following Python program.

```
myData = ["red", "yellow", "green", "blue", "grey", "orange"]
FOR item in myData:
    if len(item) > 4
        print item)
```
[3]

15 The following program should take 10 numbers as input from the user and output the quantity of numbers that are greater than 0.

```
moreZero = -1
for counter in range(0, 9):
    number = int(input("Enter a number"))
if number = 0:
    moreZero = moreZero
print("There were", moreZero, "numbers entered greater than 0"
```
The program contains at least one error.

a   Complete the trace table for this program when the user enters the data:

−2   10   −15   −3   5   152   33   −1   8   22

moreZero	counter	number	Output

[5]

b   Use your table to identify the errors in the program. Edit the algorithm to correct the errors. [4]

16 Write a program in Python to:

- ask the user to enter a number to look for in the array
- take the number as input
- count how many times that number appears in the array
- output how many times that number appears the array.

Use this statement to declare the data in the array:

```
arrayNumbers = [1, 5, 4, 3, 7, 6, 3, 5, 7, 9, 8, 5, 3,
1, 2, 4, 9, 9, 0, 8, 5, 7, 6, 5, 3, 2, 1, 3, 4, 2]
```
[8]

2 ▶ Managing data

› 2.1 Spreadsheets and analysing data

In this topic you will:

- learn about the benefits of using models to represent real-life systems

- learn to evaluate how useful a model is for representing a real-life system

- understand that a model needs to be tested with a variety of data in many ways to see how it handles different scenarios

- use the IF conditional statement in your spreadsheet to choose between two or more options

- learn how to use cell ranges in a spreadsheet

- learn how to use the MIN function to select the smallest values from a list

- learn how to use the MAX function to select the largest values from a list

- learn how to use the COUNT function to count cells in a spreadsheet.

Key words

built-in function

cell range

COUNT function

COUNTA function

COUNTIF function

filling

MAX function

MIN function

model

nested IF statement

parameter

replicating

simple IF statement

syntax

Getting started

What do you already know?

- You know how to use a spreadsheet to model a real-life system by using what-if analysis to compare different scenarios.

- You know how to create or use a simple spreadsheet to perform simple arithmetic operations such as addition, subtraction, multiplication, division and so on.

Now try this!

Japan is one of the countries in the world that has experienced a lot of strong earthquakes. The higher the magnitude of an earthquake, the stronger the earthquake.

Zara's mum is an architect working on designing a very tall building in Japan. She is concerned about the possibility of higher-magnitude earthquakes striking the country again, bringing down the building. Using the what-if analysis, help Zara's mum determine what magnitude of earthquake could bring down the building.

Open Source file **2.1_skyscraper.xlsx** using suitable spreadsheet software, and analyse the data.

Continued

- In cell B2, using what-if analysis, enter the values to determine the smallest earthquake magnitude that can make the building fall if it is 800 meters high and has a foundation depth of 5 meters. The result will be displayed in cell E2.

- Compare your results with that of a partner next to you. Who has the smallest magnitude that can bring down the building?

Stay safe!

When downloading a spreadsheet from the internet, take extra care and avoid opening suspicious links within the spreadsheet, if there are any.

Evaluating the use of models in real life

A **model** is a representation of an object or system in the real world. Models enable people to explain or study how the real-world object or system works. Models can be physical or non-physical. A physical model, such as a robotic car, can represent a real-life automated self-driving car. Models such as computer-based 3D models or mathematical and financial systems are non-physical. Models can be used to predict and explain how real-life objects will behave when placed in certain situations.

There are many reasons why we need models. One is that it is not easy for humans to create things perfectly the first time. Before we build real-life systems, we must experiment, test and analyse them thoroughly. Doing this will ensure that no one is put at risk if our ideas fail.

Unplugged activity 2.1

You will need: a pen and paper

With a partner, list examples of real-life systems that we can represent using models. Discuss why using models might be a good idea in those situations.

Models make it easy to visualise (picture in your mind) and explain processes and relationships between different parts of a system before you build it. When you evaluate models for use in real life, you need to think about the value that those models bring. You should ask yourself questions such as, 'When is it a good idea to use a model before building a real-life system for the first time?'

Figure 2.1: Learners inspecting a model car

Benefits of using models

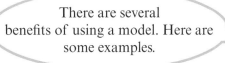
There are several benefits of using a model. Here are some examples.

1 **Cost of creating a model**

It is not always the case that a real-life system will work perfectly the first time. Big projects such as architectural and engineering designs like bridges, skyscrapers and aeroplanes would be too costly to create without assessing them first using models. If the model fails, rebuilding a new model would cost a lot less than the cost of rebuilding a new real-life project.

2 **Safety when models are used**

Some real-life systems are very complex. It is not easy to understand how they work or to use them safely without exposing people or equipment to danger through untested methods. For this reason, you can use models to help you test real-life systems in various situations and to assess their performance and safety.

3   **Testing and exploring 'what-if' questions**

You can modify the conditions of a model to see how it performs in different situations. For example, in a science experiment, you can use 'what-if' questions to raise or lower the temperature of a chemical reaction to see how a model handles different temperatures.

Drawbacks

On the other hand, using models can be challenging. This is because it is difficult to model or represent every aspect of real life accurately.

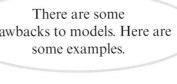

There are some drawbacks to models. Here are some examples.

1   **Limited time to perform all tests**

It requires a lot of time to test and perfect a model so that it represents a real-life scenario accurately.

2   **Cost and other budget limitations**

For some models, thorough testing under different circumstances requires a lot of money. For example, models in research work such as space explorations, military innovations and so on may require huge budgets, which may not be easily available. As a result, not every area of interest in the model is explored.

3   **Limited knowledge or detail about the subject area**

To accurately model a real-life phenomenon (something that happens) or object, all the information about that phenomenon or object must be readily available. However, sometimes there is not enough research or knowledge about the system to be modelled, so it is quite difficult to represent it using a model.

4   **The setting or environment to test the model**

Some models may behave in a different way when placed in environments they were not designed for. Consider a model that simulates the boiling point of water. At sea level or lower altitude, water's boiling point is different from its boiling point at higher altitudes, such as the top of a mountain. Similarly, the boiling point of pure water is 100 degrees Celsius. However, if you add an impurity to the water, such as salt, the boiling point becomes slightly higher.

Did you know?

A model is only as good as the data it handles. If the model is given unusual data that it is not designed to use, no one knows exactly how it will behave. For this reason, it is essential to test your models in as many scenarios as possible to get a clear picture of how it behaves in every possible situation.

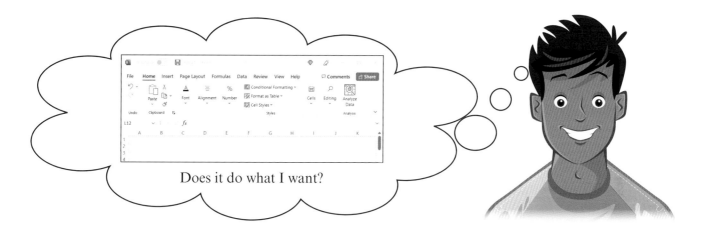

Does it do what I want?

Analysing data in a spreadsheet model

When creating a spreadsheet model, it is essential to analyse and manipulate the spreadsheet data to make it more meaningful to users. There are several ways you can analyse data in a spreadsheet. In this section, we will learn how to use the functions IF(), COUNT(), MIN() and MAX() to analyse data in a spreadsheet.

You will have previously learnt about functions and formulas.

1   Can you remember what a function is?

2   Can you remember the definition of a formula?

3   Discuss the difference between a function and a formula with the person next to you.

We can use functions as part of a formula – all functions are used within a formula, but not all formulas contain functions.

Remember that spreadsheet formulas are like a sort of programming language. Because of this, we need to obey certain rules when writing formulas. These rules include:

*   using double quotation marks around text strings "like this"
*   using brackets (like this) to group certain parts of the formula together so that calculations and logical operations are performed in the correct order.

Questions 2.1

1   Read each of the following statements about functions and
    formulas and state whether each one is True or False.

    a   All Excel formulas start with an = symbol.

    b   A function can take one or more parameters.

    c   All functions return a value when given parameters.

    d   Arun typed the formula =D9*E9 in cell F9. The formula
        multiplies the contents of cells D9 and F9.

    e   The function =SUM(A1,A2,A3) adds and multiplies values
        A1, A2 and A3.

2   What will be the first statement to be executed in this formula?

    =4/5-2(3+6)

3   The diagram below shows a screenshot of a spreadsheet.
    Identify which part is the formula bar: A, B, C or D.

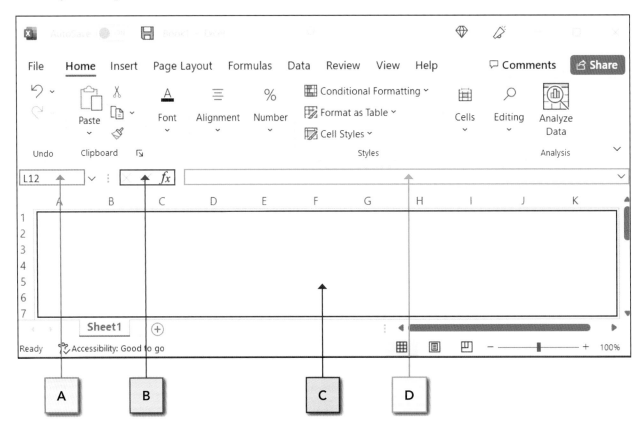

Figure 2.2: Different parts of a spreadsheet program

IF function

Marcus is excited to join a new football club. The coach for the club, Mr Brown, is very strict and won't let club members play if they haven't brought their football boots. Marcus remembers this rule at lunchtime and checks his sports kit to see if he remembered his football boots.

IF Marcus has his football boots, he can play football. IF Marcus does not have his football boots, he cannot play football.

We can write this information using the built-in IF function.

A **built-in function** is a function developed by the spreadsheet software developers and made available in the software for anyone to use. Examples of built-in functions include SUM(), AVERAGE(), COUNT(), COUNTIF() and many more. It is called 'built-in' because you only need to provide values or parameters in the function brackets for it to work.

We will talk more about the parameters on the next page.

An IF function is used to choose between one or more options that meet a particular condition in your spreadsheet. There are two types of IF statement: **simple IF statements** and **nested IF statements**. You learnt about how IF statements work in previous learning. In this topic, we go further to look at how we can use nested IF statements in spreadsheets.

A simple IF statement is one that is used when you have only two options to choose from.

The syntax for a simple IF statement is

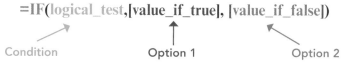

=IF(logical_test,[value_if_true], [value_if_false])

Condition   Option 1   Option 2

The word **syntax** refers to the way a formula or statement is arranged so that it is acceptable or meets the rules of a particular language. Every language has its syntax, which could include rules such as spelling and grammar. You came across the term syntax in earlier learning.

Let's look at the parts of the IF statement syntax in detail:

- The *logical_test* is the condition or question whose answer can result in either Yes (True) or No (False).

- The *value_if_true* represents the option that should happen if the answer to the logical_test is Yes or True.

- The *value_if_false* represents the option that should happen if the answer is No or False.

So, in Marcus's case, it would be:

$$=IF(Has\_boots= \text{"Yes"}, \text{"Marcus plays football"}, \text{"Marcus doesn't play football"})$$

Condition   Option 1: If True   Option 2: If False

The values passed to the IF function in the brackets are known as **parameters** and are separated by commas. Parameters are the items of information that we want to use in a function. These parameters can be numbers, text, cell references or another function like in a nested formula. Notice that if a parameter is text, you need to put double quotation marks around it, "like this". We will learn more about this when we look at nested IF statements.

In Marcus's case, three parameters passed to the IF function would be:

1   Has_boots="Yes"
2   He can play football
3   He cannot play football

We can represent this information in a spreadsheet model using the IF function and cell references, as shown below.

	A	B	C
1	**Player name**	**Has boots?**	**Outcome**
2	Marcus	Yes	Can play football
3			

Figure 2.3: Marcus can play football if he has his boots

- Column A shows the player information (for example, in cell A2).
- Column B shows if the player has their boots (for example, in cell B2).
- Column C displays the outcome based on whether Marcus has his boots or not.

The IF function was typed in cell C2, but in Figure 2.3, we cannot see the function or formula, just its outcome. One way you can show formulas used in a spreadsheet is to enable the Show Formulas feature. Follow the steps below to do this:

1   Click on 'Formulas' on the Main Menu tab.
2   Under the 'Formula Auditing' section, click on 'Show Formulas'. Depending on the size of your spreadsheet window, you might not see the complete phrase 'Show Formulas'. Instead, you might see just the 'Show Formulas' icon as shown in Figure 2.4.

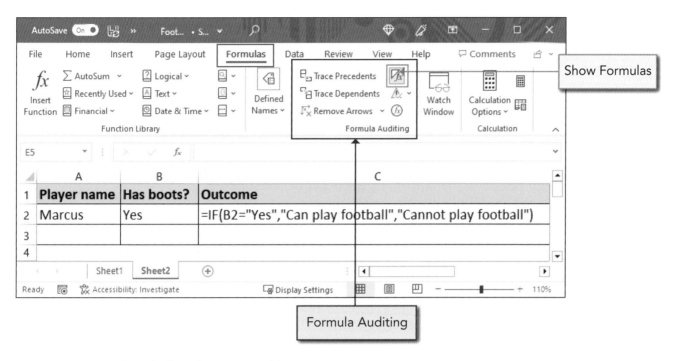

Figure 2.4: How to show the formulas in a spreadsheet

This formula is used to determine the outcome.

=IF(B2="Yes","Can play football","Cannot play football")

The parameters are:

1   B2="Yes" (This is the condition which can result in either Yes or No)

2   "Can play football" (This is the option if Marcus has his boots)

3   "Cannot play football" (This is the option if Marcus does not have his boots).

Replicating formulas and values in a spreadsheet

One of the many things you will be doing when working with spreadsheets is **replicating** formulas or values. The word replicate means to make an exact copy of something. Thus, replicating a formula or value means copying and pasting that formula or value into other cells.

Formula replication saves time as it means you don't have to retype the same formula in other cells. There are several ways to replicate a formula in a spreadsheet. The most common method is by **filling**. This method allows you to replicate a formula into several cells that are next to the first one, all at the same time and in any direction: down, up, left or right.

To replicate a formula by filling:

1   Select the cell with the formula to replicate.

2   There is a small square in the bottom right corner of the selected cell – this is called the fill handle. Hover the mouse on the fill handle until the mouse cursor changes to the **+** symbol.

3   Click and hold using your left mouse button and drag down, up, left, or right to fill the formula into the desired cells.

4   Release the button.

Suppose we want to replicate the formula in cell C2 in Marcus's example to display the correct outcome in cells C3 to C8. We can fill these cells with the formula as follows:

1   Select cell C2.

2   Hover the mouse on the fill handle until the mouse cursor changes to the **+** symbol, as shown in Figure 2.5.

3   Click and hold your left mouse button and drag to cell C8.

4   Release the button.

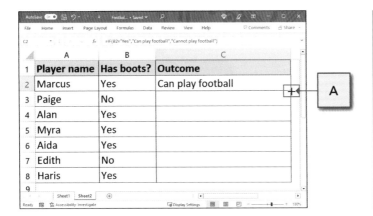

Figure 2.5: Selecting the cell to replicate

Figure 2.6: Replicated cells

Practical task 2.1

You will need: a desktop computer, laptop or tablet with spreadsheet software and Source file **2.2_football_club.xlsx**

Mr Brown has selected a list of football club members to represent the school in a competition. For safety purposes, his spreadsheet of member data contains information about any allergies the members have. Mr Brown would like to add a column to simply state whether a member has any allergies or not so that he can see quickly who does and who doesn't have allergies. He has asked Zara to help him add this data. To do this, Zara needs to:

Help me update this spreadsheet!

1   Create a new column for the yes/no allergies data.
2   Format the cell with the same formatting used in the rest of the spreadsheet.
3   In the new column, use a formula to display "No" if the player has no allergies, or otherwise display the text "Yes".
4   Replicate the formula so that the yes/no data is displayed for all club members.
5   Save the spreadsheet.

Task A

1   Open Source file **2.2_football_club.xlsx** and examine it.
2   Insert a new column after the *Allergy details* column and call it 'Allergies Y/N'.
3   Format this new column with the same formatting as the rest of the table.
4   In cell E2, use an IF function to determine whether a person will have 'Yes' or 'No' in the new column depending on what is in the *Allergy details* column.

	A	B	C	D	E
1	**First name**	**Last name**	**Age**	**Allergy details**	**Allergies Y/N**
2	Paige	Johnston	14	none	=IF(D2="none","No","Yes")
3	Alan	Sullivan	15	none	
4	Myra	Douglas	12	penicillin	
5	Aida	Craig	13	none	

Figure 2.7: Football club spreadsheet with new Allergies Y/N column

Continued

Hit Enter on your keyboard and check that the value in cell E2 is now "No".

5   Now fill the formula in cell E2 down the column so that the yes/no data is displayed for all the club members.
   - Select cell E2 in the file **2.2_football_club.xlsx**.
   - Hover the mouse on the fill handle of cell E2.
   - Click and hold using your left mouse button and drag down to cell E11, then release the mouse.

6   Save the spreadsheet.

Question

We know that the syntax for an IF statement is:

=IF(logical_test,[value_if_true],[value_if_false])

Option 1

Option 2

In the formula you have used in cell E2, what are the logical_test, the value_if_true and the value_if_false?

Task B

Football club members are required to pay a certain amount of money to participate in the competition. Each member will get a discount based on their age. If a member is younger than 14 years, they get a 15% discount. If they are 14 years or older, they get a 10% discount.

1   Open the file **2.2_football_club.xlsx** if it is not already open.
2   Insert a new column after the *Allergies Y/N* field and call it 'Discount percent'.
3   Format the cell with the same formatting used in cells A1 to E1.
4   In cell F2, enter a formula to display the percentage discount the person will receive.
5   Replicate this formula so that the percentage discount is displayed in all the cells in the range F2:F11.
6   Save the spreadsheet.

How would you ensure that the data being entered into a model is accurate? Are you aware of available tools or techniques that can help you verify and validate data during data entry?

Nested IF statement

Now let's look at how we can use a nested IF statement in a spreadsheet model. Suppose three teams (Red, Blue and Green) will compete in the football tournament. Each team is for a different age group: the Red team is for 11 and 12 year olds, the Blue team is for 13 and 14 year olds and the Green team is for 15 and 16 year olds. Players who are too old to join the Red or Blue team will automatically play for the Green team.

Marcus needs to be put in the appropriate team. We can use a nested IF statement to choose one of the teams for Marcus. The term **nested IF statement** means you have one or more IF statements enclosed in other IF statements. The enclosed IF statements will be in the place of either the value_if_true or value_if_false of another IF statement.

The syntax of a simple IF statement is:

=IF(logical_test,[value_if_true],[value_if_false])

Option 1

Option 2

For a nested IF statement with three options, the general syntax will become:

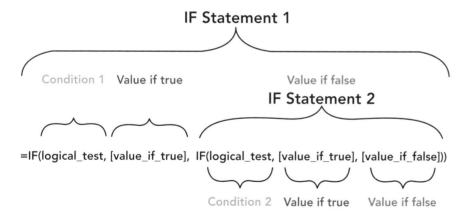

We can see that **IF statement 1** has three parts. The condition, the **value if true** and the **value if false**. Similarly, **IF statement 2** also has three parts but starts from the **value if false** place of **IF statement 1**.

Note that the second **IF statement** is only executed when the condition of **IF statement 1** turns out false.

Let's use a nested IF statement to determine which team Marcus will play for.

=IF(Age<13,"Red",IF(Age<15,"Blue","Green"))

This information can be represented in a spreadsheet using cell references, as shown below.

	A	B	C
1	First name	Age	Team
2	Marcus	14	=IF(B2<13,"Red",IF(B2<15,"Blue","Green"))
3	Alan	15	
4	Myra	12	

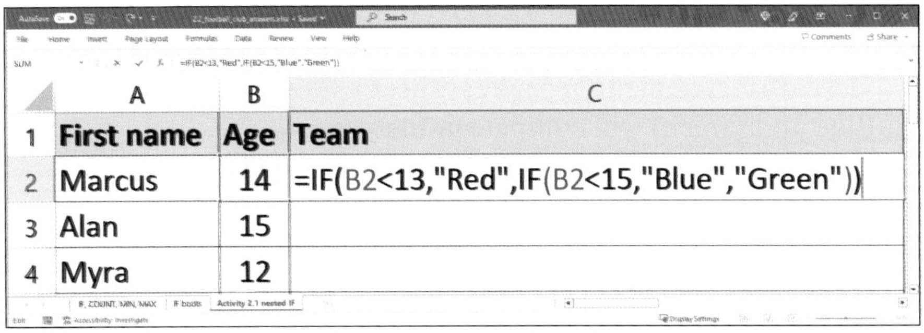

Figure 2.8: Formula for choosing the correct team

In cell C2, the false part of one IF statement is replaced with the start of another IF statement. This process can be repeated for as many options as we have. This is why it is called a nested IF statement. Each F statement 'nests' inside another IF statement.

If neither of the two conditions are true, the last option ("Green") will automatically be selected. This means that each player will automatically play for team Green if they don't play for team Red or Blue. You do not need another IF statement to test for team Green as it will be the only option if the player does not meet the conditions for team Red or Blue.

The general rule is that if you have n options to choose from, you will need n–1 IF statements. n means 'any number'. For example:

- If you have three options to choose from, then you need two IF statements.
- If you have four options, then you will need three IF statements.
- You will need four IF statements if you have five options.

The final output will be displayed as shown below.

	A	B	C
1	First name	Age	Team
2	Marcus	14	Blue
3	Alan	15	
4	Myra	12	

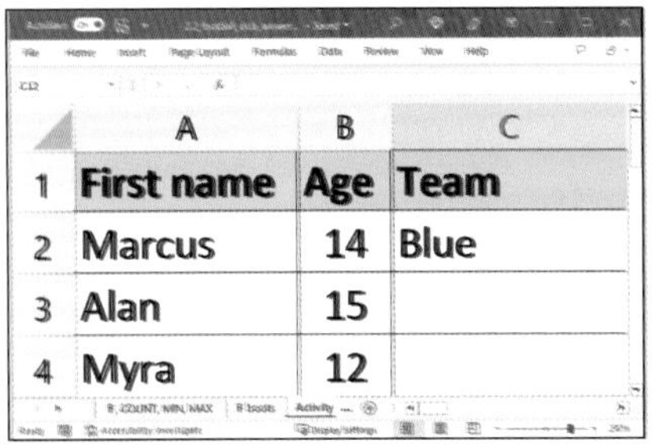

Figure 2.9: Team allocation based on age bracket

Activity 2.1

You will need: a desktop computer, laptop or tablet with spreadsheet software

1   Try recreating this spreadsheet and experiment by changing the value in the Age column to 11 or 15.
2   What happens if the age value is left blank? Why?
3   How could we improve this formula so that anyone who is not aged 11 to 14 is put in the Green team? (You do not need to try to do this, just think about how it could be done.)

Practical task 2.2

You will need: a desktop computer, laptop or tablet with spreadsheet software and Source file **2.2_football_club.xlsx** with Practical task 2.1 completed

Sofia has noticed that not many learners with allergies are playing in the tournament and says so to Mr Brown. Mr Brown wants to encourage as many learners as possible to participate, especially those with allergies or health conditions. He has revised the discounts to represent both the allergy status and the age of the learners. Learners with allergies who are 13 years old or younger will get a 20% discount, and those above will get a 15% discount. All other learners will get a 10% discount. You are required to update this information in Source file **2.2_football_club.xlsx**.

Open Source file **2.2_football_club.xlsx** and examine the contents.

1   Create a new column called 'Discount percent' in column F after the *Allergies Y/N* field if it is not already created.
2   Format the heading for this column to the format shown in cells A1 to E1.
3   Place in cell F2 a formula to display an appropriate discount for the learner using the information above.
4   Replicate this formula to display the discounts for all the learners in the range F2:F11.
5   Save the spreadsheet with the same file name.

SUM function and cell ranges

The SUM function adds together all the values in cells that you specify. This function is particularly useful when you want to add up the values in several cells.

In a typical spreadsheet, you will be working with multiple cells. You can access each of these cells using cell references, for example cell A2, cell E4, cell F9 and so on.

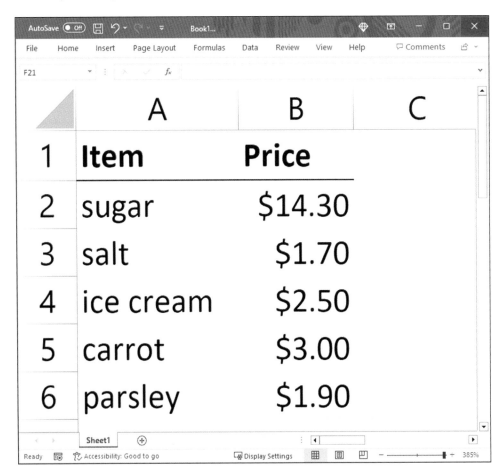

Figure 2.10: List of items and their prices

Suppose you want to find the total of a list of prices in column B. You can use the function SUM() and provide the values or cell references to be added, separated with commas, like this:

=SUM(B2,B3,B4,B5,B6)

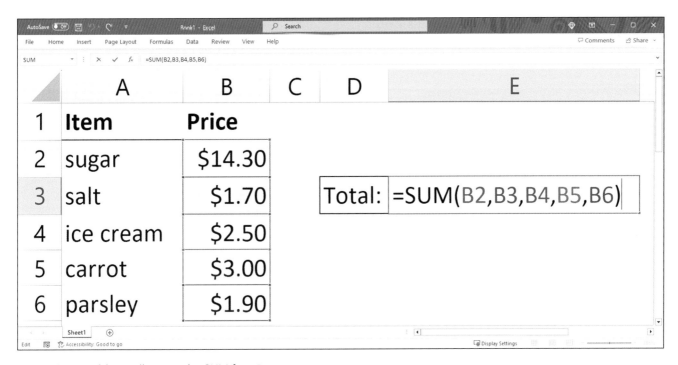

Figure 2.11: Adding cells using the SUM function

Alternatively you can use a simple formula to add cell values together, like this:

=B2+B3+B4+B5+B6

However, as the number of cells to sum up increases, it can become tiresome to reference each cell using one of these two methods. This is where using a **cell range** becomes useful. Cell ranges reference a group or grid of cells instead of just one cell. For example, the cell range in Figure 2.11 is B2 to B6. We can express the 'to' in a spreadsheet using a colon (:).

Let's find the total price of the items using a cell range by following these steps:

1   Select the cell where you want to add the formula and type the symbol =. Remember, all Excel formulas must start with an equals sign.

2   Type your formula as usual until you get to the part where you need to reference a range of cells.

3   After typing the open bracket, click and hold on the cell you want the range to start from (for example, cell B2).

4   Drag your mouse cursor in any direction (down, up, left, right, up) until you get to the desired cell (for example, cell B6 if you dragged down).

5 Type the closing bracket and press Enter.

6 This allows you to select a grid of cells known as the range or table, as shown in Figure 2.12.

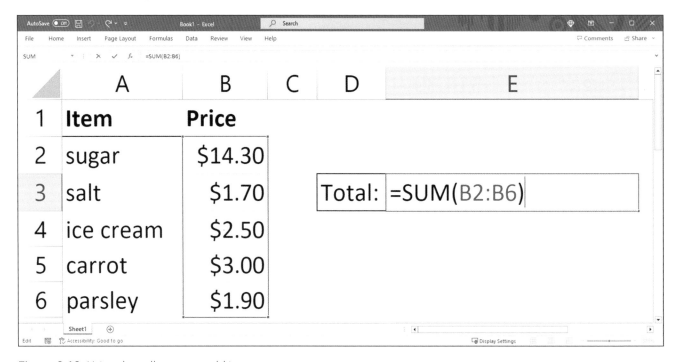

Figure 2.12: Using the cell range to add items

So the formula to calculate the sum of the prices is now given as

=SUM(B2:B6)

B2:B6 means B2 to B6. You can type this rather than selecting the cells if you prefer.

• B2 refers to the cell with the first value in the range.

• B6 refers to the cell with the last value in the range.

Cell ranges are widely used in spreadsheets. They are much simpler than the other two methods we mentioned. They are used in several formulas other than SUM(), as you will see in the next section.

MIN function

Suppose you were given a list of values and were asked to determine which of those values is the smallest. How would you do this? You would compare each value with all the other values and take note of the smallest value from each comparison.

In a spreadsheet, you can do this using the MIN() function. The **MIN function** finds the minimum or smallest value from a list of values. The syntax is:

=MIN(number1,number2,number3,[number4],…)

- the parameters *number1*, *number2* and so on are the items from which we want to calculate the minimum value
- the parameter *[number4]* is in square brackets to show that it is optional
- the three dots '…' before the closing bracket mean the list can continue depending on the available values.

Suppose we want to determine the smallest price from a list of prices shown in Figure 2.13.

We can use the MIN() function and pass to the function the values or cell references of the prices separated by commas. In the example below, B2, B3, B4, B5 and B6 are all passed to the MIN() function.

=MIN(B2,B3,B4,B5,B6)

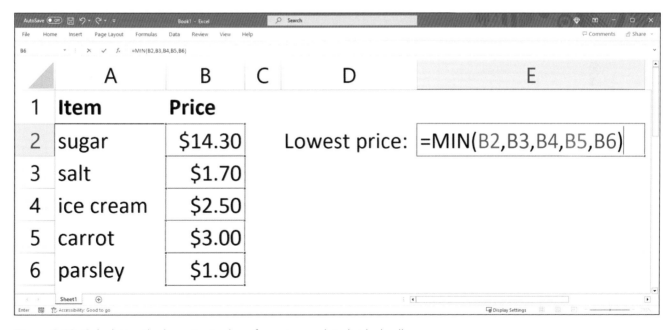

Figure 2.13: Calculating the lowest price by referencing each individual cell

This syntax is useful if you do not have too many values. However, as the number of cells from which the minimum value is to be calculated increases, it becomes challenging to do this. The most efficient method to use would be to reference the range of cells, for example:

=MIN(First_Cell:Last_Cell)

In our example, we can calculate the minimum or lowest price like this:

=MIN(B2:B6)

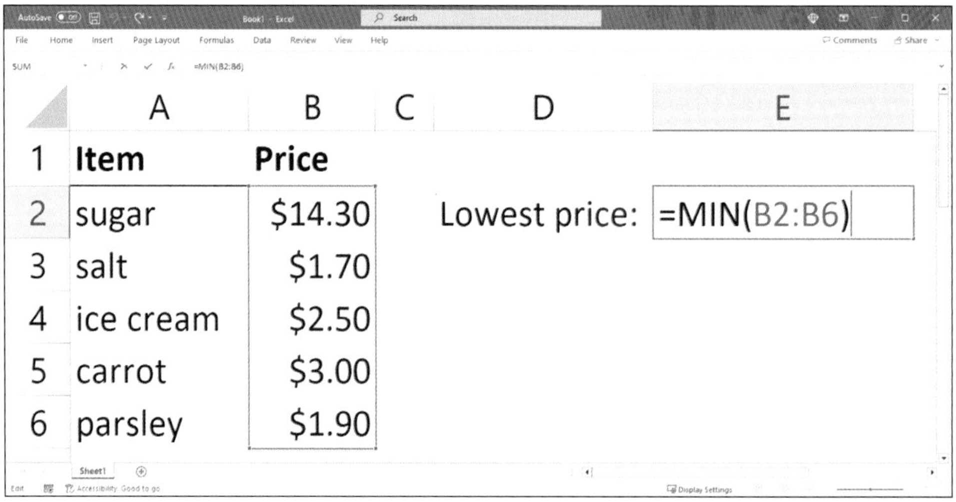

	A	B	C	D	E
1	**Item**	**Price**			
2	sugar	$14.30		Lowest price:	=MIN(B2:B6)
3	salt	$1.70			
4	ice cream	$2.50			
5	carrot	$3.00			
6	parsley	$1.90			

Figure 2.14: Calculating the lowest price using the cell range

Cell B2 is the start or first value while cell B6 is the stop or last value. Figure 2.15 shows the final output after using the MIN function.

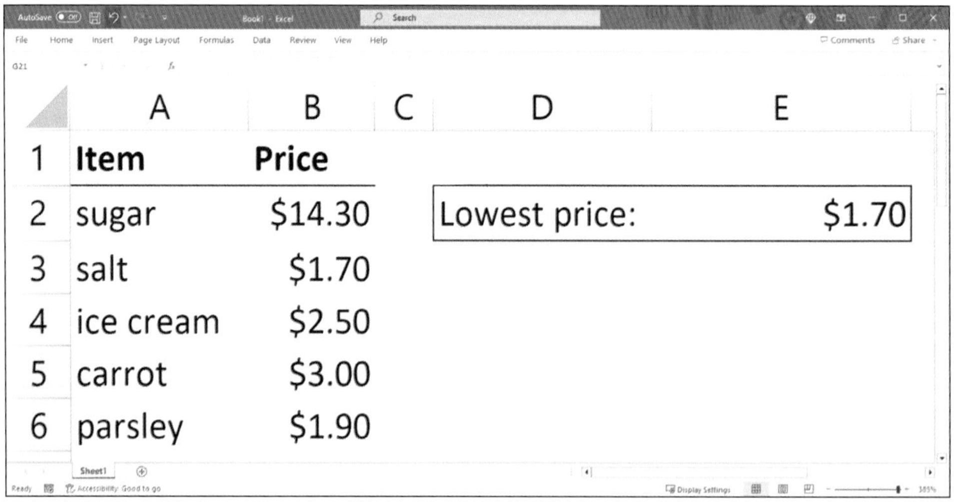

	A	B	C	D	E
1	**Item**	**Price**			
2	sugar	$14.30		Lowest price:	$1.70
3	salt	$1.70			
4	ice cream	$2.50			
5	carrot	$3.00			
6	parsley	$1.90			

Figure 2.15: Minimum value calculated using the MIN function

MAX function

The **MAX function** is the opposite of the MIN function. It is used to find the largest number from a given range of values or cells.

The syntax of the MAX function is very similar to that of the MIN function:

=MAX(number1,number2,number3,[number4],...)

Using the example of the prices in Figure 2.14, we can find the largest price using this formula:

=MAX(B2,B3,B4,B5,B6)

As we saw with the MIN function, if the number of cells in the range is too many, it becomes tiresome to use individual cell references. The most efficient method would be to use a range of cells. This can be shown as:

=MAX(First_Cell:Last_Cell)

As before:

*   First_Cell refers to the cell with the first value in the range, for example B2.

*   Last_Cell refers to the cell with the last value in the range, for example B6.

Unplugged activity 2.2

You will need: a pen and paper

Using the cell range method, can you write down the formula to determine the highest price for the list in Figure 2.14?

Unplugged activity 2.3

For this activity, the class will need to be divided into two groups. In your head, pick either 'MIN' or 'MAX'. If you picked 'MIN', go to the left side of the classroom. If you picked 'MAX', go to the right side of the classroom. Don't worry if one group looks bigger than the other!

You and your group members will need to select one learner to represent the group. If you are in the 'MIN' group, your group representative will act as the MIN function, and if you are in the 'MAX' group, your representative will act as the MAX function.

Continued

Now, the MIN function group representative will extract the shortest learner from the other group and bring them to their group.

The MAX function group representative will extract the tallest learner from the other group and bring them to their group.

Group members can suggest to their representative which learner they should extract from the other group.

This process should be repeated until all short people are in one group and all tall people are in the other.

Note: Group members cannot return to their original group once they have been chosen to join the other group.

Practical task 2.3

You will need: a desktop computer, laptop or tablet with spreadsheet software and Source file **2.2_football_club.xlsx** with Practical tasks 2.1 and 2.2 completed

1 Open Source file **2.2_football_club.xlsx** and examine the contents.
2 In cell I7, write a function to determine the age of the youngest club member.
3 In cell I8, place a function to display the age of the oldest club member from the given ages.

COUNT functions

Suppose we want to determine the total number of learners going on Mr Brown's trip. How would we do that? We could manually count the number of rows representing each learner, but what about if we want to know the number of learners of a certain age or allergy status going on the trip? We would have to manually count the number of rows for all the learners meeting a particular condition one at a time. However, this would be a bit challenging, especially if there were a lot of learners on the list and the spreadsheet data was not sorted into any order. This is where the COUNT functions become very useful.

There are several variants of the COUNT function, including:

1   COUNT
2   COUNTA
3   COUNTIF
4   COUNTIFS
5   COUNTBLANK and more.

Each variant has a specific purpose and type of data it can count. However, in this section, we shall look at the first three only as they are the most used.

This can save a lot of time!

The **COUNT function** counts a range of cells containing numeric data or values.

The syntax of the COUNT function is:

=COUNT(Value1,Value2,Value3,…)

Value1, Value2 and Value 3 must be numeric data. The COUNT function will miss out non-numeric data. Usually, if you use the COUNT function to count non-numeric data, you will get a result of zero.

Just like the MAX and MIN functions, using a range of cells is more efficient if you have many values in the list. This is shown as:

=COUNT(First_Cell:Last_Cell)

•   First_Cell refers to the cell with the first value to count.
•   Last_Cell refers to the cell with the last value to count.

Using Source file **2.2_football_club.xlsx**, we want to determine the total number of learners going on the trip. We can use the COUNT function, but we have to provide a range of cells with numeric values; otherwise, we would get an incorrect result. Can you think of a suitable column we should use in this case to calculate the total number of learners using the COUNT function?

In cell I4, enter the function:

=COUNT(C2:C11)

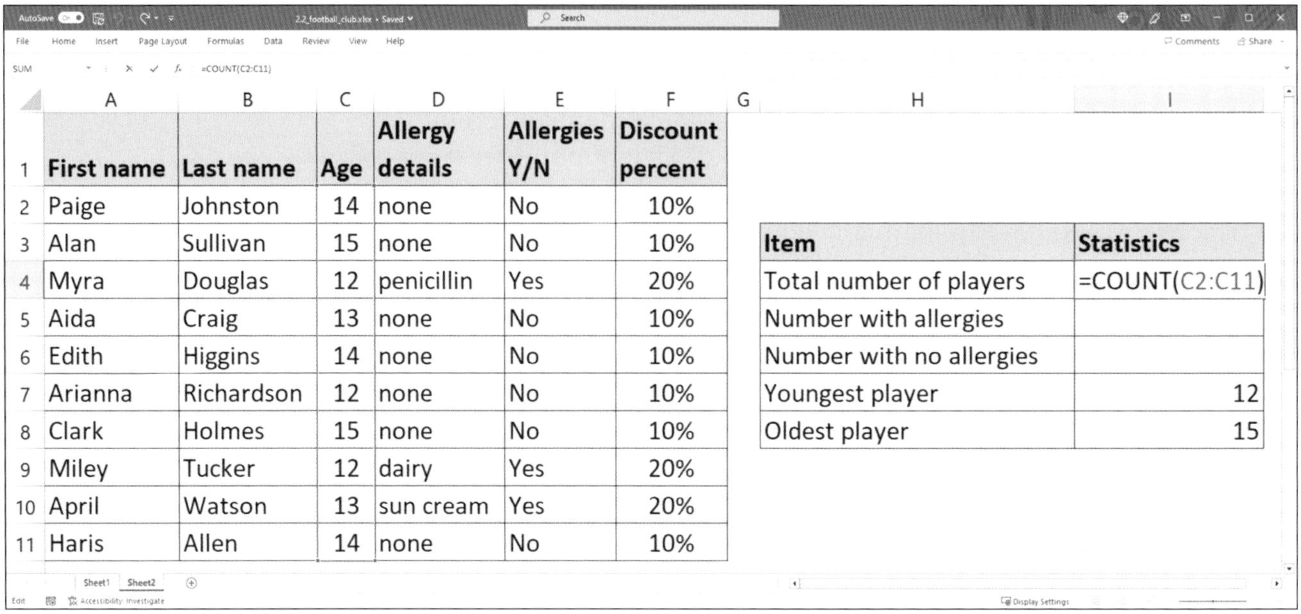

	A	B	C	D	E	F
1	**First name**	**Last name**	**Age**	**Allergy details**	**Allergies Y/N**	**Discount percent**
2	Paige	Johnston	14	none	No	10%
3	Alan	Sullivan	15	none	No	10%
4	Myra	Douglas	12	penicillin	Yes	20%
5	Aida	Craig	13	none	No	10%
6	Edith	Higgins	14	none	No	10%
7	Arianna	Richardson	12	none	No	10%
8	Clark	Holmes	15	none	No	10%
9	Miley	Tucker	12	dairy	Yes	20%
10	April	Watson	13	sun cream	Yes	20%
11	Haris	Allen	14	none	No	10%

Item	**Statistics**
Total number of players	=COUNT(C2:C11)
Number with allergies	
Number with no allergies	
Youngest player	12
Oldest player	15

Figure 2.16: Calculating the total number of players using COUNT

When you hit the Enter key on your keyboard, the value returned will be 10. This means that there are ten club members on the spreadsheet.

COUNTA and COUNTIF functions

Other variants of the COUNT function include COUNTA and COUNTIF.

COUNTA

The **COUNTA function** counts the number of cells in a range that contain a value. The values may be numeric or text. It is important to note that the COUNTA function does not include blank cells when counting a range of cells.

The syntax for the COUNTA function is very similar to the COUNT function:

=COUNTA(Value1,Value2,Value3,…)

You can also use a range of cells

=COUNTA(First_Cell:Last_Cell)

We noted that when we used the COUNT function, we could only use numeric data. However, with COUNTA, we can use columns containing text or mixed data (both numbers and text).

In Source file **2.2 football_club.xlsx**, we can determine the total number of learners on the list using any column, as long as it has no blank cells, using either

=COUNTA(A2:A11) or

=COUNTA(C2:C11)

Both of these functions would produce the same result, which is the total number of cells in the range.

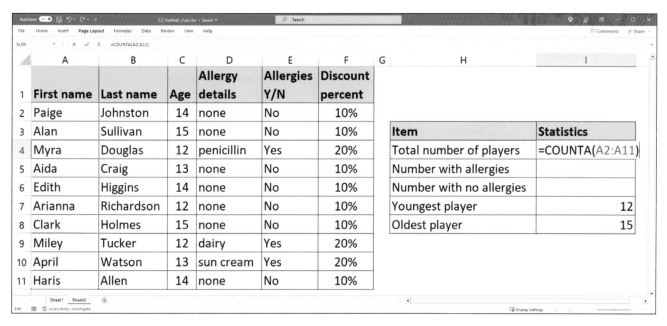

Figure 2.17: Calculating the total number of players using COUNTA

COUNTIF function

The **COUNTIF function** is a conditional count that counts the number of cells that meet a given condition. For example, we can count the number of football club members above a certain age or the number of club members with allergies.

The syntax for the COUNTIF function is:

=COUNTIF(cell_range,criteria)

- The cell range is the set of cells you want to get your value from.
- The criteria are the condition or conditions you have set, which the values in the range of cells must meet.

Let's find the number of players with allergies in Source file **2.2_football_club.xlsx** list and insert the formula in cell I5.

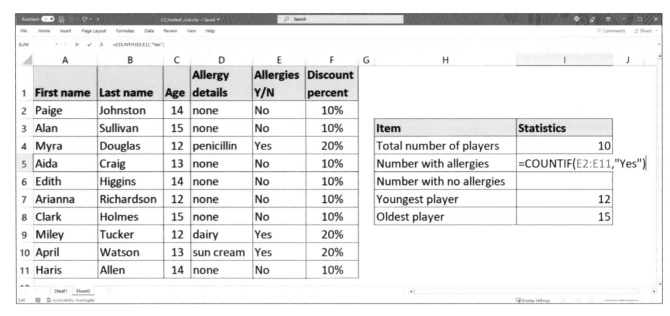

Figure 2.18: Calculating the total number of players with allergies using COUNTIF

Unplugged activity 2.4

You will need: a pen and paper

How would you work out the number of players with no allergies? Write down the formula.

Practical task 2.4

You will need: a desktop computer, laptop or tablet and Source file **2.3_test_results.xlsx**

Some learners sat tests for maths, English and computer science. The results for each test were recorded on a spreadsheet.
You will perform data analysis on the learners' results using the skills you have acquired working through this topic.

1   Using a suitable software package, open Source file **2.3_test_results.xlsx** and examine the contents.

2   Merge cell I2 and J2 so that the heading is centred over two columns.

Continued

3   Format the heading to be bold with a light grey background.

4   Format the table I2:J7 to apply a border to all the cell gridlines in the table.

5   Insert a function in cell J3 to calculate the highest mark in the maths test.

6   Insert a function in cell J4 to calculate the lowest mark in the English test.

7   Insert a function in cell J5 to calculate the number of marks which were greater than 80 in the three tests.

8   Insert a function in cell J6 to calculate the number of marks which were less than 40 in the three tests.

9   In cell J7, enter a formula to display the total number of learners in the spreadsheet.

10 Save your spreadsheet.

Practical task 2.5

You will need: a desktop computer, laptop or tablet with spreadsheet software and Source file **2.4_tuck_shop.xlsx**

Arun and his friends are running the school tuck shop this term. Arun has started to create a spreadsheet model to help him track the sales in the tuck shop but he has not finished it. You will help Arun finish creating the spreadsheet model.

Open Source file **2.4_tuck_shop.xlsx** and study the contents. The file shows items that have been sold over the past week.

Task A

1   In cell D4, enter a function to calculate the total revenue (income) from sales of biscuits for that week.

2   Replicate the formula entered in cell D4 so that it calculates the total revenue for each item.

3   In cells D15 to D19, insert appropriate functions or formulas to display the values of the items mentioned in cells A15 to A19.

4   Format all the currency values with the $ symbol correct to 2 decimal places.

5   Save your spreadsheet.

Continued

Task B

Arun would like to start a members' club, which would enable regular customers to get a 20% discount in the tuck shop. He wants to model a scenario where all tuck shop customers are members, based on the past week's sales.

1   Copy the existing tab in your spreadsheet onto a new tab so that you have two worksheets in your workbook.

2   Copy the 'Price per item' column and paste it into a new column to the right of the existing table. Rename this column 'Baseline price per item'.

3   To the right of this column, in a cell, write the heading 'Members' club active?'

4   In cell H4 (in the 'Members' club active?' column) enter the text 'Yes' or 'No' to indicate if a customer is a member of the club.

5   Change the value in cell C4 to a suitable formula to calculate the price for biscuits if the members' club is active, and if the members' club is not active.

6   Fill your formula down the column and check that it is correct in a few different cells.

7   Now change the 'yes' to 'no' in the 'Members' club active?' cell and see what happens.

    a   How has the total revenue changed?

    b   If all customers become members and sales numbers don't change, is it worth Arun starting the members' club?

    c   What are the limitations of this model?

    d   What would make it more realistic and useful?

Note: Your formula should refer to the 'Baseline price per item' column and the cell you typed 'yes'/'no' or 'true'/'false' into. You will need to use an absolute cell reference for this cell. Remember: this means putting $ before the letter and number in the cell reference to fix that reference to the correct cell when the formula is filled down the column.

Self-assessment

Think about what you have been able to do with ease on this topic. Did you find any aspect of this topic challenging? How did you work around that challenge?

Summary checklist

- ☐ I can evaluate how useful a model is for representing a real-life system.
- ☐ I understand a model needs to be tested with a variety of data in many ways so that I can see how it handles different scenarios.
- ☐ I can use conditional statements in a spreadsheet to choose between two or more options.
- ☐ I can confidently use cell ranges in a formula or function.
- ☐ I can use a formula to find the minimum and maximum values from a given range of cells.
- ☐ I can use a formula to count the number of cells in a range.
- ☐ I can use a formula to count the number of cells in a range that meet specified criteria.

> 2.2 Creating real-life systems and evaluating pre-existing spreadsheets

In this topic you will:

- create spreadsheets that model simple real-life systems
- understand essential features involved in the design of a spreadsheet model
- evaluate how suitable a pre-existing spreadsheet is for a given purpose.

Key words

layout

real-life system

suitability

Getting started

What do you already know?

- A computer model is a representation of a real-life system or situation.
- Various formulas are used to perform arithmetic and logical operations in a spreadsheet.
- To perform arithmetic operations, you can use functions such as:
  - SUM( )
  - COUNT( )
  - MAX( )
  - MIN( )
- The IF( ) function is useful for creating selection statements in a spreadsheet.

Continued

Now try this!

Get into small groups. Your teacher will give each group a spreadsheet model to look at. Open the file and examine it, looking at the formulas and changing a few of the values to see what the model does.

- Can you work out the model's purpose (what the model is for)?

- What are the features of the model that make it work?

- What are the features of the model that make it easy to understand and use?

Introduction to creating simple real-life systems

This section will look at creating spreadsheet models of **real-life systems**. A real-life system is any system that enables a user to engage with events or occurrences in the real world. Examples of real-life systems include air conditioning systems, flight control systems, transport systems and financial systems.

Deciding on a purpose

Firstly, you should think about the purpose of the spreadsheet. What will it do? What will people use it for?

There are many real-life systems you can create using spreadsheet models. Some of these include:

- school registers
- school results tracking systems
- monitoring systems
- business data storage applications
- accounting and calculation applications
- budgeting and spending applications
- calendars
- meeting agendas and many more.

When you have decided what your spreadsheet will do, you need to have an idea of:

- what data it will need to store
- what formulas and calculations it will perform on this data in order to do its job.

In other words, what will the column or row headings be, and what will the functional features of the spreadsheet be? Functional features are things like formulas and graphs. These will be the elements that enable your spreadsheet to do its job. If your spreadsheet fails to do the correct calculations, it will be pointless! For this reason, a model must perform the tasks it is designed for efficiently, using relevant data.

When you have an idea of the data and features you will use, you can start creating your model.

Creating the structure of the spreadsheet model

Layout

When creating the structure of a spreadsheet model, it is essential first to decide which information will go where – what should go in the rows and what should go in the columns. It is often helpful to decide this at the same time as you start creating your spreadsheet's layout. Layout refers to the way things are arranged or laid out on the spreadsheet. The layout of a spreadsheet model largely depends on the purpose of the model. We can decide which cells will be our row headings or column headings, how many columns or rows we need and so on. Trying different arrangements can help you decide on the best one.

Some spreadsheets will only have column headings, also known as field names, as shown in Figure 2.19. Other spreadsheets might have only row headings, as shown in Figure 2.20, and some spreadsheets will have both row and column headings.

	A	B	C	D	E	F
1	January	February	March	April	May	June
2						
3						
4						
5						
6						
7						
8						

Figure 2.19: Spreadsheet structure with layout showing column headings

	A	B	C	D	E	F
1	Day 1					
2	Day 2					
3	Day 3					
4	Day 4					
5	Day 5					
6	Day 6					
7	Day 7					
8						

Figure 2.20: Spreadsheet structure with layout showing row headings

Design features

When creating your spreadsheet's structure, it is important to use the available design features to make the information as clear as possible to the audience (the people using the spreadsheet). Use features such as the ones below to present your model clearly and in an attractive way. Think about:

- colours – you can use a colour theme if you need several different colours
- font size, type and style
- object and text alignments
- cell borders
- row heights
- column widths
- merging cells.

For example, coloured cell fills or text colours can be useful for drawing attention to certain rows or columns, or marking out certain rows as different. You can also use bold formatting to make certain information stand out.

You looked at formatting a spreadsheet in earlier stages. The information you covered will be helpful when creating and formatting the structure of a spreadsheet for your real-life system model.

Activity 2.2

You will need: a desktop computer, laptop or tablet with spreadsheet software and Source file **2.5_drama_club_register.xlsx**

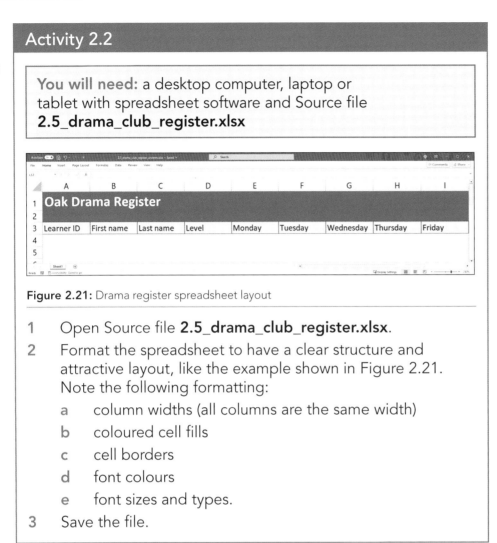

Figure 2.21: Drama register spreadsheet layout

1   Open Source file **2.5_drama_club_register.xlsx**.
2   Format the spreadsheet to have a clear structure and attractive layout, like the example shown in Figure 2.21. Note the following formatting:
   a   column widths (all columns are the same width)
   b   coloured cell fills
   c   cell borders
   d   font colours
   e   font sizes and types.
3   Save the file.

Creating the functional part of a spreadsheet model

In order to create a model of a real-life system, once the structure, layout and basic design is there, you need to start entering the data, formulas, functions and other spreadsheet features. You might not have thought about these in much detail when you were deciding what the spreadsheet model's purpose would be. Now you need to consider more precisely what information you need.

Adding data

When you create a system from scratch, you will often have to add data to it. In the case of a spreadsheet, you can enter the data manually by typing it or importing it directly from already prepared text files, such as a comma-separated values (CSV) file.

Practical task 2.6

You will need: a desktop computer, laptop or tablet with spreadsheet software and Source file **2.5_drama_club_register.xlsx**

Zara collected learner attendance details for the drama club rehearsals on a piece of paper. A drama club register structure was created using a spreadsheet. However, the model does not work yet because no formulas have been added. You will help Zara create a working drama club register to help her manage club attendance.

The details of the attendance for the week are shown in the table below. The character 'P' indicates that a learner was present, and the character 'A' means that a learner was absent.

1 Open Source file **2.5_drama_club_register.xlsx**.

Learner ID	First name	Last name	Level	Monday	Tuesday	Wednesday	Thursday	Friday
1234	Alex	Mumba	Beginner	P	P	P	P	P
1245	Felista	Kamiya	Beginner	P	A	A	P	A
1342	Agness	Tapiwa	Intermediate	A	P	P	P	P
1345	Melissa	Ngwira	Beginner	P	P	A	A	P
1355	Jeff	Arinze	Intermediate	P	P	P	P	A
1366	McDonald	Banda	Intermediate	P	P	P	P	P

Table 2.1: Drama club register

2 Add the data in Table 2.1 to the drama club register.

3 Check your data for any data entry errors.

4 Insert a new column with a suitable column heading after the 'Friday' column, which will be used to count the number of times a learner was present in the week.

5 Insert another column with a suitable column heading after the column created in step 4, which will be used to count the number of times a learner was absent in the week.

Continued

6   In cell J4, enter a function to calculate how many days a learner was present in the week.

7   In cell K4, enter a function to calculate how many days a learner was absent in the week.

8   Insert a new column after the absent column created in step 5 and call it 'Achievement point'. This column will be used to highlight learners who deserve achievement points for excellent attendance.

9   In cell L4, insert a formula which will display the text 'Award' if a learner's attendance is four days or more. If the learner does not deserve the award, leave the cell blank.

10 Replicate the formulas entered in steps 6, 7 and 9 so that attendance and award is calculated for every learner.

11 If you have not already done so, format the register so that it has a professional look using appropriate font sizes and styles, background colours, cell merging, borders, alignments and so on.

12 Save the spreadsheet.

Did you know?

Before spreadsheet computer programs were created, spreadsheet models used to be done on paper. This meant that every time a person wanted to change a number, they would have to erase that number, write a new number in and do all the calculations all over again. It took a lot of people a long time to do.

The first spreadsheet program was VisiCalc. It was written by Dan Bricklin and Bob Frankston for the Apple II computer in 1979. Dan Bricklin came up with the idea when he was doing a finance course at Harvard University and had been given an assignment to use a ledger sheet to create a financial model for a merger.

Figure 2.22: Screenshot of VisiCalc running on an Apple II computer

Putting it all together

Now that we have walked through the different steps of creating a model for one kind of purpose, let's look at another example model that has a different purpose.

Ms Zhang wants to create a simple automated learner result-tracking system using a spreadsheet. The system will hold learner results for her biology class.

Ms Zhang has asked Sofia to help create the automated results-tracking system. In this system, learners will do three quizzes, two assignments, two tests and one exam before the end of the term. The system will state whether each learner has passed the term.

Table 2.2 shows the requirements for the assessments.

Assessment	Marks	Total Marks
Quiz 1	10 marks	
Quiz 2	10 marks	40 marks
Quiz 3	20 marks	
Assignment 1	30 marks	
Assignment 2	30 marks	60 marks
Test 1	50 marks	
Test 2	50 marks	100 marks
Exam	75 marks	75 marks

Table 2.2: Breakdown of marks for assessments

The following is the breakdown of the weighting of each kind of assessment.

- The quizzes contribute 10% to the overall grade.
- The assignments contribute 20%.
- The tests contribute 30%.
- The final exam makes up 40%.

Weighting of an assessment means that if you get full marks in that assessment, it will give you a certain percentage of your overall mark. For example:

- The tests contribute 30%.

This means if you get full marks in both tests, you get 30% overall. Each test is worth 15% of your overall grade. The final exam has the highest weighting, as it is worth 40% of the total grade.

The system should also generate a term grade for each learner based on their overall score in all the assessments. The grade boundaries are shown in Table 2.3.

Overall Mark (%)	Grade
85 and above	A+
Between 75 and 84 inclusive	A
Between 65 and 74 inclusive	B
Between 50 and 64 inclusive	C
Between 40 and 49 inclusive	D
Below 40	E

Table 2.3: The grade boundaries of each grade

What is the purpose of your model?

Remember, before you can start entering data into your spreadsheet, you need to think back to what you want it to do. This will guide you regarding what information you need and what the outcome(s) should be.

In our example, what we want the model to do is:

- be a simple automated learner result-tracking system.

This system needs to track the results of the assessments and give an overall mark for *each* learner, stating whether each learner has passed or failed the term.

What inputs do you need?

Once you know what your model will do, you must list the inputs you need. In our example, Sofia will list:

- the name of each learner
- the results of three quizzes
- the results of two assignments
- the results of two tests
- the result of one exam.

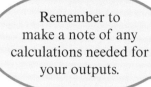

Remember to make a note of any calculations needed for your outputs.

What outputs do you need?

Once you know what your model will do, you must list the outputs you need. The system Sofia is creating will output:

- the total for each set of marks (the overall total of the three quizzes, the overall total of both assignments, and so on)
- the overall mark for the whole term for each learner
- whether the learner has passed or failed.

Often there are calculations or formulas needed for each output. It is useful to make a note of what these are for each item on your list.

Anything else?

There are often other things in the model that you need to consider. Make a list of these as well.

In our example, you need to be aware of:

- what full marks are for each assessment
- what the weighting is for each assessment.

Practical task 2.7

You will need: a desktop computer, laptop or tablet with spreadsheet software and Source file **2.6_learner_tracker.xlsx**

Now you have worked out what is needed for your model, create the automated results-tracking system. The learners' results are all collected in Source file **2.6_learner_tracker.xlsx**.

Firstly, open Source file **2.6_learner_tracker.xlsx**.

Continued

	A	B	C	D	E	F	G	H	I	J	K
1	Learner ID	Last name	First name	Quiz 1	Quiz 2	Quiz 3	Assignment 1	Assignment 2	Test 1	Test 2	Exam
2	1235	Allen	Paige	8	10	18	20	26	40	42	51
3	1237	Barrett	Ryan	7	8	16	25	24	38	40	61
4	1239	Davis	David	8	8	15	22	28	35	37	63
5	1241	Ellis	Sienna	9	8	18	21	25	39	41	68
6	1243	Fowler	Dexter	6	9	17	16	25	41	43	55
7	1245	Gibson	Byron	8	8	16	23	29	40	42	45
8	1247	Harrison	Henry	4	5	15	24	25	26	28	39
9	1249	Kelly	Adam	9	7	18	22	28	45	47	50
10	1251	Kelly	James	5	8	16	26	27	25	27	60

Figure 2.23: Examining the learner tracker file

We can see that we already have the learner names, their results for quizzes 1, 2 and 3, assignments 1 and 2, tests 1 and 2 and the exam.

We need to add the information that the tracker needs to show, starting with the total marks and the weight of each assessment. Let's start with the quizzes.

1. Create a new column after column F and call it 'Quiz total'. This column will hold a learner's total score for the three quizzes.
2. Use the SUM function in cell G2 to calculate the total mark for the three quizzes.
3. Now that we have calculated the total mark of the three quizzes, we need to calculate the weight of the quiz total as the percentage it contributes to the overall mark. Create another column after column G and call it 'Quiz weight (%)'.

   The quizzes contribute 10% to the overall mark, so we will use the expression:

   =Quiz total/Total mark*10

   where:

   - Quiz total is the total score that each learner gets on all three quizzes
   - Total mark is the total available marks for the quizzes from Table 2.2 (40 marks)
   - 10 is the available percentage that the quizzes contribute to the overall mark.

Continued

4 In cell H2, enter the formula, replacing the red and blue elements with the correct cell references or values.

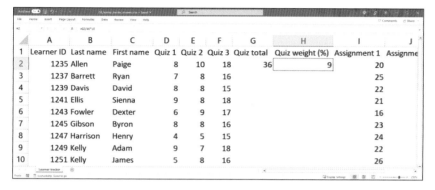

Figure 2.24: Calculating the weight of the quizzes as a percentage

We can see from Figure 2.24 that if a learner scores 36/40 on the quizzes, they get a 9% contribution to the overall mark.

5 Now fill the formulas in cells G2 and H2 down the columns to calculate the values for all the learners on the spreadsheet. Format all the values as whole numbers (no decimal places) and adjust the column widths so that all of the data is fully visible.

Now calculate the weights for the assignments, tests and exam.

6 Create a new column after the 'Assignment 2' column and call it 'Assignment total'. Insert a formula to calculate the total marks for the two assignments and fill it down the column.

7 Create a new column after the 'Assignment total' column and call it 'Assignment weight (%)'. Insert a formula to calculate the weight of the two assignments. This is calculated by dividing the assignment total mark by the total available assignment marks (60) multiplied by the weight (20). Fill the formula down the column.

8 Use similar steps to calculate the weight of the tests and exam using appropriate column headings.

9 Create a new column after the 'Exam weight' column created above and call it 'Overall mark (%)'. Insert a formula in this column to calculate the overall mark. This is calculated by adding together the quiz weight, assignment weight, test weight and exam weight. Fill the formula down the column.

Continued

10   Create a new column after the 'Overall mark (%)' column and call it 'Overall grade'. Use a nested IF statement to determine the grade the learner will receive based on the data in cell S2 and the given grade boundaries. Fill the formula down the column.

11   Format all the cells so that the numeric values are whole numbers (no decimal places).

12   In cells D24 and D25, enter the appropriate functions to determine the highest and lowest overall marks.

13   Save the spreadsheet.

Self-sssessment

After completing Practical task 2.7, how confident do you feel about creating a spreadsheet that models a real result-tracking system? Did you find it easy to calculate the weight of the tests and exam? If not, why is that so?

Assessing the suitability of a spreadsheet for a given purpose

Suitability means how appropriate or right something is for a situation. A spreadsheet is suitable when it does what it is intended to do. When evaluating or assessing a spreadsheet, you need to:

- examine the requirements (what the spreadsheet is meant to do)
- check that the spreadsheet does what it is supposed to do
- test the spreadsheet thoroughly (to check that every feature is doing what it is supposed to do).

You must check or evaluate all formulas to ensure they produce the correct results. You should also look at the non-functional aspects of the spreadsheet, asking yourself questions such as:

- How easy is it to use and read the spreadsheet?
- Are the instructions, if any, clear?
- Can I make any improvements?

Let's look at how we can evaluate a spreadsheet.

Arun is doing business studies in another class. His coursework this term is to think of a business he can run and create a spreadsheet to help him manage his staff.

Arun dreams of running an airline company with several flights within and outside Europe. He has asked you to help evaluate his spreadsheet and recommend any improvements he can make.

The requirements are that the system should:

- be well presented and easy for everyone to read
- use US dollars ($) correct to two decimal places
- calculate the total salary paid to all staff per month
- calculate the total number of pilots employed, including trainee pilots
- calculate the number of pilots who earn less than $2,000
- state the number of pilots above the age of 25
- state the number of pilots who work part-time.

Arun has asked his friend Marcus to look at the spreadsheet and suggest improvements. Marcus needs to look at the formulas, appearance and formatting of the spreadsheet.

To evaluate a spreadsheet's suitability, Marcus needs to check its functional and non-functional features.

- Functional features include correct formulas and proper data formats.
- Non-functional features include suitable text background and foreground colours, font sizes, images and layout.

Marcus opens the spreadsheet and examines it. You can also open Source file **2.7_pilots_data.xlsx** and examine it.

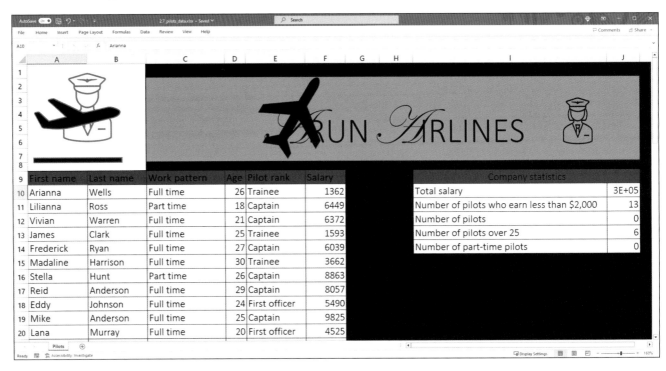

Figure 2.25: Arun's spreadsheet for evaluation

Marcus writes down the following notes for Arun:

- The title text has good contrast with the background colour. However, some people might not like the combination of black and orange.
- The plane icon covers the first letter of the airline's name, making it difficult to read. Maybe move the plane icon to the left or remove it, since there is already a plane icon in the top left corner.
- The formula to count the number of pilots is wrong: =COUNT(E10:E64). Column E contains text, and the COUNT function only counts cells with numeric values. Use COUNTA instead of COUNT for the same range.

Practical task 2.8

You will need: a desktop computer, laptop or tablet with spreadsheet software and Source file **2.7_pilots_data.xlsx**

Open Source file **2.7_pilots_data.xlsx**.

1   Evaluate the rest of Arun's spreadsheet, referring to all the requirements mentioned. Write down your analysis, using bullet points to describe what changes you recommend.

2   Now make all the changes you and Marcus have listed so that the spreadsheet fulfils all of the requirements and all the data is correct.

Questions 2.2

1   Name three examples of spreadsheet models people use in everyday life.

2   Fill the gaps in these steps for creating a spreadsheet model. The first letter of each missing word is provided for you.

a   Decide what the p_____ of your spreadsheet will be.

b   Think about what d_____ it will need to store (inputs), what c_____ it will perform and what the spreadsheet will o_____.

c   Create the l_____ of the spreadsheet, filling in the c_____ and r_____ headings. Use appropriate d_____ features to make the model easy to use.

d   Add your data and your f_____.

e   Check that all calculations w_____ as they should, and that the model fulfils its p_____.

3   Which features of a spreadsheet are more important and which are less important? Write the following features in order of importance from most important to least important. Give reasons for your answers.

tidy layout	correct formulas	correct data
nice colours	easy to use	

Practical task 2.9

You will need: a desktop computer, laptop or tablet with spreadsheet software

Figure 2.26: It's pizza time!

Marcus's uncle runs Pizza Pizzaz! – a company that sells pizza and drinks. Its main products are:

- Margherita pizza $1.80
- Vegetable pizza $2.00
- Meat pizza $3.00
- Seafood pizza $2.60

Marcus helps his uncle out at weekends. Marcus has said he'll build his uncle a spreadsheet model to help him plan the selling price for each of the products.

Marcus's uncle has told Marcus he needs to know:

- the cost to make
- the selling price
- the profit if 20 of each pizza is sold
- the total revenue
- the total profit.

Continued

Pizzas are sold at four times the price they cost to make.
For example, if a Margherita pizza costs $0.50 to make, it is sold at $2.00.

1   Make a list of everything you need to include in your spreadsheet:

    a   the purpose of the spreadsheet (be specific)

    b   inputs

    c   outputs (including calculations)

    d   anything else.

2   Using your lists, create your spreadsheet.

    a   What is your total revenue?

    b   What is your total profit?

Now you have created your spreadsheet model, we need to test that it works. You can use some of the data analysis tools you learnt earlier.

3   Marcus's uncle wants to sell each pizza at five times the price that it costs to make. The cost to make each pizza stays the same.

    a   What is your total revenue?

    b   What is your total profit?

4   Marcus is raising money for his youth club.
They want to buy a minibus and need $200 more.

Marcus's uncle says he will give all the profits raised next Saturday to the youth club. Pizza Pizzaz! is doing a special offer on Margherita pizzas next Saturday. They will cost $1.50.

If Pizza Pizzaz! sells 20 of each of the other pizzas (at five times the price that it costs to make them), how many Margheritas will they have to sell to raise the $200?

Peer assessment

Swap your spreadsheet with a partner.

Using the criteria given above, evaluate your partner's spreadsheet by writing in a separate document the things that work well and the things your partner can improve.

Continued

Make sure you:

- examine the requirements of the spreadsheet – does it do what it is supposed to?
- test the spreadsheet thoroughly – does everything work?
- check the formulas to ensure they produce the correct results.

Activity 2.3

You will need: some coloured pens and paper, a desktop computer, laptop or tablet with word-processing software

Zara has missed this lesson and you've said you will help her to catch up. Create a leaflet that she can stick in her book explaining how to evaluate the suitability of a spreadsheet and what to look for and consider.

What discoveries have you made whilst working on this topic? Are there specific challenges you faced? What strategies did you use to overcome them?

Summary checklist

- ☐ I can use spreadsheets to create models of simple real-life systems.
- ☐ I can use and explain essential features to consider when designing a spreadsheet model of a real system.
- ☐ I can evaluate a spreadsheet for a given purpose.
- ☐ I can test formulas in a spreadsheet to assess if they are working correctly.

› 2.3 Creating databases

In this topic you will:

- learn about the types of database
- learn how to create a relational database
- learn how to create complex searches in a relational database
- learn about big data and where it can be applied.

Getting started

What do you already know?

- A database is a collection of data organised in a way that makes it easy to store, retrieve and manipulate. In a database, you can set field names and data types.

- A database uses a **primary key**. This contains a unique piece of data for each record. The primary key ensures that each record is different from all the other records in at least one field.

- You should be able to perform simple validations on a database.

- You can search through an existing database using a single criterion, such as < or >.

Key words

attribute

big data

data redundancy

database

deletion anomaly

delimiter

flat file

foreign key

multiple criteria

orphan

primary key

referential integrity

relational database

update anomaly

wildcard

Continued

Now try this!

The table below shows the structure of a database table.

1   Identify the data types for each **attribute** (field name).

Attribute/field name	Data type
Learner ID	
First name	
Last name	
Age	
Height	
Do you like to read?	
Pocket money	

2   Which attribute or field name would you recommend to become the primary key and why?

Different types of databases

Figure 2.27: Paperwork and filing cabinets

Figure 2.28: Sofia opening a database

So far, you have learned that a **database** is an organised collection of data that allows data to be searched, retrieved and manipulated. A database can be paper-based, such as files in cabinets in an office (Figure 2.27) or electronic, such as spreadsheets on a computer (Figure 2.28).

A spreadsheet is an example of a **flat file** database. A flat file is created using only one table. However, the problem with using flat files is that they become difficult to manage as the quantity or volume of data increases. This is because the data items become so dependent on each other that whatever you do to one part of the data affects another. This means that activities such as deleting, updating or inserting new data into the spreadsheet can become challenging.

To overcome these challenges, we need to use another type of database known as a **relational database**. A relational database is a database made up of two or more tables that are joined together using a type of link called a relationship. Let's look at some problems caused by flat files and how a relational database can solve these problems.

Sofia has created a single table to store and manage classes and teachers.

Learner ID	First name	Last name	Class	Teacher	Department	Teacher phone
1	Alex	James	9B	Mr Brown	computing	+97155336254
2	Ndulo	Gems	9B	Mr Brown	computing	+97155336254
3	Mikel	Antenos	9B	Mr Brown	computing	+97155336254
4	Barbara	Juventus	9B	Mr Brown	computing	+97155336254

Table 2.4: Single table created by Sofia

If three more new learners join the class, Sofia will have to type in all the learner details and repeat the same information about the class and teacher.

Learner ID	First name	Last name	Class	Teacher	Department	Teacher phone
1	Alex	James	9B	Mr Brown	computing	+97155336254
2	Ndulo	Gems	9B	Mr Brown	computing	+97155336254
3	Mikel	Antenos	9B	Mr Brown	computing	+97155336254
4	Barbara	Juventus	9B	Mr Brown	computing	+97155336254
5	Marios	Bendis	9B	Mr Brown	computing	+97155336254
6	Gentos	Bandilas	9B	Mr Brown	computing	+97155336254
7	Benjamin	Andrea	9B	Mr Brown	computing	+97155336254

Table 2.5: Three learners added to the class

Sofia will keep repeating or duplicating the same information about the class and teacher for each new learner. This process can be tiresome if multiple learners join the class. This problem with flat files is known as **data redundancy**. Data redundancy means unnecessary replication of the same data in multiple places.

Let us look at the second scenario. If, at the end of the term, Mr Brown leaves the school to join another school, Sofia must now update the spreadsheet with information about the new teacher, Mr Ahmed. The problem is that Sofia will have to replace every instance of Mr Brown's name, department, and phone number with Mr Ahmed's information.

Learner ID	First name	Last name	Class	Teacher	Department	Teacher phone
1	Alex	James	9B	Mr Ahmed	science	+97150478526
2	Ndulo	Gems	9B	Mr Ahmed	science	+97150478526
3	Mikel	Antenos	9B	Mr Ahmed	science	+97150478526
4	Barbara	Juventus	9B	Mr Ahmed	science	+97150478526
5	Marios	Bendis	9B	Mr Ahmed	science	+97150478526
6	Gentos	Bandilas	9B	Mr Ahmed	science	+97150478526
7	Benjamin	Andrea	9B	Mr Ahmed	science	+97150478526

Table 2.6: Updating the table with new teacher information

If Mr Brown taught hundreds of learners, this information would need to be changed for every learner one at a time, which would be very tiresome. This kind of problem can lead to update anomalies. An anomaly is something that happens that is unexpected or unusual. An **update anomaly** is when different instances of the same data in a database become inconsistent with (different from) each other because only some of the instances are updated.

Lastly, suppose the learner Barbara Juventus leaves the class, and her record must be deleted from the spreadsheet. This will cause information about Mr Ahmed to be deleted alongside Barbara Juventus's details, as shown in Table 2.7.

Learner ID	First name	Last name	Class	Teacher	Department	Teacher phone
1	Alex	James	9B	Mr Ahmed	science	+97150478526
2	Ndulo	Gems	9B	Mr Ahmed	science	+97150478526
3	Mikel	Antenos	9B	Mr Ahmed	science	+97150478526
5	Marios	Bendis	9B	Mr Ahmed	science	+97150478526
6	Gentos	Bandilas	9B	Mr Ahmed	science	+97150478526
7	Benjamin	Andrea	9B	Mr Ahmed	science	+97150478526

Table 2.7: Deleting the learner Barbara Juventus from the table

If all the learners left the class and their records were deleted, then the spreadsheet would be empty, and we would have lost vital information about Mr Ahmed too. This is known as a **deletion anomaly** – the loss of valuable data when other data is deleted.

Learner ID	First name	Last name	Class	Teacher	Department	Teacher phone

Table 2.8: Table empty after deleting all learners

We can see that a flat file has limitations when it comes to managing inter dependent data. However, we can represent the same spreadsheet information using a relational database. We need to split the single table into two tables: a learner table and a teacher table. Then we need to create a relationship between the two tables, as shown in Figure 2.29.

Learner table

Learner ID	First name	Last name	Class	Teacher ID
1	Alex	James	9B	123
2	Ndulo	Gems	9B	123
3	Mikel	Antenos	9B	123
4	Barbara	Juventus	9B	123
5	Marios	Bendis	9B	123
6	Gentos	Bandilas	9B	123
7	Benjamin	Andrea	9B	123

Teacher ID	Teacher	Department	Teacher phone
123	Mr Brown	computing	+97155336254

Teacher table

Figure 2.29: A relational database structure

Notice that we have introduced a new column in each table called 'Teacher ID'. This column will help us join or link the two tables so that we do not lose the teacher information when we delete it from the first table. The Teacher ID in the teacher table is the primary key for that table. The Teacher ID is also used in the learner table, where it is a **foreign key**. A foreign key is a field in a table that is a primary key (unique entry) in another table. Using a foreign key creates a relationship between the two tables.

If a new learner joins the class, we only need to type the learner details in the learner table and provide the Teacher ID. If a new teacher joins the school, we enter the information in the teacher table, and that information will automatically be updated in the linked learner table. This is what makes relational databases powerful when it comes to data manipulation.

Unplugged activity 2.6

You will need: a pen and paper

The local zoo keeps a database of all their animals, what they are called, how old they are and how much they weigh.

The zoo has another database that keeps track of what food they have in stock so they know when to order some more.

Animal
Name
Age
Weight

Table 2.9: Animal database

Food
Food type (meat/veg)
No. of bags left

Table 2.10: Food database

The zookeeper needs to know which animals eat which foods.

With a partner, think about how you would link the two databases. Copy the two tables onto paper and add any extra fields that are needed to link them.

Creating a relational database using a database package

A relational database is like a folder containing multiple tables. We can represent the learner and teacher tables in a database software application and create a relationship between them. Microsoft Access is a good example of a database package that can be used to create a relational database.

You can create a database and add tables to it in two ways.

1 Create the database, then create the tables from scratch and type the data into each table manually.

2 Create the database, then import existing tables from other files into the database.

The first method is useful if you do not have a lot of data to type into your database tables. The second method is the most common and useful if you have a lot of data. Tables are prepared using other applications such as spreadsheets or word processors and are saved in a format that can be imported into a database.

Practical task 2.10

You will need: a desktop computer, laptop or tablet with database software and Source files **2.8_learner_table.csv** and **2.9_teacher_table.csv**

Sofia has asked Marcus to help her organise the class information. Marcus has decided to create the database using database software. He will need to import tables into his database and set appropriate data types for the tables. Then he will create a relationship between the tables.

Task A

1 Using suitable database software such as Microsoft Access, create a new database and save it with the name *School_information*.

2 Import the table from Source file **2.8_learner_table.csv** into your database. Set the data types for each field in the table as shown in Table 2.11.

Continued

Field name	Data type	Format
Learner_ID	number	integer
First_name	short text	
Last_name	short text	
Class	short text	
Teacher_ID	number	integer

Table 2.11: Data types for learner table fields

3   Set the field 'Learner_ID' as the primary key.

Solution

1   Open your database software and select 'Blank database' on the Microsoft Access 'Home' screen. Give the database the name *School_information* and create the database.

2   Before we import the table, we first need to close the default table that was made when we created the blank database. You can right-click on the tab (Table1) and select 'Close' from the menu or click on the X symbol next to Table 1.

    a   Go to 'External Data' on the main menu.

        i   Select 'New Data Source' from the ribbon.

        ii   Select 'From File' from the drop-down menu.

        iii   Select 'Text File' from the side menu, as shown in Figure 2.30. You can also import Excel, HTML documents and XML files.

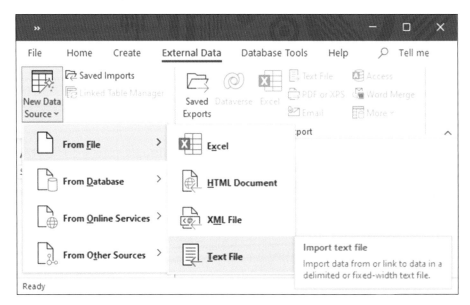

Figure 2.30: Importing a text file into Microsoft Access

Continued

b   This opens a new window to allow you to browse the computer and locate the file.

   i   Click on 'Browse' and find Source file **2.8_learner_table.csv** in your work area.

   ii   Make sure to leave the 'Import the source data into a new table in the current database' selected.

   iii   Click on 'OK'.

   Ensure the file you want to import is not open or being used by another application, such as Microsoft Excel, otherwise, you will encounter an error.

c   The 'Import Text Wizard' window will open. This will guide you through the steps to successfully import the Source file **2.8_learner_table.csv**.

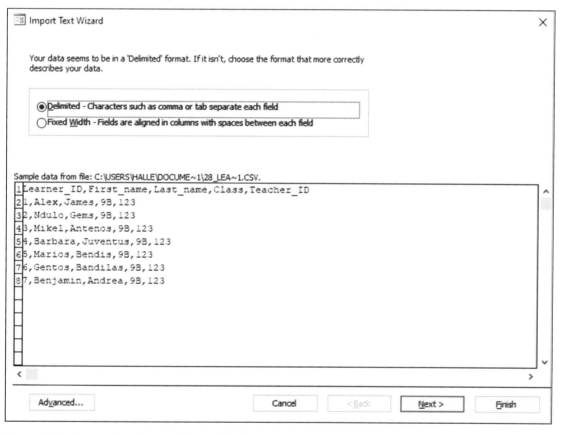

Figure 2.31: Setting the data to delimited before importing

Continued

Microsoft Access will detect the format of the data in the file. Since the learner table is a comma separated value file (CSV), each field or column in the file is separated by a comma, as shown in Figure 2.31. The comma between the columns is known as the **delimiter**. A delimiter is any symbol that separates two items of data. For example, the delimiter in a date could be a slash (/) symbol or a hyphen (-), so 20/04/2022 or 20-04-2022.

Leave 'Delimited' selected and click 'Next'.

d   On the window that appears, tick the checkbox 'First Row Contains Field Names', as shown in Figure 2.32, and click 'Next'. (If you don't tick this box, the program will assume that the first row is a record like all the other rows and there will be errors importing the table.)

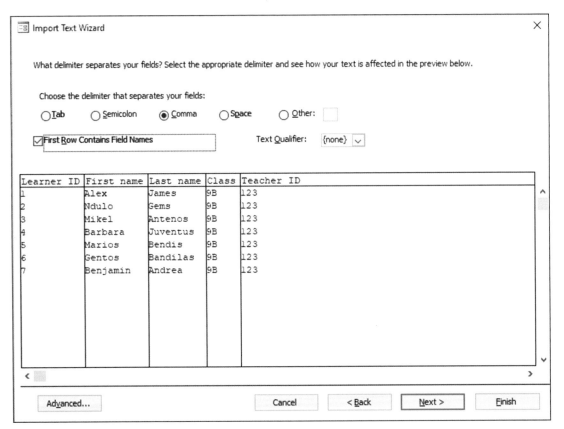

Figure 2.32: Setting the column headings using the delimiter

e   The next window is where you will set the data types for each field. Set the fields as shown in Figure 2.33 using the data types given in Table 2.11. In Microsoft Access, 'Short Text' supports text up to 255 characters, whereas 'Long Text' can accommodate longer sentences and paragraphs.

Continued

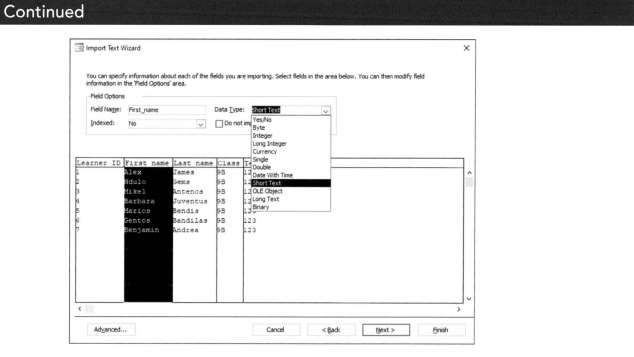

Figure 2.33: Setting the data types for fields

f   Click 'Next'. The next window is where you can set the primary key for your table. Select the radio button 'Choose my own primary key' and ensure 'Learner_ID' is set as the primary key from the drop-down list, as shown in Figure 2.34. You can also set the primary key in the table's Design View.

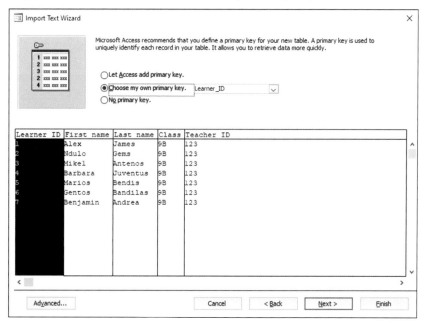

Figure 2.34: Setting the primary key for the table

Continued

g   Click 'Next' and then 'Finish' to complete the importing process.
     Figure 2.35 shows the imported table.

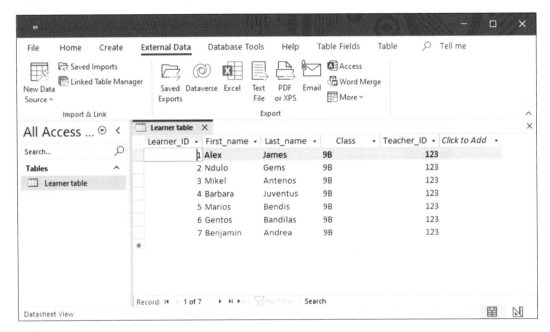

Figure 2.35: Imported table in datasheet view

Task B

1   Import Source file **2.9_teacher_table.csv** as a new table into the
     School_information database.

a   Set the data types for each field in the table, as shown in Table 2.12.

Field name	Data type	Format
Teacher_ID	number	integer
Teacher_name	text	short text
Department	text	short text
Teacher_phone	text	short text

Table 2.12: Data types for teacher table fields

b   Set the 'Teacher_ID' as the primary key for this table.

c   Save the database with the same name.

Question

• Explain why the 'Teacher_phone' field has been set to have the data type
  'Text' instead of 'Number'.

Creating a relationship between tables

Now we will create a relationship between the learner table and the teacher table. We first need to identify two fields we can use to link the two tables. The two fields must have the same data, and one of the fields must be a primary key in one table.

Practical task 2.11

> **You will need:** a desktop computer, laptop or tablet with database software, the *School_information* database created in Practical task 2.10 and Source file **2.10_class_table.csv**

Create a relationship between the 'Teacher_ID' field in the learner table and the 'Teacher_ID' field in the teacher table.

Task A

To create a relationship between two tables, first you need to close any open tables in Microsoft Access.

    a   Click on 'Database Tools' on the main menu and select 'Relationships'.

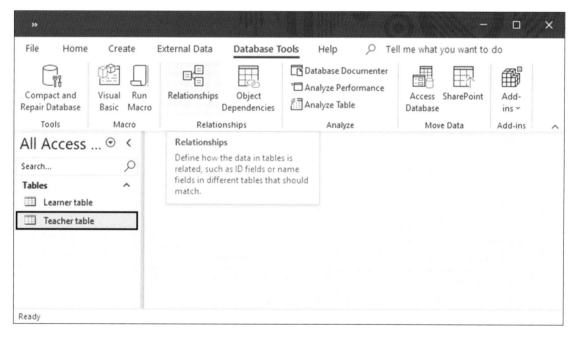

Figure 2.36: Opening the 'Relationships' window

Continued

b Select the tables you want to use to create the relationships and click on 'Add Selected Tables'.

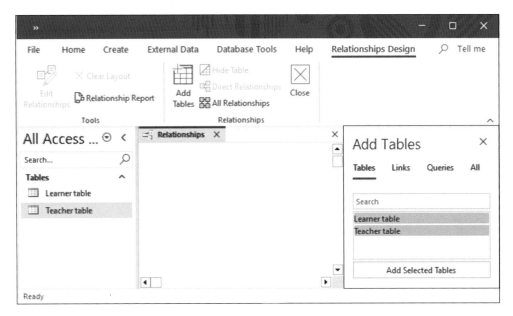

Figure 2.37: Selecting tables to use for the relationship

c In the window that appears, select the field 'Teacher_ID' in the learner table. Click and hold, then drag and drop it onto the 'Teacher_ID' field in the teacher table.

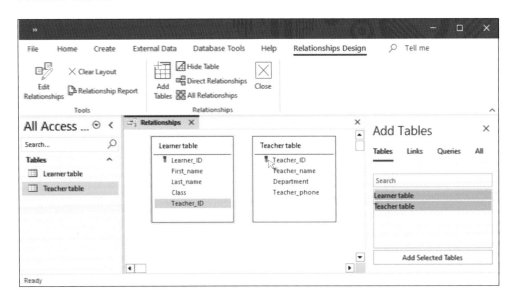

Figure 2.38: Selecting the fields for the relationship

Continued

d   The 'Edit Relationships' window will be displayed. Make sure that 'Enforce Referential Integrity' is ticked. **Referential integrity** is when all references are valid, that is, every record you add to one table has corresponding data in the linked table.

A record that isn't linked to corresponding data in another table but should be is called an **orphan**. Ticking 'Enforce Referential Integrity' makes sure that there are no orphans.

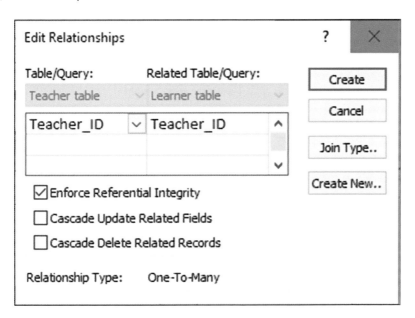

Figure 2.39: Enforcing referential integrity

There are some occasions when it is not possible to enforce referential integrity. In this case, just leave it unchecked and go on to implement the relationship.

Continued

e   Click on 'Create' to finish creating the relationship. The linked tables should look like the ones in Figure 2.40.

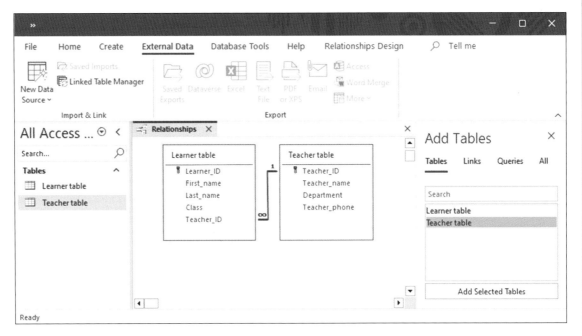

Figure 2.40: Relationship between the two tables

Task B

Now, let's see if you can create a relationship between tables on your own.

1   Import Source file **2.10_class_table.csv** into your database.
2   Identify and set suitable data types for each field in the class table.
3   Identify which field would be suitable to be the primary key in the table and set it as the primary key.
4   Create a relationship between the class table and the learner table using 'Class_code' in the class table and then 'Class' in the learner table.
5   Save your database with the same name.

Practical task 2.12

You will need: a desktop computer, laptop or tablet with database software and Source files **2.11_learner_data.csv** and **2.12_jobs.csv**

Zara interviewed several learners of different age groups and asked what they want to be when they grow up. She also researched the weekly income each job is likely to provide. Zara now intends to create a database to help her manage the collected information. She has organised the data into two tables stored in Source files **2.11_learner_data.csv** and **2.12_jobs.csv**. Help Zara to import the tables, set properties for each attribute (another word for field name) and create relationships between the tables.

1   Using a suitable software package, create a new database called *Careers*.

2   Import the file **2.11_learner_data.csv** into your database as a new table.

3   Set the data types for each attribute in this table to the values shown in Table 2.13.

Field name	Data type	Format
Learner_ID	number	integer
First_name	text	
Last_name	text	
Age	number	integer
Job_ID	text	

Table 2.13: Data types for learner data table fields

4   Set the 'Learner_ID' field as the primary key and name the table 'Learner data'.

5   Import Source file **2.12_jobs.csv** into your database as a new table.

Continued

6   Set the data types for each attribute to be the values shown in Table 2.14.

Field Name	Data Type	Format
Job_ID	Text	
Description	Text	
Weekly_earning	Currency	$ symbol to two decimal places

Table 2.14: Data types for jobs table fields

7   Identify which column would be suitable as the primary key for the jobs table and set it as the primary key. Name the table 'Jobs'.

8   Create a relationship between the 'Job_ID' field in the learner data table and the 'Job_ID' in the jobs table.

Creating complex searches in a database

A database is where you store information that will be used later. A database can hold vast amounts of data, which may not all be required at a particular time. Therefore, you must know how to search for specific information in a database. For example, when you visit a doctor for a medical check-up, the doctor might want to check your medical history before they can attend to you. The doctor will then have to search a database containing thousands of medical files to find yours.

Some searches can be simple, such as searching for a client by their last name. On the other hand, some searches can be complex. This is because they may involve searching for data using **multiple criteria**. Multiple criteria means we are searching for data that meets more than one condition.

Figure 2.41: Doctors searching through patients' medical histories

Unplugged activity 2.7

This should be a class activity. The class will be treated as a database, and your teacher will extract learners from the database that meet a specified criterion. Everyone should be seated initially.

1   All the learners who can speak English should stand up.

2   Of the learners standing up, those that speak another language other than English should continue to stand up. The rest of the learners should sit down.

3   Those native to the continent you are in should continue to stand up among the learners standing. The rest of the learners, who are from another continent, should sit down.

4   All the learners who have travelled to more than five cities on this continent should continue to stand up. The rest of the learners should sit down.

5   All learners who have spent more than four days in at least two countries should continue to stand up. The rest should sit down.

Creating complex searches using multiple criteria

Using multiple criteria enables us to refine the results of a database search. In Unplugged activity 2.7, you searched for learners in the class who met several criteria. As you increased the number of conditions a learner needed to complete before being selected, fewer learners were standing up. This is an example of a complex search using multiple criteria.

In real life, databases involve multiple criteria, such as filtering data by age, date of birth, last name and height. In this section, we will create complex searches in a database using multiple criteria.

Practical task 2.13

> **You will need:** a desktop computer, laptop or tablet with database software and Source file **2.13_dreams.accdb**

Zara collected and stored data about learners' dream jobs and the country they would love to travel to in their first year of employment. She has assigned each learner a fake employee ID (*Emp_ID*) to help her uniquely identify each learner. She now wants to analyse this data by performing searches on the database using multiple criteria. She would like you to help her create a query in the 'Learner dreams' table to search for learners:

- who are native English speakers
- who are less than 12 years old
- whose dream job starts with the letter A.

Zara only wants to see the learner's first name, last name, age and dream job in the results.

Task A

1   Open Source file **2.13_dreams.accdb** and examine the tables.
2   Go to the 'Create' tab on the main menu and to the 'Queries' group on the ribbon as shown in Figure 2.42.

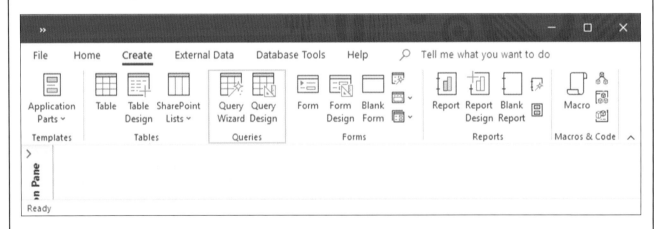

Figure 2.42: The 'Queries' group

Continued

3   Now let's create a query to find learners who are native English speakers and are less than 12 years old.

You can use the 'Query Wizard' or 'Query Design' to build your query. In this example, we will use the 'Query Wizard', so click on it to load the next window and select 'Simple Query', then click 'OK'.

4   Under 'Table/Queries', select the table from which you want to extract the data (in this case the table called 'Learner dreams'). Then select the required fields from the list shown below. For this question, you have been asked to display the learner's first name, last name, age and dream job. So, you need the fields 'First_Name', 'Last_Name', 'Native_English_Speaker', 'Age' and 'Dream_Job'.

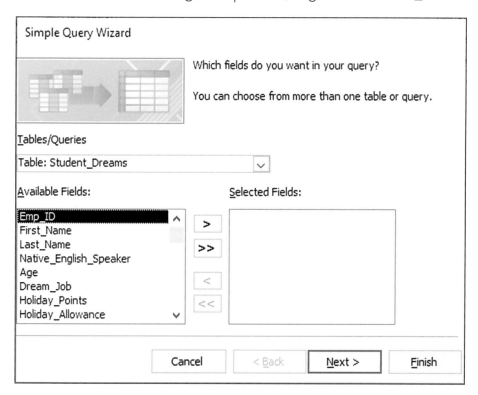

Figure 2.43: Selecting table and fields to use for the query

Continued

5   To select a field, either double-click it from the list of 'Available fields' or select it and click on the single >. The double arrows >> allow you to add all of the fields. To remove a field from 'Selected Fields', use the opposite arrow <. The double arrows << allow you to remove all of the fields. Complete the selection of the fields 'First_Name', 'Last_Name', 'Age', 'Native_English_Speaker' and 'Dream_Job'. These are the fields we will use for the query. Now, click 'Next'.

6   Click 'Next' in the window that appears. You can set the title or name of your query. Select 'Modify the query design' and click 'Finish'.

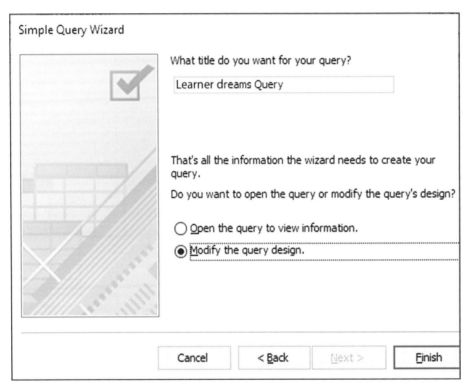

Figure 2.44: Options for finishing off the query wizard

Continued

7   We now have a query created on the screen that loads, but we have not specified the criteria. If this query is run as it is, it will display all the learners in the 'Learner dreams' table. If the screen in Figure 2.45 isn't showing, and you see the table showing all the learner data instead, click on the 'Design View' button on the 'Home' menu.

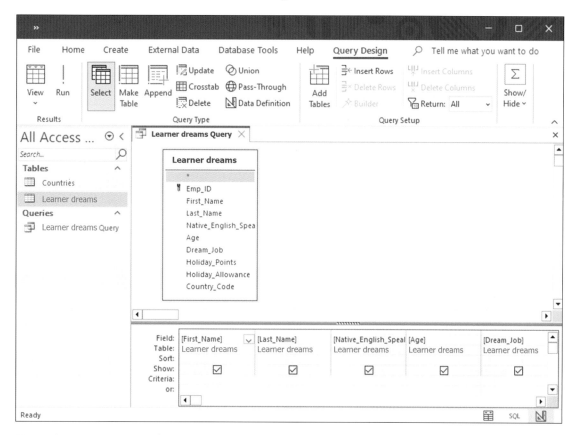

Figure 2.45: Design view of query

8   We need to specify the criteria: 'Native_English_Speaker=Yes', 'Age<12' and 'Dream_Job' that starts with the letter 'A'. Notice that the 'Native_English_Speaker' field is not among the fields that must be shown, so we should untick the 'Show' box. Type 'Yes' (without quotation marks) in the 'Criteria' row for 'Native_English_Speaker'. Then, set 'Age' to be less than 12.

Continued

9 Lastly, we need to set the dream job to start with the letter 'A'. To do this, we need to use a **wildcard** such as *. A wildcard in computing is a special character used as a placeholder for another character. Table 2.15 shows an example of how to use wildcards to search for a sequence of characters.

Wildcard *	Meaning
C*	should start with the letter C, followed by any character or none
CA*	should start with the letters CA, followed by any character or none
*D	should start with any characters and end with D
C*T	should start with C followed by any characters but should end with T

Table 2.15: Using wildcards

Figure 2.46 shows how we can use a wildcard to retrieve only the dream jobs that start with the letter 'A'.

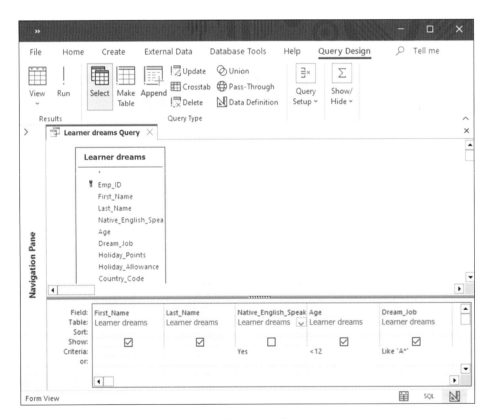

Figure 2.46: Adding multiple criteria to the query design

Continued

Now click 'Run' to display the output from the query.

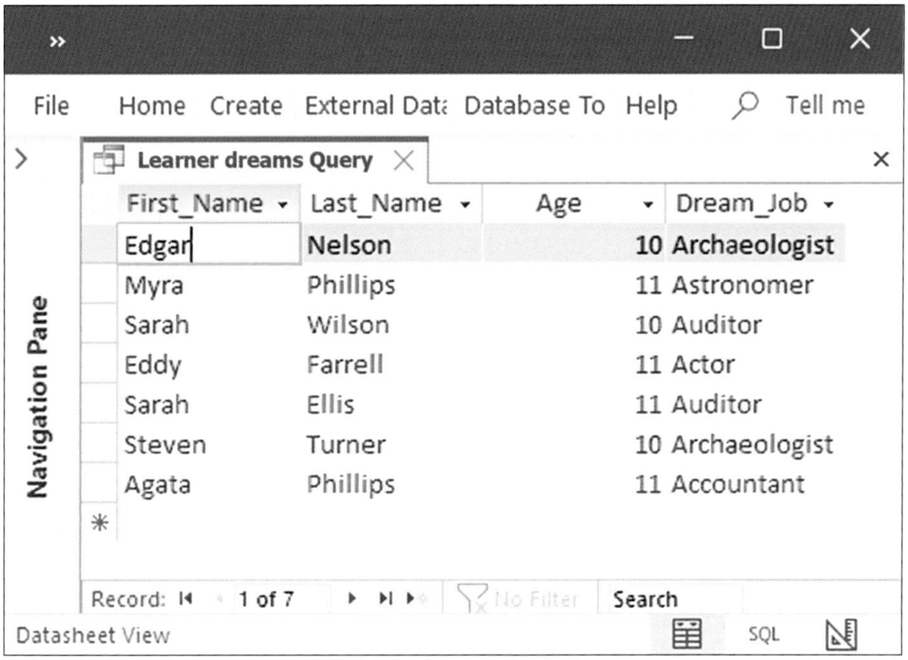

First_Name ▾	Last_Name ▾	Age ▾	Dream_Job ▾
Edgar	Nelson	10	Archaeologist
Myra	Phillips	11	Astronomer
Sarah	Wilson	10	Auditor
Eddy	Farrell	11	Actor
Sarah	Ellis	11	Auditor
Steven	Turner	10	Archaeologist
Agata	Phillips	11	Accountant

Record: I◄ 1 of 7 ► ►I ► No Filter Search

Datasheet View

Figure 2.47: Displaying the outcome after running the query

Task B

Now try these on your own using data from the 'Learner dreams' table.

1   Create a query to search for non-native English speakers whose dream job involves sales. Show only the learner's last name, first name, age and dream job.

2   Create a query to search for learners older than 14 years with last names beginning with M and with a holiday allowance. Show only the learners' first names, last names and ages.

3   Create a query to search for learners whose first names start with the letter 'A' and last names do not contain the letter 'A'. The learners should have accumulated fewer than two points and should not have a holiday allowance. In this order, show only the last name, first name and age.

4   Save the database with the same name.

Creating complex searches in a relational database

You can create complex searches in a relational database using the same process you would use when dealing with single tables. The only difference is that the data in a relational database will come from multiple tables. When creating the query, you must specify the tables you want to search for data, as shown in Figure 2.48. How to do this is explained in the following section.

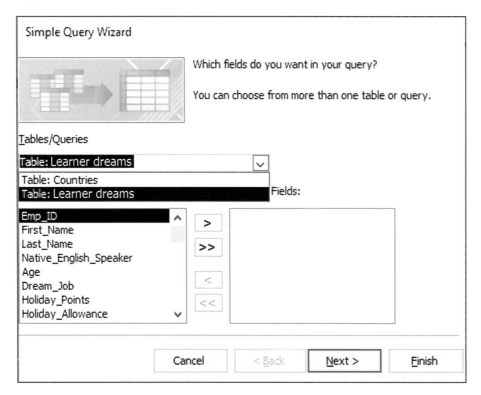

Figure 2.48: Selecting fields from multiple tables

Let's use a complex search to retrieve information from a relational database.

Practical task 2.14

You will need: a desktop computer, laptop or tablet with database software and Source file **2.13_dreams.accdb**

Zara wants to search for information about learners and their preferred holiday destinations in the first year of their dream job. The information is stored in the **2.13_dreams.accdb** database, which has two tables: 'Learner dreams' and 'Countries'. The 'Learner dreams' table holds information about the learners, and the 'Countries' table contains information about the holiday destination countries.

Using information from the two tables, Zara would like you to create a query that displays a list of all 14-year-old native English speakers who do not want to visit Switzerland. She would like the following information to be displayed in the results:

1 last name
2 first name
3 country.

The information must be in this order: last name then first name. Make sure it's not the other way around.

Task A

1 Open Source file **2.13_dreams.accdb** using database software and examine the content. There are two tables in the database.

Let's create a simple query using a query wizard to extract the required information. Notice that the information about the learners will come from the 'Learner dreams' table. The information about countries will come from the 'Countries' table. So, we need to create a query that uses both tables.

2 Go to 'Create' on the menu, then select 'Query Wizard' from the 'Queries' group.
3 Select 'Simple Query'.
4 Now select the 'Learner dreams' table from the list of 'Tables/Queries'.
5 Select the required fields 'Last_Name', 'First_Name', 'Native_English_Speaker', 'Age' and 'Country' as shown in Figure 2.49.

Continued

6 From the dropdown list of 'Tables/Queries', select the 'Countries' table and add the 'Country' field to the list of 'Selected Fields' as shown in Figure 2.49. Then, click 'Next'.

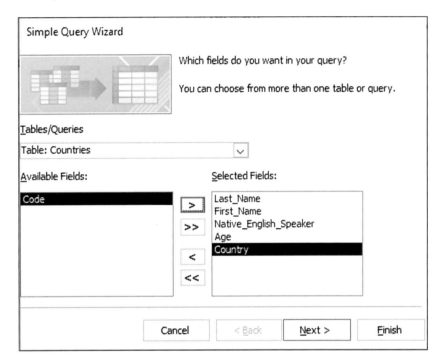

Figure 2.49: Selecting fields from the 'Countries' table

7 In the window that opens, click 'Next' again, then select 'Modify the query design'. Select 'Finish'.

8 In the query design, add the criteria to select only native English speakers using the 'Native_English_Speaker' field. Type 'Yes' (without quotation marks) in the criteria row, as shown in Figure 2.50.

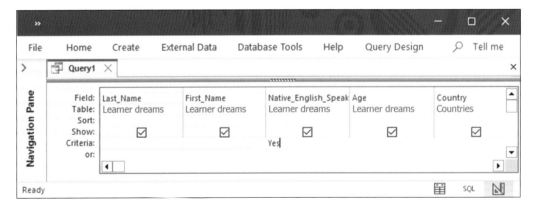

Figure 2.50: Extracting native English speakers

Continued

9 Click 'Run' to test the query. You should see a list of all native English speakers.

10 Next, we restrict the age to 14 years old. In the 'Age' field, set the criteria to =14 as shown in Figure 2.51, and then run the query. You should see a list of native English speakers who are 14 years old.

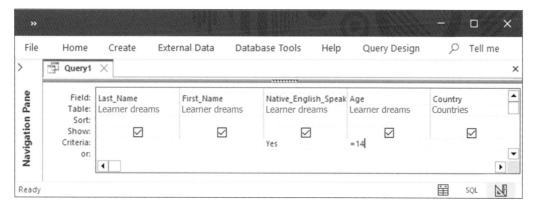

Figure 2.51: Extracting native English speakers who are 14 years old

11 Now we need to select learners who do not want to visit Switzerland. This is like choosing learners who want to visit Switzerland, except we must request the opposite result using the logical operator NOT.

If we wanted to select learners who want to visit Switzerland, we would write "Switzerland" in the 'Country' criteria. To exclude all learners who want to visit Switzerland, we can write NOT "Switzerland" (with the double quotation marks), as shown in Figure 2.52.

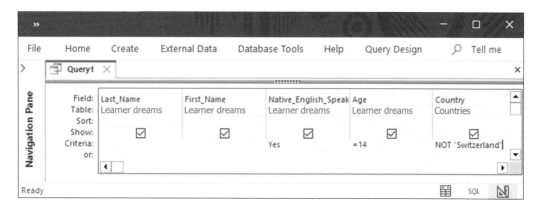

Figure 2.52: Extracting native English speakers who are 14 years old and do not want to visit Switzerland

Run the query, and all learners who want to go to Switzerland will not be shown.

Continued

12 Finally, in this order, we need to show only the fields for last name, first name and country. In the 'Show' row in the query design, untick the 'Native_English_Speaker' and 'Age' tickboxes, as shown in Figure 2.53.

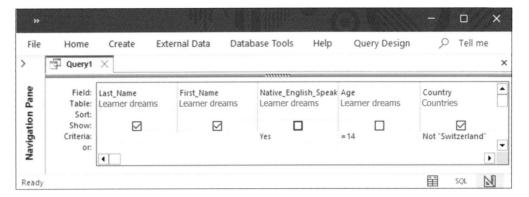

Figure 2.53: Selecting only the required fields in the query

13 The final list of learners extracted is shown in Figure 2.54.

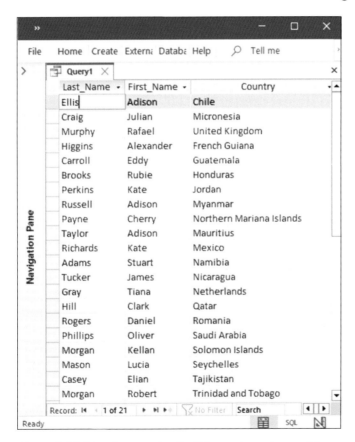

Figure 2.54: List of non-native English speakers who are 14 years old and do not want to visit Switzerland

Continued

Task B

1   Using information from the two tables, create a query that displays a list of all learners over the age of 13 who want to visit the United Arab Emirates or Tunisia. As before, show only the last name, first name and country.

2   Using information from the two tables, create a query that displays a list of learners with a holiday allowance, more than four points and who do not want to travel to a country whose name starts with the letter 'M'. Show only their first name, last name, country, points and holiday allowance in this order.

Peer assessment

Compare your solution to Practical task 2.14 to that of a friend. Did you both manage to extract the correct set of learners? If not, what did you or they do wrong, and how can you avoid making the same error in future?

Questions 2.3

1   What is the difference between a flat file and a relational database?

2   What is the main reason why relational databases are necessary?

3   What is data redundancy?

4   What is this query in the Dreams database searching for, and which fields will show in the results table?

Field:	Country	First_Name	Last_Name	Native_English_Speaker
Table:	Countries	Learner dreams	Learner dreams	Learner dreams
Sort:				
Show:	✓	✓	✓	☐
Criteria:	>"T*"			No
or:				

Big data and its application

Figure 2.55: Data server

The concept of **big data** is gaining a strong presence in the world today. Think about the amount of data stored on your phone, such as pictures, videos, emails and social media apps. You will realise that your phone deals with a lot of data. There are over 6 billion smartphone devices in the world, so you can imagine how much data is generated daily by these devices.

Big data refers to the huge volumes of complex data generated from different sources. The volume of this data is so huge that, by themselves, traditional methods of processing data are inadequate.

Activity 2.4

You will need: a desktop computer, laptop or tablet with internet access

Figure 2.56: Large amounts of data are uploaded to the internet every minute

Use a search engine to find the answers to the following questions.

1 How many photos are posted every minute on the internet?
2 What is the total size of videos posted on the internet every minute?
3 How many social media comments are posted every minute?
4 How many searches are done on the internet every minute?

Stay safe!

When searching for information on the internet, make sure you use secure websites. An unsecured website can contain malware that can harm your computer and files. Look out for the HTTPS protocol at the start of the address to check if a website is secure. You can also check for a padlock icon next to the web address.

Figure 2.57: Secure website – check for the padlock

Characteristics of big data

Big data has characteristics that make it different from ordinary data. There are five characteristics, also known as the five Vs.

Volume refers to the fact that big data deals with huge amounts of data. For example, hospitals and clinics generate a lot of data through patient records and test results every day.

Variety refers to the fact that this data comes from various sources: videos, audio files, emails, images and more. For example, in a hospital, the data can come from existing spreadsheets, X-ray images or other scans or diagnoses.

Velocity means speed – the data is generated extremely fast. Millions of people contribute to generating huge volumes of data every second. For example, during the COVID-19 pandemic, millions of people were tested for the virus, which generated vast amounts of data in a short time.

Veracity means data must be trustworthy and accurate. You must use reliable methods to collect and process data. Data inconsistencies must be eliminated before the data is used for important processes.

Value means making sense of the data generated so that people can benefit from it. For example, a quick and thorough analysis of test samples in a hospital allows patients access to better treatment and healthcare.

Application of big data

Big data is used in many areas today. Almost every industry generates and processes huge amounts of data. Retail shops like Amazon and eBay handle huge volumes of transactional data, customer data, browsing and shopping histories, order-tracking information and much more. There are many other areas where big data is used, including:

- transport
- insurance
- entertainment and media
- healthcare
- governments and their agencies
- education
- banking and finance
- technology.

Activity 2.5

You will need: a desktop computer, laptop or tablet with internet access and presentation software

Sofia is organising a group presentation about big data at school. She would like you to contribute by creating a presentation about an area or application where big data is used. The group will present this to the rest of the class at the end of the week.

1 Suggest an area of industry where big data is used.
2 Explain how the data is generated and used in that area.
3 Find images and other illustrations that can make your presentation more meaningful.
4 Videos are a wonderful way to summarise or introduce concepts to an audience. Find a video online that explains how big data is used in your chosen area and add it to your presentation.

- What are your biggest areas of strength in this chapter?
- What are your biggest areas of improvement in this chapter?
- What strategies will you use to help you master these challenges?

Summary checklist

- [ ] I understand the types of database and why we need them.
- [ ] I can create a relational database.
- [ ] I can create complex searches with two or more criteria.
- [ ] I can search through a relational database using complex searches.
- [ ] I understand the term 'big data'.
- [ ] I can list applications where big data is used.

Project: Database systems

You will need: a desktop computer, laptop or tablet with database software and Source files **2.14_patient_table.csv**, **2.15_doctor_table.csv** and **2.16_medical_history_table.csv**

Zara and Arun have just finished learning about databases and are excited to try some real-life projects.

They come across an advertisement for a competition inviting learners from another stage to create a hospital management database. The database will have related tables and queries to help doctors search for information about patients and their medical history, medicine and doctors. They have asked you and a partner to help them.

The competition organisers have provided you with three sample tables which must be linked together using relationships to create the hospital management database. The tables are:

1   Patient table (Source file **2.14_patient_table.csv**)
2   Doctor table (Source file **2.15_doctor_table.csv**)
3   Medical history table (Source file **2.16_medical_history_table.csv**)

Task 1

1   Create a database using the three tables provided. Set appropriate data types for each field and set primary and foreign keys.

2   Create queries to search for the following information from the database:

   a   privately insured patients who have been discharged – show their first name, last name, insurance type and previous diagnosis

   b   publicly insured patients who are 24 years old or younger and are currently admitted – show the doctor's title, last name and speciality, and the patient's details (first name, last name, insurance type and previous diagnosis)

   c   single patients discharged from the hospital whose first name contains the letter 'E' – show their first name, last name and the doctor's full name.

Each query should be saved with a meaningful name so it can be used again.

Task 2

Zara and Arun won the competition! They have been asked to tell the school about their competition entry in a school assembly. Your teacher wants you to help them write the presentation for the assembly. You need to explain:

1   primary and foreign keys
2   how to do complex searches.

Continued

They also want you to tell the school:

3   how many privately insured patients have been discharged
4   how old the oldest discharged patient was
5   how young the youngest discharged patient was.

To find out this information, you will need to find the correct table and open it as a spreadsheet.

Your presentation needs to explain points 1 to 5 above. You also need to tell the school:

- which functions you used to find out the answers to questions 3 to 5
- which formulas you used to find out the answers to questions 3 to 5.

You can create your presentation however you want. You could use presentation software, posters, act it out or even make up a song – as long as it contains the information required.

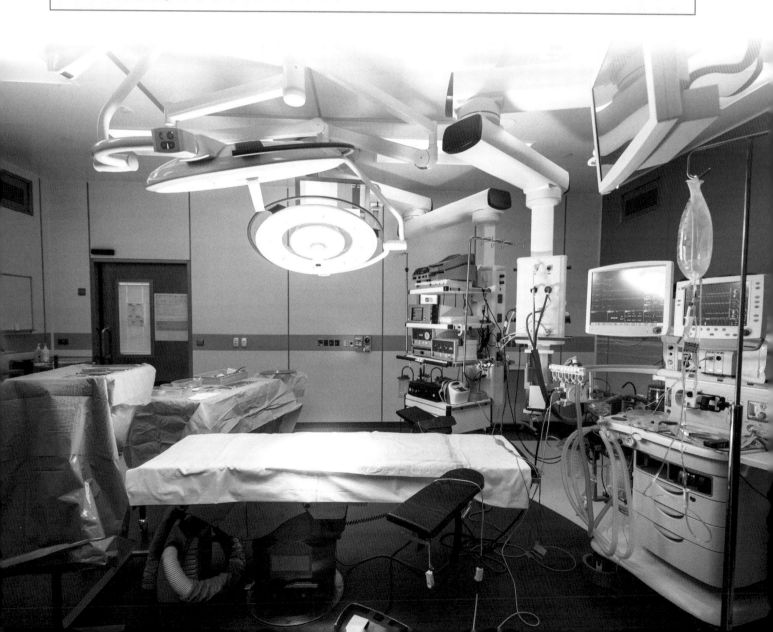

Check your progress 2

1 Models are used in many applications to simulate real systems.

   a   Explain two benefits of using models to represent real systems.   [2]

   b   Explain one challenge that may be associated with using models to represent real systems.   [1]

2 The spreadsheet below shows fruits that Arun sold at a school event. He now wants to analyse his sales.

	A	B	C	D	E	F
1	Item	Quantity (kg)	Unit price per kg	Total price		Statistics
2	apples	2.0	$1.30	$2.60		
3	guavas	2.0	$0.50	$1.00		
4	mangos	1.0	$1.90	$1.90		
5	watermelon	3.0	$3.00	$9.00		
6	peaches	1.0	$1.30	$1.30		
7	grapes	1.3	$2.60	$3.38		
8				$19.18		

Figure 2.58: Spreadsheet showing fruits that Arun sold at a school event

What will the output be if he places the following formulas in the 'Statistics' column?

a   =MAX(B2:B7) [1]

b   =MIN(D2:D7) [1]

c   =COUNTIF(B2:B7,">1") [1]

d   =IF(D8>15,"5% discount","2.5% discount") [1]

e   =COUNTA(A1:A7) [1]

3   Using the spreadsheet from question 2, write formulas to:

a   count the number of items sold [2]

b   determine the total price in cell D2 [2]

c   determine the overall price in cell D8 [2]

d   determine the smallest quantity in kg. [2]

4   Big data is now being used in many applications around the world.

a   Explain the term big data. [1]

b   State two applications where big data is used. [2]

c   State one source of data for one of the applications you mentioned. [2]

5   Sofia created a database to show test results.

Learner performance database					
Learner ID	First name	Last name	Maths	English	Geography
1234	Savanna	West	87	78	55
1235	Roman	Wright	45	85	65
1236	Alissa	Henderson	90	75	98
1237	Carlos	Grant	77	76	78
1238	Connie	Riley	79	75	85
1239	Aldus	Richardson	80	73	66
1240	Tyler	Brown	82	72	68
1241	Lilianna	Johnson	83	70	75
1242	Andrew	Martin	85	69	85
1243	Harold	Stewart	86	67	75
1244	Edwin	Roberts	88	66	89
1245	Oliver	Bailey	89	64	95
1246	Adison	Walker	91	63	99
1247	John	Brown	92	61	85

Table 2.16: Test results

a State the number of records. [1]

b State the number of fields. [1]

c Which field is suitable to be the primary key and why? [2]

6 Sofia created a query to search for information in the database.

Field:	Learner_ID	First_name	Last_name	Maths	English	Geography
Table:	Performance	Performance	Performance	Performance	Performance	Performance
Sort:						
Show:	☐	✓	✓	✓	✓	☐
Criteria:				>80	>=70	
or:						

Figure 2.59: Query to search the test results database

a State the output when the above query is executed. [4]

b Copy the query template below onto paper. Use it to write a query to search for learners who scored below 70 in English and above 90 in geography. Show only the learner's first name and last name. [4]

Field:	Learner_ID	First_name	Last_name	Maths	English	Geography
Table:	Performance	Performance	Performance	Performance	Performance	Performance
Sort:						
Show:	☐	☐	☐	☐	☐	☐
Criteria:						
or:						

Figure 2.60: Query to search the test results database

3 Networks and digital communication

> 3.1 Network topologies

In this topic you will:

- learn about the different network topologies
- learn about the advantages and disadvantages of the different network topologies.

Getting started

What do you already know?

- There are several different types of network, including personal area networks (PANs), local area networks (LANs) and wide area networks (WANs). The type of network needed depends on how many devices are in it and how large an area it covers geographically.

Key words

backbone

bridge

bus topology

data packet

hub

hybrid topology

IP address

media access control (MAC) address

network topology

node

ring topology

star topology

switch

terminator

Continued

- There are various types of network hardware, such as switches, routers, bridges and wi-fi access points.
  - Switches are network devices that connect devices in a LAN.
  - Routers are network devices that connect different networks, such as a LAN to a WAN.
  - Wi-fi access points extend a LAN so that other devices can access the LAN wirelessly.
- Digital content is stored on a server. This includes content for online streaming, such as video games and movies, and messaging services, such as emails.

Now try this!

Copy out and complete the activity by filling in the blanks with the correct term from the list below.

computers   printers   network   large   router

switch   WAN   LAN   small

A _____ is a collection of devices connected to share resources such as files and printers. You can use various devices to create a network. A _____ is a network device that connects devices such as _____, _____, access points and more in a network. This device has some level of intelligence that allows it to forward data to the correct connected device. A _____, on the other hand, is a device that connects two different networks. It has a table where it keeps the addresses of various networks.

There are several types of network. A _____ is a network that connects devices in a _____ geographical area, such as a school or building. A _____, on the other hand, is a type of network that connects groups of networks over a _____ geographical area.

Did you know?

One of the benefits of using networks is that they allow us to share data files and software between computers. Before computer networks were invented, data was saved onto floppy diskettes. The capacity of the floppy diskettes was as little as 1.44 MB and the data transfer speeds were very slow compared with modern networks.

Stay safe!

Malware can quickly spread to devices connected to a network. Every participating computer on the network should have up-to-date anti-malware software to keep the data files and system safe.

Network topologies

You have learnt about the different types of network in previous stages. In this section, we will look at **network topologies**. A network topology refers to the layout of the network in terms of how it communicates with different devices. The topolgy shows us the arrangement of devices on the network and the physical relationships between them, for example where each device is connected.

There are three network topologies. These are:

- star topology
- bus topology
- ring topology.

Other topologies can also be created by combining any of the three topologies.

Star topology

In **star topology** you connect all devices on the network to a central device, such as a **switch** or **hub**. A hub is a device that connects devices such as computers, printers and servers. However, a hub differs from a switch in that it broadcasts data packets to all devices connected to the network. A **data packet** is a small chunk of data sent across the network.

Unlike a hub, a switch has some level of intelligence. It can determine the correct device to which the data packets should be sent. Devices can connect to a switch or hub using cables. Some can connect wirelessly via wi-fi access points.

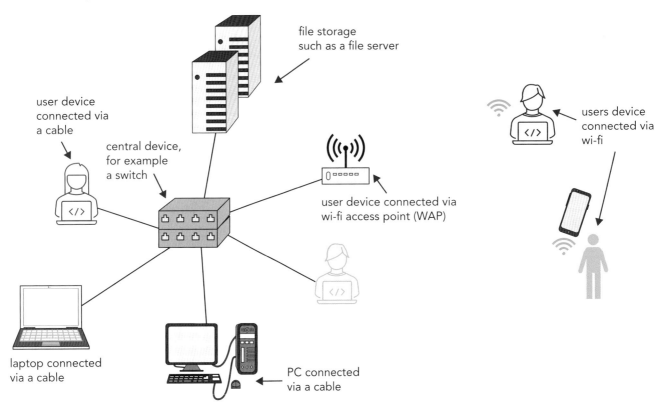

Figure 3.1: Layout of devices in a star topology

How a star topology works

Suppose Sofia wants to send a 14 gigabyte (GB) video file to Marcus using a star topology. Because the file is large, it cannot be sent as one whole file. The file must be broken into smaller chunks or packets for easier transmission. Each packet will have:

- a packet number by which it can be identified
- the sender's **IP address**
- the receiver's IP address.

An IP address is a series of numbers that is used to identify a device on the network.

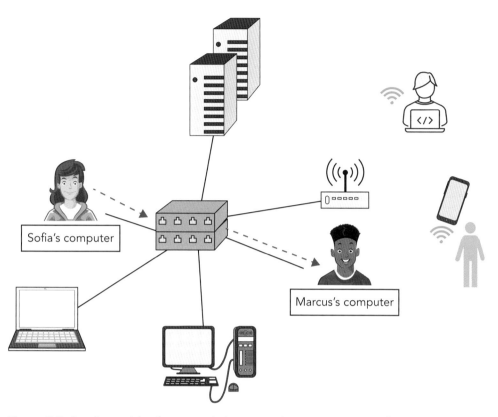

Figure 3.2: Sending a video from one device to another using a star topology

Sofia's computer sends the file in packets to the central device, which will check the packet to determine which computer on the network to send it to. The central device will compare the destination IP address in the packet to the IP address of each device. Then it will forward the packet to the computer with the matching IP address. When Marcus's computer receives all the packets, it must reassemble them in the order of the packet numbers to recreate the original 14 GB video file.

Advantages of star topology

- When one device breaks down, it does not affect the operation of other devices.
- You can manage the network from one central location. This means a network administrator can install software and manage network policies from one computer.
- It is easy to set up the network and to back up data.
- Devices can join using either an Ethernet (network) cable or wirelessly via a wi-fi access point.
- There is no limit to how many computers can connect.

Disadvantages of star topology

- When the central device breaks down, it affects the operation of the entire network. This is known as a single point of failure.
- It can be expensive to purchase cables for each device connected to the network.
- If too many computers connect, the network performance is reduced.

Bus topology

Bus topology is a network topology in a LAN in which all devices are connected to one cable. The cable runs through the room or multiple rooms, and devices connect to it to join the network, as shown in Figure 3.3.

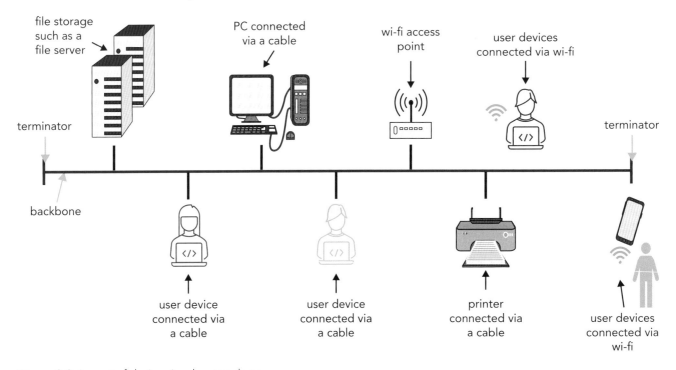

Figure 3.3: Layout of devices in a bus topology

In a bus topology, the long cable devices connect to is known as the **backbone**. The backbone is named after the long set of bones in the human skeleton known as the backbone or spine, to which other bones, like ribs, connect.

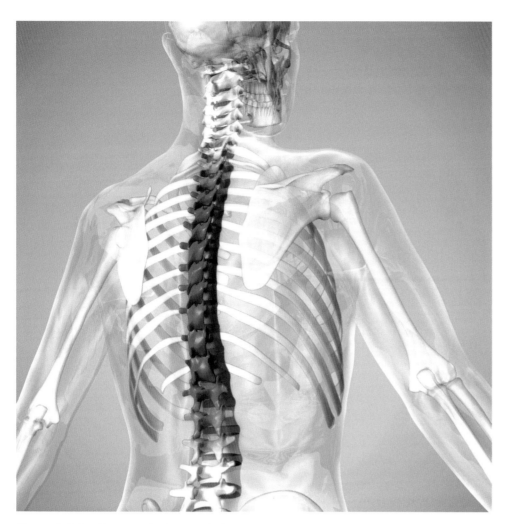

Figure 3.4: Backbone in the human skeleton

Figure 3.5: Example of coaxial cable

The backbone in a bus topology is made from coaxial cable like the one shown in Figure 3.5.

Each device joins the backbone using special connectors. At the end of either side of the backbone are **terminators**. Terminators are hardware devices that prevent signals from bouncing back to the backbone. Without terminators, there would be a lot of data collisions between old and new signals.

Coaxial cable is an electrical cable that is used primarily to carry data signals. It is made of a central inner conductor with a metal shield wrapped around it that is engineered to block signal interference.

How a bus topology works

Suppose Zara wants to send a music file from her computer to Arun, who is in the next computer room. She is connected to the bus topology using a cable, whilst Arun is connected using wi-fi, as shown in Figure 3.6.

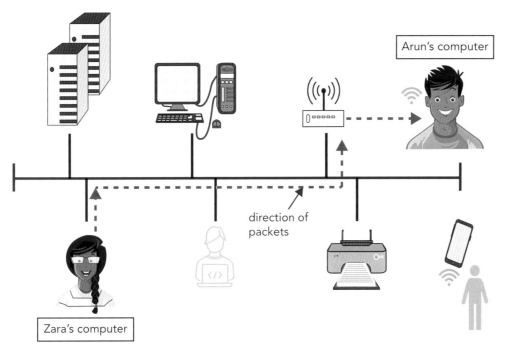

Figure 3.6: Sending a music file from one device to another in a bus topology

When Zara sends the file, the file is broken down into packets. Each packet can travel in any direction on the backbone. This causes all computers on the network to receive a copy of the packet, although they cannot open it to view the content. Each device will compare its IP address with the destination IP address of each packet. If the two IP addresses match, that device will be allowed to access the packet.

In this case, only Arun's computer will access the packets. The rest of the devices will discard the packets. This process is repeated for each packet until all the packets making up the music file are sent from Zara's computer. Once Arun's computer receives all the packets, it rearranges them in the order of the packet number to recreate the original music file from Zara.

Advantages of bus topology

- It is relatively easy to install the bus topology.
- It is relatively easy to add a new device.
- If one device fails, it does not affect the operation of other devices connected to the backbone.
- It uses fewer cables compared to the star topology. In a bus topology, cables run from the device to the nearest part of the backbone. However, in a star topology, cables run from the device to the central device, for example a switch, which could be at a distance.

Disadvantages of bus topology

- If the backbone cable breaks, the section of the network beyond the point of breakdown is affected.
- As the number of devices connected increases, the network becomes slower.
- There may be security concerns every device on the network receives a copy of the data packets.

Ring topology

Ring topology is a network topology where devices are connected one after the other to form a ring or loop. Each device has two neighbouring devices it communicates with. Ring topology is an old topology and is rarely used nowadays.

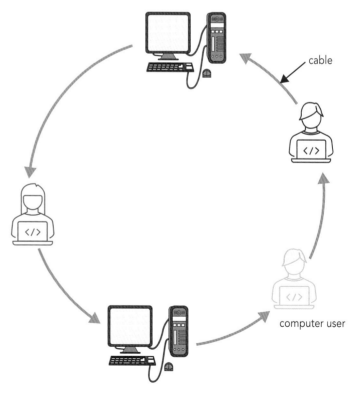

Figure 3.7: Layout of devices in a ring topology

How a ring topology works

Marcus wants to send a message to Zara. Each packet from Marcus's computer will be forwarded to all the computers in the ring before it gets to Zara.

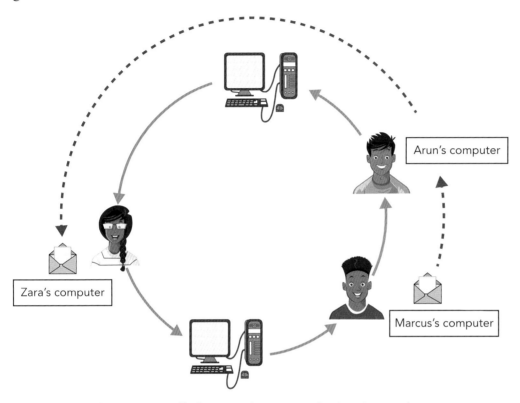

Figure 3.8: Sending a message file from one device to another in a ring topology

When the message reaches a device in the ring, the device checks the message's destination IP address and compares it to its own address. If the two addresses match, the message has successfully reached its destination. However, if they do not match, the device forwards the message to the next device in the ring. The process is repeated until the message is delivered or returned to the sender, after which the message is dropped from the ring.

Advantages of ring topology

- There is no need for a central device, which saves on costs.
- It is relatively easy to add a new device. However, this will cause an interruption to the other network users since you must turn off the network to allow the addition of new devices.
- Fewer cables are used compared with star topology. To connect a new device, the administrator only needs two short cables. Each cable will connect the new device to existing devices on either side of the new device.
- There is less chance of data packet collisions as the data is sent in one direction.

Disadvantages of ring topology

- If the ring cable breaks, the entire network is affected.
- If a device breaks or is switched off, the ring or loop is broken, and the network will not work.
- The data transmission process may be slower if too many devices are connected. This is because the data packets must pass through all the other devices before reaching the destination.

Hybrid topology

A **hybrid topology** is a topology created when two or more network topologies are joined together at a point called a **node**. A node in a network is a point of connection where wired or wireless devices can join the network.

An example of a hybrid topology is a star topology joined to a bus topology, as shown in Figure 3.9.

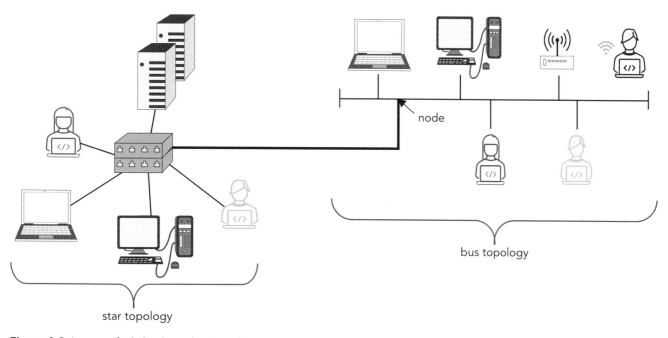

Figure 3.9: Layout of a hybrid star–bus topology

One of the immediate benefits of a hybrid topology is that it is very flexible, and you can enjoy the benefits of each network topology. However, this topology is costly and it is not easy to install. Other hybrid topologies can be created using a combination of any of the three topologies: star, ring and bus.

Unplugged activity 3.1

You will need: a pen and paper

Draw two simple hybrid topologies by combining the following topologies:

1   ring and bus topology
2   star and ring topology.

You must decide at what point (node) the second topology should join the first topology.

Unplugged activity 3.2

You will need: a pen and paper

Find out the network topology used in your computer room and draw the network topology diagram. Include in your diagram all the networked devices, such as printers, scanners and projectors.

Peer assessment

Swap your diagram with a partner. Have you both drawn the same topology? Have you both included the same devices?

If your diagrams aren't the same, discuss which elements are different and decide if you and your partner need to make any changes to your diagrams.

Bridges

Consider the bus topology below. Sofia wants to send data files to
Arun's computer. In a bus topology, data packets are broadcast to all
devices on the network. However, only the intended computer is allowed
to access the packets. Since every device receives a copy of Arun's data,
as the data moves in all directions on the bus, this causes network traffic
and slows down the network speed.

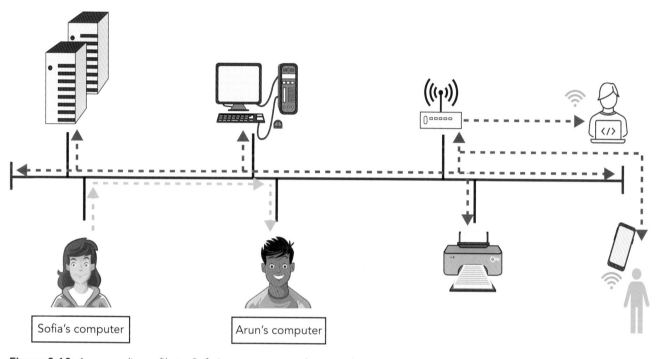

Sofia's computer

Arun's computer

Figure 3.10: Arun sending a file to Sofia's computer on a bus topology

To minimise network traffic in the above topology, you can use a
device known as a bridge. A bridge is a network device that joins two
segments in a local area network. The computers in each segment
are identified by their media access control (MAC) address. A MAC
address is a series of numbers that act as a physical address to uniquely
identify a device. You should distinguish a MAC address from an IP
address. A MAC address is a physical address created by the device
manufacturer to uniquely identify one hardware device compared
to another. On the other hand, an IP address is a logical address that
identifies a device connected to a network such as the internet. A MAC
address has two parts. The first identifies the device manufacturer, and
the second identifies the device's serial number. Most digital devices
have MAC addresses, including computers, phones, printers, smart
TVs and smart fridges.

A bridge stores a table that holds all the MAC addresses and says which segment of the network each MAC address belongs to. For example, for the network in Figure 3.11, the table would store the information shown in Table 3.1.

Device	MAC address	Segment
Arun's computer	00:00:5e:00:53:af	segment 1
Sofia's computer	01:23:45:67:89:ab	segment 1
printer	00:b0:d0:63:c2:26	segment 2
phone	00:00:0a:bb:28:fc	segment 2
Marcus's computer	00:25:96:ff:fe:12	segment 2

Table 3.1: An example table holding information about which segment devices are in

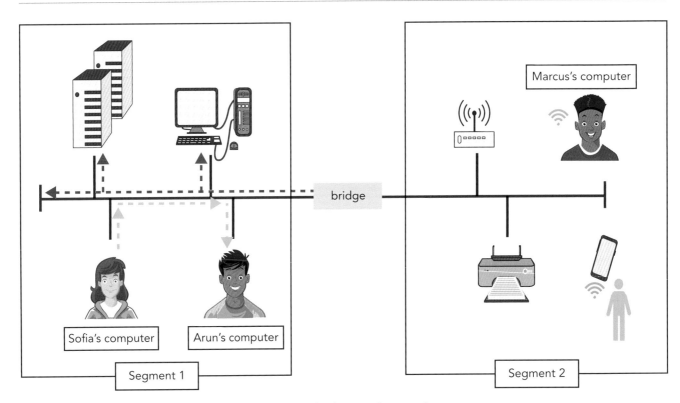

Figure 3.11: Arun sending a file to Sofia's computer via a bridge on a bus topology

Arun wants to send data to Sofia. When a bridge is used, as shown in Figure 3.11, the data packets follow this sequence:

1   Data from Sofia's computer is first sent to the bridge.
2   The bridge will check the destination MAC address and determine which segment Arun's computer belongs to. This is done by comparing the destination MAC address against a list of MAC addresses stored in the bridge's table for all the devices in the two segments (see Table 3.1).

3   The bridge will then broadcast the data packets only to devices in the correct segment. This prevents devices from the other segment from receiving a copy of Sofia's data packets, which improves the performance of the network.

Unplugged activity 3.3

You will need: a pen and paper

Look at Figure 3.11, Sofia decides to send a message to Marcus. Draw a diagram to represent how a bridge would handle the message before it gets to Marcus's computer.

How did you map the different topologies in the activities in this topic? Did you list the devices first and then draw the topology, or did you draw the topology type first and then add the devices?

Would you do it differently if you had to design a network or several networks for a place that doesn't already have a network?

Questions 3.1

Identify the network topology described in each statement.
You may choose more than one answer.

1   This network topology has a long cable that connects other computers to the network.

    A   bus topology   **B**   ring topology   **C**   hybrid topology   **D**   star topology

2   This network topology has a central device.

    A   bus topology   **B**   ring topology   **C**   WAN   **D**   star topology

3   In this topology, if one device fails, the network can still work.

    A   bus topology   **B**   ring topology   **C**   star topology

4   In this topology, if one device fails, the entire network fails.

    A   bus topology   **B**   ring topology   **C**   hybrid topology   **D**   star topology

5   In this network topology, each device is connected to two other devices that it communicates with.

   A   bus topology   **B**   ring topology   **C**   hybrid topology   **D**   star topology

6   This network topology uses terminators at the end of the cable.

   A   bus topology   **B**   ring topology   **C**   hybrid topology   **D**   star topology

7   When you combine one or more network topologies, you create this kind of topology.

   A   bus topology   **B**   ring topology   **C**   hybrid topology   **D**   star topology

Summary checklist

☐ I understand what a star topology is and how it works.
☐ I understand what a bus topology is and how it works.
☐ I understand what a ring topology is and how it works.
☐ I can explain the advantages and disadvantages of each network topology.

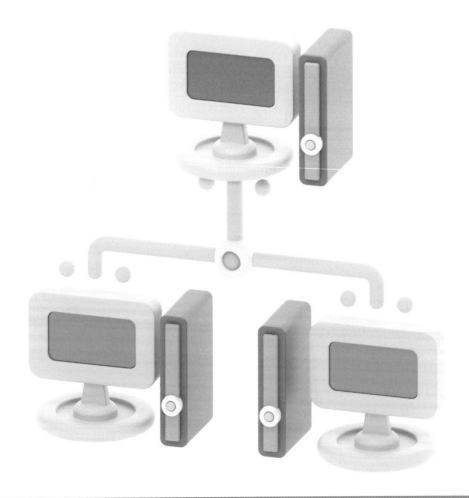

❭ 3.2 Data transmission

In this topic you will:

- understand what is meant by a protocol in computing
- understand the protocols TCP/IP and HTTP and how they are used in data transmission
- explain factors that you need to consider when designing a network.

Getting started

What do you already know?

- Data is divided into small pieces and transmitted as packets through many devices over networks to the receiving device. The data is then put back together at the destination.

- You can use fibre optic and copper cables to transmit data.
  - Fibre optic transmission is faster than copper cable transmission because fibre optic uses light impulses to send data. Copper cables use electrical signals, which travel at a slower rate than light.
  - Fibre optic has a higher bandwidth for a given transmission distance compared to copper cables.

Key words

acknowledgement (ACK)

bandwidth

client computer

client–server architecture

handshake

HTTP

protocol

protocol suite

scalability factors

server

synchronisation message (SYN)

synchronisation-acknowledgement (SYN/ACK)

TCP/IP

Continued

- There are advantages and disadvantages of using wired and wireless networks, including performance and security aspects:

  - Wired connections are usually more reliable, giving a more secure connection as they are hard to hack. They normally have a faster transmission speed for data than wireless connections.

  - However, it is more difficult to connect new devices, and they are normally more expensive to set up.

  - Adding new devices to wireless connections is easier, and they are cheaper to set up than wired connections.

  - Walls and other radio waves can interfere with wireless connections. Wireless connections can be less secure and normally have a slower transmission speed for data than wired connections.

Now try this!

> **You will need:** a desktop computer, laptop or tablet and Source file **3.1_networking_matching_exercise.htm**

Open Source file **3.1_networking_matching_exercise.htm** using a suitable web browser.

Match the key words or concepts on the left to the correct descriptions from the drop-down list. After answering all questions, click 'Check' to reveal your score.

Did you know?

The internet is made up of deep-sea fibre optic cables buried under the ocean, which connect the world's continents. Large ships on the surface of the water pull the cables to lay them in place under the ocean. Robots are then deployed underwater to bury the cable to protect them from sea creatures and fishing activities.

Figure 3.12: A cable under the ocean

Data transmission protocols

When you network devices, you allow them to share resources. These resources include data files, hardware and software. However, computers and other devices cannot talk to each other unless they agree on rules for communication. These rules are known as **protocols**. A protocol is a set of rules that control how devices can communicate, a bit like grammar in a language. There are several protocols used in digital communication.

TCP/IP protocol

TCP/IP is a **protocol suite** for data transmission. Remember that there are various kinds of protocol, all with different purposes. When we combine them, they are called an internet protocol suite. The two most important protocols are TCP and IP. TCP stands for transmission control protocol, while IP stands for internet protocol.

In the previous section, we defined an IP address as an address that identifies devices on a network. Without an IP address, it would be impossible to locate specific computers on the network or deliver data to them. TCP is a protocol responsible for data transmission on the internet. TCP works with IP to ensure the safe delivery of packets to the correct devices on the network.

Before transmitting using TCP/IP, there must be a 'handshake' between the devices intending to share data. A handshake is a technique that allows two devices to communicate before data transmission begins. The sending device sends a short message to the receiving device, indicating that it intends to send data. The receiving device sends a short message to the sending device telling it its status (whether it is ready to receive or not). The sending device can then start to transmit if possible. This allows the devices to determine what protocols and transmission speeds they will use. An example of a handshake is the TCP/IP handshake shown below.

A TCP/IP handshake is sometimes called a three-way communication. This is because:

1   The **first device sends a packet to the second device.**
2   Then the **second device responds by sending a packet to the first device**.

    The packet from the second computer includes extra information such as an acknowledgement (confirmation that what was sent has been received), the second device's status (whether it is free or not) and how the transmission will proceed.

3   When the first device receives the packet from the second device, **it must also send back an acknowledgement to the second device**.

This is how three-way communication is established.

Let us look at this using an example. Suppose Arun wants to send some data from his computer to a server on the internet.

1 **His computer first needs to establish a connection with the server.** This is done by sending a signal or packet known as a synchronisation message (SYN) to the server. A SYN is a short message to notify the server that Arun's device intends to transmit data.

2 **The server will respond by sending a synchronisation-acknowledgement (SYN/ACK) message to Arun's computer.** A synchronisation-acknowledgement (SYN/ACK) tells Arun's computer that the server acknowledges receiving his request and that the server is ready or not ready to receive data.

3 **Finally, Arun's computer must send an acknowledgement (ACK) to the server.** The acknowledgement (ACK) indicates that the computer has received the server's response and will wait or start transmission.

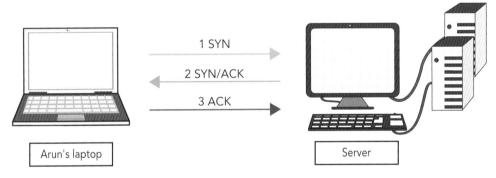

Figure 3.13: Handshake process between a laptop and a server

Unplugged activity 3.4

You will need: a pen and paper

Six statements are shown in the table below. Copy this table and mark each one true or false by ticking (✓) the relevant column.

	True (✓)	False (✓)
A protocol is a set of rules.		
Both devices must send an ACK message during a handshake.		
The first computer can send a SYN/ACK message during a handshake.		
TCP stands for transmission control process.		
TCP/IP is a protocol suite used only for security.		
TCP/IP can ensure that data is delivered to the correct computer using the IP address.		

HTTP

HTTP stands for hypertext transfer protocol. HTTP is a protocol that is used to send and receive files over the internet. HTTP can send any file such as text, images, videos and sound. It is also used to find specific documents or information on the World Wide Web (www).

Sofia wants to visit her school website to check out the recent swimming gala photos. She opens her favourite web browser on her computer and types the URL of the school website in the address bar.

Figure 3.14: Address bar showing a uniform resource locator (URL)

Sofia's computer makes an HTTP request via her browser to access the school website. At this stage, her computer becomes known as a **client computer**. A client computer is a computer that requests a service.

A computer that responds to requests from client computers like Sofia's is known as a **server**. The interaction between Sofia's computer and the server is known as **client–server architecture**. Client computers make requests to servers for services, and servers respond to clients' requests with the requested information if it is available, or with error messages if the information is not available.

When the server receives Sofia's request, it sends an HTTP response back to Sofia's computer. The web browser on Sofia's computer can interpret the HTTP response from the server and display the school web page on her browser.

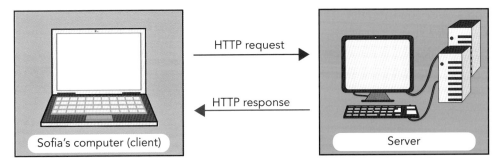

Figure 3.15: HTTP request from the client and HTTP response from the server

HTTP sends data as plain text, meaning it can be understood by anyone if intercepted.

However, a more secure HTTP version is HTTPS (hypertext transfer protocol secure).

The URL in Figure 3.16 shows an example of HTTPS.

Figure 3.16: Address bar showing HTTPS, a secure version of HTTP

You have learnt about the HTTPS protocol. HTTPS encrypts the data files before they are sent. To encrypt data means to encode or scramble it into a meaningless form so that it cannot be read without a decryption key. HTTPS can use protocols such as socket secure layer (SSL) or transport layer secure (TLS) to secure the data.

You can identify an HTTPS connection by checking for the letter 's' at the end of 'http' or a padlock icon just before the URL in the address bar.

Stay safe!

Do not send sensitive information, such as credit card details, or pay for things using an insecure HTTP connection. If the information is intercepted, the attackers can read it as plain text.

Unplugged activity 3.5

You will need: some coloured pens, a pencil and paper

Create a poster about how to recognise secure and insecure websites. Share your poster with learners from other stages to help them stay safe online.

Scalability factors to consider when designing networks

Small networks are usually built for a certain number of users. For example, in a school of 500 learners and staff, you can estimate that a maximum of 200 to 300 users will use the network at any time. So, all the devices and other network hardware will be designed with this number in mind.

However, if a school grows and takes on new staff and enrols more learners, it means there will be more users on the network. To make a network bigger, it needs to be scalable (able to change in size). When we talk about scalability factors, we are talking about the potential of the network to grow.

The following are some of the scalability factors to consider.

1 **Increased number of users on the network**

   The infrastructure and chosen network topology should support adding new computers or other devices to the network. Think of the advantages and disadvantages of the various network topologies we have looked at. For example, it is easier to set up a ring topology as you only need two connection points. However, as the number of nodes or computers on the network increases, the network becomes slower as it takes longer for the data to move across the network. Similarly, you should consider device or hardware limitations such as transmission speeds and bandwidth.

2 **The costs that come with increased users**

   As more people join the network, some of their devices will be further away from the central point of the network. Wired networks can be a maximum length of about 100 metres before the network signal or strength becomes weak. To extend a wired network, the network owner will need to buy new hardware equipment, such as wi-fi access. You might also want to break the network into two or more segments (parts) using hardware devices, such as bridges. Bridges restrict network traffic to a specific network section, leaving other parts unaffected by the traffic. We looked at a bridge in the previous topic when we talked about network topologies.

3 **The network bandwidth**

   Bandwidth means the amount of data a communication channel can carry. Bandwidth is like a road network. The more lanes there are on the highway, the higher the number of cars the road can carry at a given time. It is the same with networks: more bandwidth means more data carried by a communication channel and a faster overall transmission process. This means that more users can use the network at once.

4   Compatibility of hardware devices

The hardware used in networks must all be compatible. It must be easy to upgrade and maintain and it must work with other devices without issues. Devices can be incompatible for several reasons, including incompatible hardware, connection and transmission speeds, different protocols on each device and so on. Most organisations have policies that say they have to get all their hardware from the same manufacturer. These policies are created to minimise incompatibility and maintenance issues.

Activity 3.1

You will need: a pen and paper, a desktop computer, laptop or tablet with presentation software

In groups of three to five, visit the IT support department or equivalent in your school to conduct research on the network topology in your school. Ask the following questions and write down your answers:

1   How many people was it designed for?
2   Are there any hardware or software changes that the school would need to make if the number of staff tripled and the number of learner doubled?
3   Using suitable presentation software, make a presentation about your findings to present to the rest of the class.

Peer assessment

Think about the presentation of the group who went after you. (If your group went last, think about the presentation of the group who went first.)

*   Write down two things you liked about their presentation.
*   Write down one thing you think they could have included in their presentation or could have done differently.

What stood out for you from this topic? What did you enjoy the most? Is there anything you found challenging to understand? What steps will you take to resolve this?

Questions 3.2

1   State the difference between IP and TCP.
2   Explain what handshaking is.
3   What is the role of HTTP?
4   How does HTTPS differ from HTTP?
5   Imagine you have been asked to design a network for a small school of 100 learners and staff. Describe two scalability factors you would consider in your network design.

Summary checklist

- [ ] I know what a protocol is.
- [ ] I understand what transmission control protocol (TCP) and internet protocol (IP) are and how they work.
- [ ] I understand what HTTP is and what it is used for.
- [ ] I can explain the difference between HTTP and HTTPS.
- [ ] I can explain scalability factors that should be considered when designing networks.

> 3.3 Parity checks and network security

In this topic you will:

- understand what parity bits are
- understand the role of parity bits in error detection
- know how to calculate a parity bit
- explain the choices that need to be made when implementing network security, including accessibility, cost and the relative security requirements of different data sets.

Key words

accessibility

byte

cloud-based

even parity

machine code

odd parity

parity bit

parity block

parity check

security breach

transposition error

Getting started

What do you already know?

- Errors sometimes occur in data transmission. Some of the main reasons for this are:
  - electricity surges
  - interference in radio waves
  - crosstalk.
- One way a computer can check the data to see if an error has occurred is by using an echo check, which can be used to detect errors in transmission. During an echo check, the computer compares two data sets to see if they match.
- Firewalls play an essential role in ensuring that the traffic coming into a network meets specified rules.

  The user sets rules that the traffic must obey. Any traffic that does not meet these criteria is not allowed into the network.

Continued

- Antivirus software protects a computer against viruses that can delete, corrupt or modify computer files.

  - You must regularly scan your computer for viruses and update your antivirus software to ensure it has the latest virus definitions.

  - Viruses are constantly evolving, becoming more sophisticated and challenging to detect. Companies that create antiviruses regularly release new virus definitions, which include new rules and strategies for detecting viruses during a scan.

Now try this!

1 List one source of transmission errors.
2 Explain how an echo check can be used to detect transmission errors.

Parity checks

Understanding the role of parity bits in error detection

You have already looked at error detection methods such as the echo check. This section will look at another error detection method known as a parity check. A parity check is a method of error detection where the total number of bits in any data transmitted is either even or odd.

In earlier stages, you looked at how to represent numbers in a computer system using the binary number system.

We know that data is stored in bits, that is, 0s and 1s. One byte is made up of eight bits.

1	0	1	1	1	0	1	0

Table 3.2: One byte of code

Did you know?

Binary numbers are sometimes called machine code. Machine code is a low-level language. It is the language that computers understand. If you give the computer any high-level language (such as Python) or any language other than machine code, it must be translated to machine code for the computer to understand.

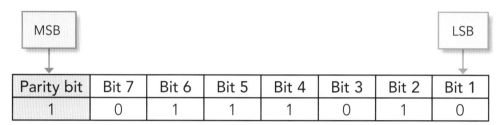

Table 3.3 shows the structure of a byte, including the **parity bit**, which is used as a check on a set of binary values.

Parity bit	Bit 7	Bit 6	Bit 5	Bit 4	Bit 3	Bit 2	Bit 1
1	0	1	1	1	0	1	0

Table 3.3: One byte of code with a parity bit

To start, let's read the bits from right to left. Or, from the least significant bit (the LSB) to the most significant bit (the MSB). Each bit in a binary number is assigned a weight based on its position, and these weights determine the column headings as shown in the table below. The LSB is the bit with the smallest weight while the MSB is the bit with the largest weight. For example, in the table below, the LSB is shown as $2^0 = 1$ while the MSB is shown as $2^7 = 128$.

Weight →	2^7	2^6	2^5	2^4	2^3	2^2	2^1	2^0
Column heading →	128	64	32	16	8	4	2	1
Binary number →	1	0	1	1	1	0	1	0

Column headings are useful when converting numbers to binary or denary. The eighth bit is the parity bit. The rest of the bits (bit 1 to bit 7) will store the data.

There are two types of parity check:

* even parity
* odd parity.

Both the sending and receiving devices must agree on the type of parity check they will use before transmission by performing a "handshake" (discussed in the previous topic). **Even parity** checks that the number of 1s in a byte is even. If the number of 1s in data (that is, bits 1 to 7) is odd, the parity bit is set to 1 to make the total number of 1s in the byte even.

Odd parity, however, determines to see that the number of 1s in a byte is odd. It sets the parity bit to 1 if the number of 1s in the data (that is, bits 1 to 7) is even.

In Table 3.3, there are four 1s from bits 1 to 7. This is an even number. Therefore:

* for an even parity check, the parity bit will be set to 0
* for an odd parity check, the parity bit will be set to 1.

Note: the parity check determines whether the number of 1s in a byte is odd or even. This does not mean that the binary number when converted to denary is odd or even. For example, there are five 1s in the table, which is odd. However, the binary number when converted to denary is 186, which is even. Remember, a denary number or decimal number is a number system that uses a base of 10, for example 0, 1, 2, 3, 4, 5, 6, 7, 8 and so on.

Unplugged activity 3.6

You will need: a pen and paper

1   Sofia sent the byte 10111011 to Marcus using even parity.
Marcus received the byte as 10111011. State whether
the transmission passed the even parity check.

Solution:

Marcus and Sofia used even parity, so the number of 1s in
the received byte must be an even number. Counting the
number of 1s in the byte gives us 6, which is even.
Therefore, the byte passed an even parity check.

Now try this on your own.

2   Marcus sent back a series of bytes to Sofia using even parity.
For each received byte, state whether the byte passed the
even parity check. Copy the table out and place a tick (✓) in
the correct column for each row.

Received byte	Passed (✓)	Failed (✓)
11001000		
01101111		
10110011		
00111100		
11111110		

Unplugged activity 3.7

You will need: a pen and paper

Sofia and Zara are sending some music files to each other using their phones. Their devices are using odd parity checks to check for transmission errors. Some bytes from the sent data are shown in the table below. State whether the received byte passes an odd parity check. Copy the table out and place a tick (✓) in the correct column for each row

	Transmitted byte	Received byte	Passes (✓)	Fails (✓)
1	10001001	10001001		
2	10101010	10101000		
3	11101110	01101011		
4	10101101	10101101		
5	00111001	01011100		

Limitations of parity checks

Parity checks can only determine if the transmission was successful by looking at the number of 1s in the byte before and after transmission. They cannot detect if there has been a swap or switch in the position of the bits during transmission.

Consider the communication between Arun and Zara in Figure 3.17. Arun sent a byte of data using even parity to Zara.

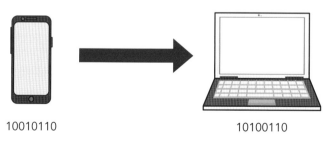

10010110   10100110

Figure 3.17: Arun sends data to Zara using even parity

The byte arrived on Zara's computer as 10100110. The devices used an even parity check, and the number of 1s in the received byte was even, so it passed the parity check. However, the data has been corrupted because some bits have been switched. You will get two different values if you convert the two binary numbers to denary, as shown in Tables 3.4 and 3.5.

- Converting **10010110** to denary

128	64	32	16	8	4	2	1
1	0	0	1	0	1	1	0

Table 3.4: Converting 10010110 to denary

= 128 + 16 + 4 + 2

= 150

- Converting **10100110** to denary

128	64	32	16	8	4	2	1
1	0	1	0	0	1	1	0

Table 3.5: Converting 10100110 to denary

= 128 + 32 + 4 + 2

= 166

This shows that the data has changed or is corrupted. This type of error results from bits switching places and is known as a **transposition error**. For example, a 1 turns into a 0 or the other way around. Transposition errors are mainly caused by human error during data entry. They can also be caused by changes in electrical voltages during transmission. One way of detecting transposition errors is using parity blocks.

Parity blocks

Parity blocks are used to detect which bits have been swapped during data transmission. When sending data, the data is transmitted in blocks. The block is made up of rows and columns. Each row contains a byte of data, and the last row contains the calculated parity byte.

	Parity bit	Column 1	Column 2	Column 3	Column 4	Column 5	Column 6	Column 7
Byte 1	1	0	1	0	1	1	0	1
Byte 2	1	1	1	1	0	0	1	0
Byte 3	0	1	0	1	0	1	0	0
Byte 4	0	0	0	0	0	1	0	0
Byte 5	1	0	0	1	1	0	0	1
Parity byte	0	1	1	0	1	1	0	1

Table 3.6: A parity block

A parity check is applied to each row and column before and after transmission. If the transmission used odd parity, then all the bytes (rows) and columns should pass odd parity. If one byte (row) fails an odd parity check, we expect one or more columns to fail the odd parity. We will add an extra column after column 7 to help us check each row.

	Parity bit	Column 1	Column 2	Column 3	Column 4	Column 5	Column 6	Column 7	Pass odd parity check?
Byte 1	1	0	1	0	1	1	0	1	✓
Byte 2	1	1	1	1	0	0	1	0	✓
Byte 3	0	1	0	1	0	1	0	0	✓
Byte 4	0	0	0	0	0	1	0	0	✓
Byte 5	1	0	0	1	1	0	0	1	✗
Parity byte	0	1	1	0	1	1	0	1	

Table 3.7: Rows of bytes being checked by an odd parity check

The first four rows (byte 1 to byte 4) in Table 3.8 pass an odd parity check. The fifth row (byte 5) doesn't pass. Let us add another row after the parity byte to help us determine if each column passes the odd parity check.

If we perform a parity check on the columns, all the columns pass the odd parity check except column 5, as shown in Table 3.8.

	Parity bit	Column 1	Column 2	Column 3	Column 4	Column 5	Column 6	Column 7	Pass odd parity check?
Byte 1	1	0	1	0	1	1	0	1	✓
Byte 2	1	1	1	1	0	0	1	0	✓
Byte 3	0	1	0	1	0	1	0	0	✓
Byte 4	0	0	0	0	0	1	0	0	✓
Byte 5	1	0	0	1	1	0	0	1	✗
Parity byte	0	1	1	0	1	1	0	1	
Pass odd parity check?	✓	✓	✓	✓	✓	✗	✓	✓	

Table 3.8: Columns of bytes being checked by an odd parity check

The intersection of the row and column gives us the corrupted bit, as shown in Table 3.9. In this case, byte 5 was switched from a 1 to a 0 in column 5.

	Parity bit	Column 1	Column 2	Column 3	Column 4	Column 5	Column 6	Column 7	Pass odd parity check?
Byte 1	1	0	1	0	1	1	0	1	✓
Byte 2	1	1	1	1	0	0	1	0	✓
Byte 3	0	1	0	1	0	1	0	0	✓
Byte 4	0	0	0	0	0	1	0	0	✓
Byte 5	1	0	0	1	1	(0)	0	1	✗
Parity byte	0	1	1	0	1	1	0	1	
Pass odd parity check?	✓	✓	✓	✓	✓	✗	✓	✓	

Table 3.9: Where the transposition error occurred

Limitation of parity blocks

Despite helping to detect which bit has been corrupted in the transmitted block, parity blocks cannot detect the exact corrupt bits in multiple rows or columns. For example, if two errors exist in a byte, that byte would still pass the even or odd parity check as before. For example:

Original byte

10101101

The byte has five 1s (an odd number).

Corrupted byte

10100001

The byte has three 1s (an odd number).

If, after transmission, two bits are corrupted, the byte will have three 1s (an odd number). Parity blocks will not find the exact bit that has been changed because they are looking for a change from an odd number to an even number of 1s.

Unplugged activity 3.8

You will need: a pen and paper

Marcus is transmitting a block of data to Arun using even parity. The block of data arrived at Arun's computer as shown here.

	Parity bit	Column 1	Column 2	Column 3	Column 4	Column 5	Column 6	Column 7
Byte 1	1	0	1	1	1	1	0	1
Byte 2	1	1	1	1	0	0	1	0
Byte 3	1	1	0	1	1	0	0	0
Byte 4	0	1	0	0	0	1	0	0
Byte 5	1	0	1	1	1	0	1	1
Parity byte	0	1	1	0	1	1	0	0

1 Add another column after column 7 to determine if each byte passes even parity.
2 Determine which byte (byte 1 to byte 5) has been corrupted.
3 Add another row after the parity byte to determine if each column passes even parity.
4 Determine which column has been corrupted.
5 Determine which bit has been corrupted.

Continued

Peer assessment

Review a friend's solution to Unplugged activity 3.8 for possible errors. Did they get it right? If not, what went wrong and how can they fix it?

Choices to be made when implementing network security

Figure 3.18: Servers on a network

The security of a network is an essential element of network design. Data should be protected from corruption, deletion or accidental loss. For this reason, organisations invest in security measures to minimise or prevent **security breaches** such as hacking. A security breach is a failure of security measures to prevent unauthorised access to a device, data, applications or networks.

Security measures to avoid security breaches may be physical or digital. Physical measures can include using access codes to server rooms and locking computers when not in use. Digital measures include firewalls, antivirus software, encryption and the authentication techniques that you have looked at in previous stages. These are all very important when considering the security of a network.

There are other things to think about as well. Decisions need to be made about things like:

- redundancy and data recovery plans
- accessibility
- cost
- training of staff.

Redundancy and data recovery plans

There should be adequate backup plans for network hardware, software and data in the event of an interruption. This can be achieved using redundant or multiple hardware devices, such as backups on external storage media or file servers located in different places. Suppose one part of the network is not working. In that case, the alternative hardware should allow minimal interruption to the network's operation.

Most organisations have subscribed to cloud-based security companies to manage their data. Using cloud-based data services means using the internet and remote servers to store and manage data. Cloud-based security companies help secure data offsite for their clients at a fee. The fee can be paid monthly or yearly as a subscription. This means that the client no longer has to worry about data security and availability.

Accessibility

When designing network security, it's crucial to consider accessibility for individuals with disabilities (for example, those with visual, hearing, cognitive, motor or mobility impairments) so they can use network resources safely and efficiently. The goal of accessibility is to ensure that every network user can experience equal participation and enjoyment in using network resources. Therefore, involving people with disabilities in the network design and testing processes can provide valuable feedback and continuous improvement.

There are various options for adding accessibility features, including:

- using alternative authentications like biometrics (fingerprints, facial recognition, voice recognition) or hardware tokens such as smart cards
- utilising user interfaces that allow easy navigation using screen readers, keyboard shortcuts and other assistive technologies
- labelling and documenting various parts of the network to assist users who need to navigate through the network sections
- ensuring training materials are accessible and, where appropriate, add alternative text for images and videos or provide video transcripts

Cost

There is a cost element that comes along with securing a network. The cost is for both software and hardware devices meant for network security. For example, you can buy a software-based firewall at a lower price than a hardware-based one. For some people, having a physical security device is ideal due to the nature of the data they want to protect (despite having to buy it at a very high price). Organisations that need physical security devices include large organisations like governments, banks and research centres, which hold very sensitive data. On the other hand, organisations like schools may use software-based security measures, which are cheaper but can provide enough security.

Training staff

Network users must be trained in the basics of security and how to protect themselves from being victims on the internet. For example, they must know how to identify fake websites, install and update antivirus software and identify phishing and pharming attacks, among other threats. Human errors cause most security breaches, so there must be resources allocated for training sessions for new network users.

If training sessions are not possible, there must be easy-to-use documents or brochures to give enough information to users about security. In some organisations, network users must sign an IT policy that outlines what they can and cannot do on the network. There are also sanctions for breaching any of the guidelines in the policy document.

Figure 3.19: Staff should be trained to spot threats

Unplugged activity 3.9

Work in a group of four.

Imagine that your group is setting up a business. It can be any kind of business. You need a secure network to run this business. As a group, think about and write down the choices you would make when implementing network security. Why did you choose what you did?

Questions 3.3

1   What is a parity check?

2   What are the types of parity check and what do they check for?

3   State two limitations of parity checks.

4   For each received byte, state whether the byte would pass an odd parity check.

	Received byte	Passes (✓)	Fails (✓)
a	11100001		
b	01110101		
c	11100101		
d	00111100		
e	00111101		

5   For each block below, determine:
    a   whether you need to do an odd parity check or an even parity check
    b   which byte (byte 1 to byte 5) has been corrupted
    c   which column has been corrupted
    d   which bit has been corrupted.

	Parity bit	Column 1	Column 2	Column 3	Column 4	Column 5	Column 6	Column 7
Byte 1	0	0	1	0	1	0	1	1
Byte 2	0	1	1	0	1	1	0	0
Byte 3	1	1	0	1	0	1	1	0
Byte 4	0	1	1	0	1	0	0	1
Byte 5	0	0	0	0	1	1	0	0
Parity byte	1	1	1	1	1	1	0	0

Summary checklist

☐   I understand what parity bits are.
☐   I can explain the two types of parity check.
☐   I can determine if a byte is corrupted during transmission using an even or odd parity check.
☐   I understand what parity blocks are and how to use them.
☐   I can explain the choices to be considered when implementing security measures on a network.

Project: Teach the class

Arun and Zara have joined the school's computer club this year. They have been doing a project on networks and the computing teacher has asked them to lead a lesson to teach the rest of their class about networks and how data is shared. They have asked you to help.

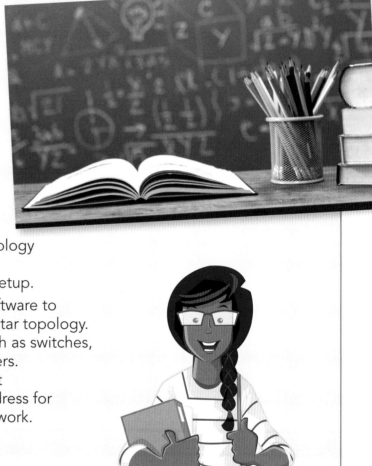

Task 1: Explain the different network topologies

Arun is going to explain about networks. He would like you to:

- Create a poster showing the different network topologies. Explain what topology your computer classroom has and why this is the best topology for this setup.

- Use free online network simulation software to create a network of 20 devices using star topology. Your network should have devices such as switches, desktop computers, laptops and routers. Choose appropriate cables to connect the devices. Set an appropriate IP address for each device so that it can join the network.

Task 2: Explain data transfer and error detection methods

Zara is going to teach the class about how data is transferred and needs your help in explaining error detection methods.

- Create a presentation for your class about error detection methods. Choose at least two error detection methods and explain how they work.

- Add visuals to your presentation such as videos, pictures or animations to make your presentation interesting and educational.

Ask your teacher if you need support with adding things to your presentation.

Check your progress 3

1 Which topology uses a single long cable to connect devices to form a network?   [1]
   a   WAN
   b   bus
   c   terminator
   d   ring

2 This is a central device that connects devices. It has some intelligence that allows it to forward data packets to the correct device. What is it?   [1]
   a   router
   b   switch
   c   hub
   d   bridge

3 The diagram shows a network segment.

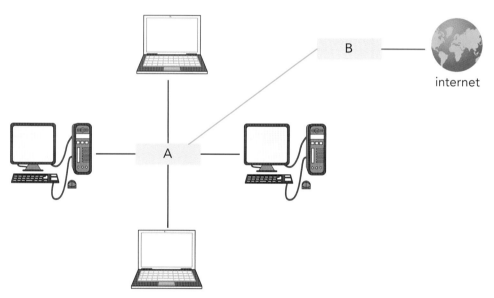

   a   Identify the device labelled A.   [1]
   b   Identify the device labelled B.   [1]
   c   What type of network topology is shown in the network segment?   [1]
   d   State two advantages of using this topology over other topologies.   [2]
   e   State one disadvantage of using this topology over other topologies.   [1]

4 The table below shows data received after transmission using even parity.

Add the correct parity bit to make the transmission of each byte pass an even parity check. **[3]**

Parity bit							
	0	1	1	0	1	1	1
	1	1	1	0	0	0	1
	1	0	0	1	0	1	1

5 The following block of data was part of a movie Sofia downloaded. Unfortunately, the data is corrupted.

	Parity bit	Column 1	Column 2	Column 3	Column 4	Column 5	Column 6	Column 7
Byte 1	1	0	1	0	0	1	1	1
Byte 2	0	1	1	1	0	0	1	1
Byte 3	1	1	1	1	0	1	0	0
Byte 4	0	0	0	1	1	0	0	0
Parity byte	1	0	0	0	0	1	1	1

The computer performs an odd parity check.

a Which column is corrupted? **[1]**

b Which byte is corrupted? **[1]**

c Explain how you would determine which bit is corrupt. **[1]**

d State which bit is corrupt (1 or 0). **[1]**

6 Protocols are used in many communication devices.

a Define the term protocol. **[1]**

b State two protocols that can be used during data transmission. **[2]**

c Explain the role of one of the protocols mentioned in question 6b. **[1]**

7 How does HTTPS help protect data transmitted over the internet? **[2]**

8 Mention two choices to consider when implementing network security. **[2]**

4 Computer systems

> 4.1 Computer design

Getting started

What do you already know?

- A computer system or device is made up of hardware and software. The hardware and software have different features that contribute to how the device does its job.

- People decide which hardware and software they want by looking at its cost, evaluating its design and deciding whether it does the job they need it to do in the best way possible.

Key words

- accessibility
- biometrics
- early adopters
- emerging technologies
- ergonomic
- ergonomics
- Internet of Things
- minimum viable product (MVP)
- prototype
- technology
- user experience

> **Continued**
>
> **Now try this!**
>
> You may have heard some of the key words in this topic before. Look at each one and write down what you understand it to mean. If you're not sure, guess!
>
> After you have written down a definition of each word, discuss with a partner what the words mean. Did you have the same ideas? If not, who do you think is right?

Design factors

The design of a computer device is very important. A computer device should:

- be easy for the user to use
- look attractive to the user
- be appropriate for the user's needs.

You are going to learn how to look at the design of a computer device and identify improvements that can be made.

There are three main factors that we should consider when looking at the design of a digital device. They are:

- user experience
- accessibility
- ergonomics.

User experience

The way a person feels when they use a device or application is called the **user experience**. It is important that device manufacturers and software companies make sure their products are easy for everyone to use. If their software or devices aren't a pleasure to use for a wide range of people, people won't buy them! Therefore, the user's interaction with the device needs to be as easy and pleasant as possible.

Sofia has a new mobile phone. She takes the phone out of the packaging and turns it on. She starts to use the new device and has some thoughts.

Figure 4.1: It's important for a device to be easy and fun to use

- I like the colour.
- The screen is nice and bright.
- The interface looks very simple to use.
- I can easily see where I would find my photographs.
- The buttons are easy to press.

All the things that Sofia is thinking about are part of the user experience.

Unplugged activity 4.1

You will need: a pen and paper

Think of five other features that Sofia could comment on that are about the user experience of a mobile phone.

Peer assessment

Compare your five user experience features with a partner. Which of the features they thought of did you find most interesting? Share this with your partner.

Accessibility

Accessibility is how easy something is to use (or access) for a person with a disability or special needs. It is important for companies to make sure that as many people as possible can use a device easily, including those who have difficulties with their sight, hearing, movement or learning. As with user experience, this focuses on the user's interaction with the device.

Arun has a friend who is partially sighted – she cannot see as well as other people. Arun is helping his friend find a tablet computer that is accessible for her needs. Arun has found a device he thinks has good accessibility features for his friend. He tells her, "This tablet looks great! You can use voice commands and change the screen colour."

Figure 4.2: It's important for devices to be as accessible as possible so that everyone can use them

There are lots of things that can be included in a device to improve its accessibility. Some of these are:

- the ability to change the colour of the background and text to make it easier to read (for example, a dark mode)
- speech-to-text software that allows the user to speak words into the device and have the text appear on screen
- the ability to use voice commands to tell the device to do things
- larger buttons that can easily be pressed by users with reduced movement skills
- a colour-corrective screen for users who are colour blind
- simplified gestures, for example instead of having to pinch the screen to zoom in, the user can double-tap it
- a vibrate function to allow a user with a hearing impairment to feel that a notification has been received.

Activity 4.1

You will need: a desktop computer, laptop or tablet with infographic software

Zara is volunteering at a games club for people with different disabilities. Zara knows people at the games club like to play games on their electronic devices. Zara decides that she would like to display a poster in the club about the different accessibility features that can be included in a device. She would like you to create the poster.

Zara has given you the option to focus your poster on one particular device, for example a mobile phone, or on a range of different devices.

Self-assessment

Zara wants you to make sure that your poster is eye-catching and easy to read. Display your poster on your computer screen and stand a few steps back from your computer. Think about the following questions.

- Is it easy to read everything on your poster?
- Is everything nicely spaced out on your poster?

Ergonomics

Ergonomics is the science of designing things to be efficient, safe and comfortable to use. In everyday language, when we talk about things being **ergonomic**, we usually mean they have been designed to fit the natural position of the human body so that using them is a comfortable and pleasant experience.

Figure 4.3: An ergonomic mouse

For example, an ergonomic computer mouse is designed to fit into the natural shape of the hand so that it can be used for a long time without causing pain or injury. The buttons are easy to press and in the perfect position for the fingers to use repeatedly without discomfort.

Marcus has a new laptop computer. He is really pleased with the ergonomics of his new laptop. It feels very comfortable to sit with the laptop on his lap and use it. It has an inbuilt wrist rest that supports his wrists and helps to stop them hurting when he types for long periods of time. The laptop is also lightweight, so it doesn't hurt when it rests on his lap, and it fits perfectly in his bag to allow him to carry it around.

Unplugged activity 4.2

You will need: a pen and paper

Think about buying a new mobile phone. What ergonomics would be important to you? What features would the device need to have to make it the best device for you? Write down your thoughts and then share them with a partner. Do you value the same things in a mobile phone?

Designing a device that is suitable for all users can be a very difficult job. People come in all different shapes and sizes and often want very different things from a device. There are lots of things that a designer needs to consider and they will normally base their decisions on the people they most want to use the device. For this reason, it is often possible to look at a device and think about improvements that would make the device more suitable for you.

Activity 4.2

You will need: a desktop computer, laptop or tablet with presentation software

Think about a device that you use on a daily basis. Create a presentation that:

- shows how you feel about your experience of using the device
  (What do you think is good about it? What do you think is not so good?)
- shows what kinds of accessibility features your device has
- shows how you feel about the ergonomics of your device.

In your presentation you should also include three improvements that you would make to your device if you could. Say why each of them would improve the device for you.

Peer assessment

Swap your presentation with a partner. Ask your partner for their exercise book. Write down the following checklist in your partner's exercise book:

- The presentation contains information about user experience.
- The presentation contains information about accessibility.
- The presentation contains information about ergonomics.
- The presentation contains three improvements.
- The presentation looks smart and professional.

Look at your partner's presentation and complete the checklist for it. You should also complete these two sentences in your partner's exercise book about their presentation:

- I think the best improvement you have suggested is …
- I think this is the best improvement because …

Emerging technologies

Technology is the application of scientific knowledge to practical situations in order to achieve a task. Examples of technology include all sorts of things we use every day, such as electronic toothbrushes, cars, computers and software. Emerging technologies are new or developing technologies, or new ways of using existing ones. Here are some examples of emerging technologies:

- Artificial intelligence (AI) is a simulation of human intelligence within a computer system. AI has regular new developments.

Figure 4.4: Facial recognition software on a smartphone

- 5G is a wireless communication technology with very fast data transmission speeds.

- **Biometrics** technology uses the measurements of human features for security and personalisation. There are regular new developments, especially in areas such as facial recognition.

- Nanotechnology is a relatively new technology that involves manipulating individual atoms and molecules to create useful structures and substances.

Did you know?

One exciting nanotechnology currently in development is graphene. Graphene is a material made of sheets of carbon atoms arranged in a honeycomb structure. Graphene is excellent at conducting electricity, is very flexible and has a high surface area.

In testing, batteries made with graphene have been able to store four times as much energy as existing batteries at less than a quarter of the cost. A smartphone with a graphene battery would be able to last for a week on a 15-minute charge! Graphene batteries will also last much longer before wearing out, meaning that in the future, an electric vehicle could use the same battery for many decades.

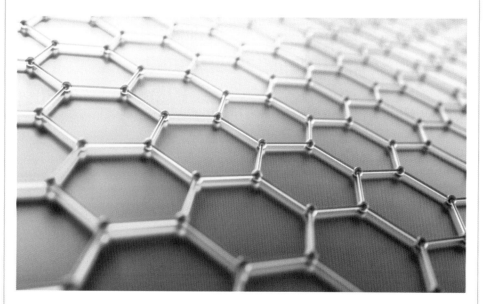

Figure 4.5: The structure of a sheet of graphene – each sheet is only one atom thick

Emerging technologies can be used to improve the design of a device, as well as improve a device's security and user experience.

For example, a laptop could incorporate biometrics scanners and AI software to make it more secure. The user could scan their fingerprint or their face in order to log in instead of needing to input their password or PIN. Login details can be stolen, but it is almost impossible to fool a computer's biometric-recognition AI into believing that someone else's face or fingerprint belongs to you. The AI has been trained to recognise fakes using millions of examples.

Figure 4.6: A device's biometric recognition means that a user can scan their fingerprint to log in instead of typing in a password

Using biometrics not only increases security, but it also makes logging in much quicker and easier for the user, as they don't have to remember their login details or spend time typing them in. Modern mobile phones already include fingerprint scanners to increase security, particularly when using banking apps. Cash machines in some countries have started using facial recognition software to authenticate users and make financial transactions as secure as possible.

It is important that software and hardware companies keep up with the latest technologies when designing new versions of their products. If they don't, developments in technology will overtake them and customers will buy from other companies instead.

5G capabilities could be added to new devices to increase the speed at which the devices are able to send and receive data, and to make sure the devices stay useful and desirable in an era when more and more things are becoming 'smart'.

The **Internet of Things (IoT)** is one reason why the 5G network is needed. The IoT is all the machines and objects (things) in our lives that contain sensors, processors and the ability to send and receive data via the internet. IoT devices include smart coffee machines, baby monitors, central heating thermostats and robot vacuum cleaners.

All these things need to send and receive a *lot* of data all the time, and more and more of them will be made in the coming years, so the world needed a new communication network to carry huge amounts of data efficiently at high speed.

Prototypes

When designing a new device, a hardware company will create an early model of the product called a **prototype**. A prototype is a first attempt at making a product that the company thinks will meet users' needs and expectations. A prototype may not have all the features or the exact design that the final product will have, but it will have some of the main ones.

Companies will usually have made some assumptions about what customers want. Although designers will be testing the prototype themselves, they will also often ask potential customers to use the prototype. The customers will then give feedback (say what they like and dislike about it) to test whether the design team's assumptions were correct.

Figure 4.7: Customers will use the prototype of a device and provide feedback that the company can use to improve their product

Then the team will make changes to the design in response and may create a new prototype for people to test. They will repeat this process until they settle on a final design with a complete set of features.

Sometimes a prototype might concentrate on a certain aspect of the device. For example:

- a **visual prototype** will have the look, shape, feel and weight of the final device but none of the functions
- a **proof-of-principle prototype** usually only has certain key features of the device
- a **working prototype** will have almost all of the functionality of the final device.

When companies make prototypes, especially early ones, they usually use quicker build methods and cheaper materials than the ones they will use for the finished product. This way, they can explore different shape and style options without spending too much money.

Figure 4.8: The iPod mini inspired one experimental design for the original iPhone

One big benefit of creating prototypes is that the designers can get an idea of the user experience of a device. This will often reveal issues that weren't obvious when they were discussing ideas and looking at drawings of the design. Prototyping will often lead to design teams rejecting designs that don't work well and following a different design instead. For example, one early iPhone prototype had a shape similar to the iPod mini, but when the designers held it to their ear as if making a phone call, the sharp edges hurt their ears, so they rejected this design.

It is not always the best idea for a company to prototype repeatedly until the product is exactly how they want it before releasing it for sale. Sometimes a company will just aim to release a minimum viable product (MVP). An MVP is an early version of a product (very similar to a fully working prototype) that has enough of the desired features to satisfy people who want the product as soon as possible. These customers are keen enough to buy the product as soon as it is released and then provide feedback for the company to use to further develop it. Customers like this are called early adopters. They are often more accepting of the product's flaws and are more willing than the average customer to give their opinions to help with the product's development.

The advantage of releasing an MVP is that the company gets paid for its work developing the device so far and doesn't waste money on more development before it knows whether it will be a success. However, there are also big risks: if the MVP is awful and customers hate it, it may damage the company's reputation so much that it never recovers.

Activity 4.3

You will need: a desktop computer, laptop or tablet with internet access and word-processing software

The original iPhone was released in 2007 as an MVP. Before it was released, it went through many, many prototypes over several years, some of which looked very different from the final product! Use the internet to research:

- how Apple developed the original iPhone design
- what the different prototypes were like
- how each main kind of prototype helped the design team make decisions that led them to the final design.

Activity 4.4

You will need: a desktop computer, laptop or tablet

A video game company wants to design and manufacture a new games console. Their first games console, the G BOX, was really successful. The company is giving you a sneak peek at their prototype of their new games console: the G Box Extreme. They would like your feedback on how it can be improved.

Here is the prototype:

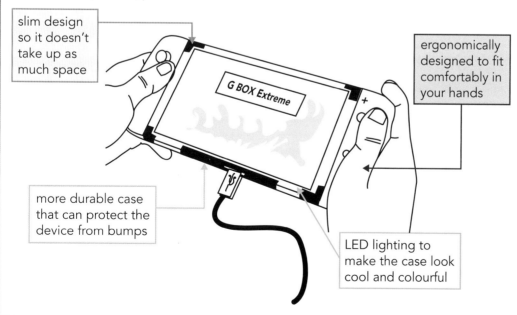

slim design so it doesn't take up as much space

ergonomically designed to fit comfortably in your hands

G BOX Extreme

more durable case that can protect the device from bumps

LED lighting to make the case look cool and colourful

Continued

Write an email to the company to tell them your feedback about what you think of the user experience, accessibility and ergonomics of their prototype. They would like at least one suggested improvement. The company also wants to make sure the new games console is successful, and they think including an emerging technology in the device would help. They would like you to suggest an emerging technology that could be included.

How did you judge what the user experience of the device was like?
How did you decide what improvements to suggest?

Questions 4.1

1   What is user experience?

2   Give two examples of accessibility features on a tablet device.

3   Why is it important that devices are ergonomic?

4   Give two examples of emerging technologies.

5   Explain why prototypes are useful for identifying what improvements can be made to a device's design.

Summary checklist

☐ I understand why a computer device should be easy for the user to use, look attractive and be appropriate for the user's needs.

☐ I can explain why user experience, accessibility and ergonomics are all important factors when designing a digital device.

☐ I understand how emerging technologies can be used to improve the design of a device.

☐ I understand how to identify improvements to the design of a digital device.

> 4.2 Computer architecture

In this topic you will:

- learn that a computer stores a list of instructions that are processed one at a time

- learn and understand the fetch-decode-execute cycle.

Getting started

What do you already know?

- All computer data goes through the steps: input, process, output. We give the computer the data (input), the computer processes it, then outputs data.

- The CPU (central processing unit) is the part of the computer that processes all data so that we can use the computer to do tasks.

- A computer has two types of storage: primary memory and secondary storage. RAM is primary memory that temporarily stores data for programs being used right now. ROM is primary memory that permanently stores the instructions used to boot up the computer.

- Computers represent all kinds of data in binary form (combinations of 1s and 0s). Binary numbers can be used to represent different types of data, such as numbers, characters, images and sounds.

Continued

Now try this!

Get into small groups of three or four. Each person should take a small piece of paper and write down a short, simple action someone should do. Here are some ideas:

- draw a square
- make a silly face
- write down your favourite colour.

Now put all these pieces of paper in a container such as a box or a pencil case, and place the container on the table.

One person in the group should be chosen to take the following steps:

1   Take one piece of paper out of the container.
2   Read the action on the paper out loud.
3   Perform the action.
4   Repeat these steps until all the pieces of paper have been taken out of the container and all the actions have been completed.

Now in your group, discuss the answers to these questions:

1   If the person doing the actions was a piece of computer hardware, which piece do you think they would be?
2   Which piece of computer hardware would the container be?
3   If the writing on the paper was stored in a computer, what would it look like?

Instructions and computers

'Switch on your computer!' is an instruction you might hear your teacher say. An **instruction** is a command to do something, or information about how something should be done. You use instructions in your daily life to tell people what you need. You also receive instructions from other people as they tell you what they need.

This means that instructions and how they are used are important in our lives. They are also important for a computer. For this reason, the instructions that we give to a computer need to be very clear.

If your friend says to you 'make me a sandwich', they are giving you an instruction.

However, from this instruction, can you immediately make your friend a sandwich? You might be able to as you may already know what kind of sandwich your friend would like. But what if they wanted something different? How would you know this from the simple instruction to make a sandwich? You may also make a sandwich very differently from the way that your friend makes a sandwich. They may not like the way that you make a sandwich.

To be able to carry out the instruction your friend gives you, you need a series of smaller instructions. For example:

•   use wholemeal bread
•   the filling should be cheese.

This is exactly the same for a computer. A computer needs a series of instructions to carry out a task. It processes each of these instructions one at a time to carry out the task. For example, if a computer was asked to make a sandwich, the instructions could be:

1   Take a slice of wholemeal bread.
2   Butter the slice of bread.
3   Add the cheese filling to the slice of bread.
4   Take another slice of wholemeal bread.
5   Butter the slice of bread.
6   Put the second slice of bread on top of the cheese filling.

Can you see any problems with these instructions? Is there anything missing?

Instructions we give to a computer must be detailed and specific, otherwise the computer does not know exactly what to do. It's a bit like if someone didn't know what a sandwich was and tried to follow these instructions. They might not end up with a sandwich at all. They might not know that they should place the bread on a flat surface to butter it. They might not know that buttering means spreading a thin layer of butter all over the surface of the bread. They might butter both sides of the bread. They might use their fingers to butter it!

As humans, we use a lot of knowledge and clues from our experience and the situation around us to help us understand instructions we receive. A computer cannot do this. It only has the instructions it is given at the time. When software gives instructions to the hardware of a computer, it has all this detail built in.

Unplugged activity 4.3

You will need: a pen and paper

Write an improved list of instructions for making a cheese sandwich. Make it as detailed and specific as possible so that someone who had no idea what a sandwich was would make the sandwich correctly.

Peer assessment

Swap your set of instructions with a partner's and compare them. Did your partner include steps that you did not? Did you include different details? Give your partner a score out of 5 for their instructions. 5 means the instructions cannot be improved. 1 means they need a lot of improvements.

If your partner included useful steps or details that you did not think of, add extra steps or details to your list to improve it further.

Why do we need to give the instructions to the computer one at a time?

Think back to the Getting started activity. The person doing the actions was playing the role of the CPU in a computer – the processor. Would it have been possible for the person doing the actions to take out two pieces of paper, read them both at the same time and perform both actions at the same time? No – the person only has one brain and one set of eyes and hands, so they needed to do the actions one by one.

This is why we must give instructions to a computer one at a time. A single-core CPU only has one 'brain' and cannot process more than one instruction at once. A core is the processing unit within a CPU.

Did you know?

You may have heard of dual core or quad core processors. These are CPUs with more than one core processing unit. Multi-core CPUs can perform some actions at the same time, as each core can work on different instructions.

However, instructions still need to be given one by one because some CPUs only have one core. Providing instructions one by one also ensures they are performed in the right order. If the order got jumbled up, the results might not be correct (imagine trying to butter the bread before you took it out of the packet!).

Continued

Even in multi-core CPUs, sometimes one core will need to wait for the output from another core in order to perform the next instruction.

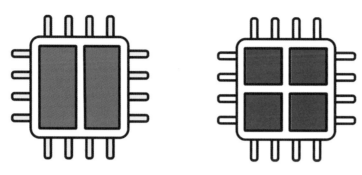

Figure 4.9: Dual core and quad core CPUs

Unplugged activity 4.4

You will need: a pen and paper

Get into pairs. Write a detailed set of step-by-step instructions to tell your partner how to draw a simple picture of something real, such as a car, a flower or a ladder. You should not tell them what the image will be or give them any clues. The instructions should only be about which lines and shapes to draw, for example how long they should be, what angle they should be at, whether they should be straight or curved.

For example, your instructions might look something like this:

1   In the middle of the page and slightly to the right, draw a rectangle that is wider than it is tall.

2   Draw four small circles under the rectangle, touching the bottom edge of the rectangle.

3   Next to the rectangle, on the left of it, draw another rectangle that is taller than it is wide and slightly taller than the first rectangle. This rectangle should almost touch the first rectangle, and its bottom edge should be aligned with the bottom edge of the other rectangle.

4   Draw two small circles under this rectangle, touching the bottom edge of the rectangle.

Continued

5   Inside the smaller rectangle, touching its left edge, draw an even smaller rectangle that takes up the top left-hand quarter of the rectangle.

If you followed these instructions, you would (hopefully!) end up with something like this:

When you are happy with your instructions, swap instructions with your partner and follow them. After your partner has followed your instructions, look at what they have drawn. See if they can guess what the picture is supposed to be. How accurate their drawing is will tell you how good your instructions were!

How did you know what details to include in your instructions?
How could you improve the way you write instructions next time?

The fetch-decode-execute cycle

You know that all computer data is binary (1s and 0s). When we talk about computers storing data, we mean all kinds of data, including instructions. A computer can tell which sections of data are instructions and which ones are other types of data. The instructions for a program currently being used are stored in RAM.

Every time a computer processes an instruction it performs a cycle called the **fetch-decode-execute cycle**. The CPU **fetches** (gets) the instructions, **decodes** them (works out what they mean) and then **executes** the instructions (carries them out). This set of steps is a cycle because it repeats over and over again – a cycle is a set of processes that goes round and round. After one instruction has been fetched, decoded and executed, the cycle starts again and the CPU fetches the next instruction.

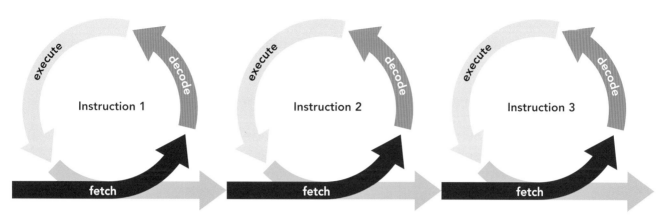

Figure 4.10: The fetch-decode-execute cycle

Table 4.1 shows what happens during each part of the cycle.

Part of the cycle	Description
Fetch	The CPU fetches an instruction from RAM.
Decode	The CPU decodes the instruction. Each instruction has a special code that is stored as binary. The special code limits the amount of data that needs to be stored. For example, the code to carry out a mathematical operation such as multiply could have the code 101. When the CPU decodes the code, it will know what action to carry out.
Execute	The CPU does the action the instruction tells it to. The cycle then repeats until there are no more instructions.

Table 4.1: What happens at each stage of the fetch-decode-execute cycle

For example, the computer is given an instruction to multiply the numbers 2 and 10. The steps for this would be:

1   Fetch the values 2 and 10 from RAM into the CPU.
2   Fetch the special code for the multiply instruction from RAM into the CPU.
3   Decode the code for multiply. The CPU now knows it needs to multiply the values.
4   Execute the instruction by multiplying the value 2 by 10.

Activity 4.5

> **You will need:** a desktop computer, laptop or tablet with internet access and word-processing or infographic software

Your school would like you to create an infographic or labelled diagram for the revision section of the school website, to help learners revise the fetch-decode-execute cycle. You could do some internet research to explain the cycle in more detail. Make sure your graphic:

- explains how the cycle works and how it repeats
- explains which components are involved
- uses images or diagrams to show how the process works.

Questions 4.2

1   Why does a computer need instructions to be:
   a   precise and detailed
   b   in the correct order
   c   given one at a time?
2   Where are instructions for the current program stored?
3   What form are computer instructions in?
4   What does decoding mean?
5   Explain the fetch-decode-execute cycle in one sentence.

Summary checklist

- ☐ I know that a computer stores a list of instructions that are processed one at a time.
- ☐ I understand why a computer needs instructions one at a time and in the correct order.
- ☐ I understand why a computer needs instructions to be precise and detailed.
- ☐ I know and understand the fetch-decode-execute cycle.

> 4.3 Computer software

In this topic you will:

- understand which tasks the operating system does
- learn how to describe examples of utility programs
- understand that there are different types of translator
- understand the main characteristics of compilers and interpreters.

Getting started

What do you already know?

- An operating system is system software that provides an interface between humans and computer hardware and allows us to run application software.

- The operating system manages everything involved in the interaction between the computer and the outside world, such as how memory and storage are used.

- Utility software is system software that helps maintain the computer and make sure that everything is working correctly.

Key words

compiler

defragmentation

device driver

high-level programming language

interpreter

low-level programming language

machine code

resources

source code

system software

translate

translator

utilities

utility software

Continued

Now try this!

Copy out the table and write each of the following things in the correct column, depending on whether you think they are an operating system or a type (or function) of utility software. There are three things in the list that do not fit into either column, so be careful!

- defragmentation
- iOS
- Linux
- device driver
- graphics card
- firewall
- Ethernet
- Android
- encryption
- Windows
- WLAN
- antivirus

Operating system	Utility software

The operating system

You already know what an operating system is, what its purpose is and some of its basic functions. Probably the most obvious reason why we as *users* need computers to have operating systems is to provide an interface to allow humans to interact with the computer's hardware. The operating system allows us to run software so that we can achieve tasks.

But why does a *computer* need an operating system?

A computer needs an operating system to manage its **resources**. Resources are things that someone or something uses to help it do its job. In a shop, resources are things like stock, money and staff. In a computer or electronic device, resources include things like:

- power
- memory
- storage
- hardware devices.

The operating system carries out several tasks to do with managing all these resources. Zara has written these tasks down in her notebook.

Memory management

File management

Device management

Power management

User accounts

Security

Memory management

While a computer is operating, data is constantly being transmitted between the RAM (short-term, temporary memory) and the CPU. The operating system is responsible for managing the movement of the data between the memory and the CPU and making sure that all the necessary processes have enough memory to run.

For example, Arun is using a chat app on his smartphone to have a conversation with Marcus. Then, Arun gets a notification from his photo app saying that his brother has added some new photos, and Arun wants to have a look at them. He opens the photo app while the chat app is still running. The photo app asks the operating system for some memory. His phone's operating system must quickly:

1 check how much memory there is in total

2 check how much memory the chat app is currently using

3 check how much memory there is available for the photo app data.

If there is not enough memory available all in one place in the RAM, the operating system will tidy up or move the data in memory to create a free space big enough for the photo app data. It does all of this in a fraction of a second!

File management

When you create a file on a computer, such as a document or an image, and you save that file, the operating system is responsible for storing that file's data in an appropriate place in secondary storage. The operating system keeps track of all your files and folders and tells you where they are, how big the files are, when they were created and what kinds of files they are. If you want to move or copy a file from one folder to another, or delete or rename it, the operating system is what reorganises the stored data to enable you to do these things.

Device management

Device management means managing the data the computer sends to and receives from devices that are connected to it or built into it, such as keyboards, mice, screens, microphones, speakers, printers, graphics cards, sound cards and network cards. The operating system works with a type of utility software called a device driver to communicate with each hardware device. You will learn about device drivers later in this topic.

Figure 4.11: Device management on a tablet can tell you whether your headphones are working or not

The operating system manages devices by:

- keeping track of the location and status of each device, for example whether it is plugged in or not working
- keeping track of any data a device needs to use
- deciding which processes need to use which devices
- alerting the user when device software needs updating.

Power management

The ability for devices to use power efficiently is important, as consumers and businesses don't want to spend more on electricity than they have to. Efficient use of electricity is particularly important for battery-powered devices such as laptops, tablets and smartphones, since a battery can only store enough power to last from a few hours, to a day or two. For these reasons, power management is a very important aspect of the operating system's role.

The operating system must constantly make decisions that use the available power in the most efficient way, especially if the battery is running low. The operating system can conserve energy by:

- turning off parts of the hardware that are not currently being used

- automatically turning on battery saver mode, which reduces the user experience to a lower quality to lengthen the amount of time the battery will last (for example, the OS might lower the brightness of the screen and reduce the amount of time before the screen goes to sleep after the device is left without any user input)

- putting the whole device into sleep mode after a certain amount of time.

Figure 4.12: Smartphones often have a 'low power' mode to reduce the amount of power being used

User accounts and security

Your school has probably given each person in your class a user account. You might also have a user account for each member of your family on your home computer. Whenever you want to use the computer, you have to log in with your username and password. The operating system is responsible for managing these accounts. This involves:

- keeping the data for each user's account separate and secure by preventing unauthorised access (you must enter the correct password to access it)

- allocating the right amount of each resource to each user account, such as secondary storage space

- setting different access levels for different types of user – for example, administrators can access all areas of a network and change settings on the system, whereas a learner's account only has access to certain drives and cannot change many settings.

Figure 4.13: Some websites and apps require users to verify their identity by entering a one-time password they received via another device

Activity 4.6

> **You will need:** a desktop computer, laptop or tablet with internet access and presentation software

Create a short presentation to explain what an operating system does, the resources it manages and the tasks it performs. Look for extra facts online and include these in your presentation. Include:

- definitions of any key words
- pictures to help with your explanations
- at least two extra pieces of information that you learnt from your research.

The operating system in a computer is one example of **system software** – software that manages the computer hardware's operations and provides a platform for other software to run. Another example of system software is utility software.

Utility software

You have previously learnt that **utility software** is like a computer's housekeeper. It helps maintain the computer and make sure that everything is working correctly. Utility programs (often just known as **utilities**) do this by cleaning, tidying and reorganising stored data. Has your photo app ever found photos it thinks you won't need any more and asked you if you want to delete them? This is an example of utility software.

You are now going to learn about some specific examples of utility software.

Device drivers

What do you think about when you hear the word 'driver'? You probably think of a person driving a car. The driver of the car is responsible for enabling the car to do its job in the right way.

A **device driver** is a specific software program that controls a specific hardware device. It has a similar job to the driver of a car – it enables a connected hardware device to communicate with the computer so that the connected device can do its job.

The role of the device driver is to make sure the external hardware and the computer understand each other. Imagine you walk into a room of people who all speak a language you don't speak. How are you going to understand each other? You will need someone who can **translate** (convert information from one language to another) between all of you so that you can communicate. This is like the job of a device driver – it makes sure that communications between the external hardware and the computer are in a language that is understood.

Figure 4.14: Without a device driver, a printer and computer cannot understand each other

For example, the computer in Figure 4.14 has a new printer connected to it. Without a device driver, the printer cannot understand what the computer is saying to it. It's like the computer is speaking English but the printer only understands French.

With a device driver, the printer understands what the computer is saying to it and is able to do its job.

Figure 4.15: The device driver translates instructions from the computer so that the printer can understand them

Many parts of a computer need drivers. Some common examples are:

- printers
- modems
- graphics cards
- network cards
- sound cards.

Defragmentation software

The hard drive of your computer can be a very messy place. Sometimes, when a file is stored in a computer, there isn't a space big enough to store the whole file in one place, so the file is split into different parts or 'fragments', which are stored in different places. Fragmented files are harder for the computer to find and will open more slowly.

Defragmentation means putting pieces of a file back together again. Defragmentation software reorganises everything stored on the hard drive so that parts of the same file are stored in one place, making them easier to find. So how does it do this?

Zara has a new hard drive in her computer. The hard drive is nice and tidy as she hasn't yet stored any files on it. Each cell represents a blank section of the hard drive.

Zara uses her computer to download her favourite song. She saves this onto her new hard drive. It takes up the first three cells on the hard drive. The colour blue is used to show the music file.

B	B	B							

Zara then uses her computer to complete her homework project. She has to create a presentation. She saves the presentation file onto her computer. It takes up the next five cells on her hard drive. The colour orange is used to show the presentation file.

B	B	B	O	O	O	O	O		

Zara now uses her computer to download her favourite movie. She saves it onto her hard drive. It takes up the next four cells on her hard drive. The colour green is used to show the video file.

B	B	B	O	O	O	O	O	G	G
G	G								

Zara next uses her computer to write a report for her teacher. She saves the report onto her hard drive. It takes up the next three cells on her hard drive. The colour pink is used to show the text file.

B	B	B	O	O	O	O	O	G	G
G	G	PN	PN	PN					

Zara next decides that she no longer needs the presentation file as she has now given her homework to her teacher. She deletes the file from her hard drive.

B	B	B						G	G
G	G	PN	PN	PN					

Zara now decides to download her favourite computer game. This is a very large file that she saves onto her hard drive. It takes up eight cells on the hard drive. The computer looks for the first available cells to save the file. It saves part of it into the place that stored the presentation file. This isn't large enough to store the whole file though, so it stores the rest at the end. The colour yellow is used to represent the computer game.

B	B	B	Y	Y	Y	Y	Y	G	G
G	G	PN	PN	PN	Y	Y	Y		

Zara now decides she doesn't like the song she downloaded and that she no longer needs the report she handed in to her teacher. She deletes these files from her hard drive.

			Y	Y	Y	Y	Y	G	G
G	G				Y	Y	Y		

Zara has a large project to complete for school. She saves the project file onto the computer. It takes up seven cells on the hard drive. The computer looks for the first available cells to save the file. It saves part of it where the song was stored, part of it where the report was stored and the rest at the end. The colour purple is used to represent the project file.

PR	PR	PR	Y	Y	Y	Y	Y	G	G
G	G	PR	PR	PR	Y	Y	Y	PR	

Zara's hard drive is now getting a bit messy. Some of the files that she has stored are split up and saved in different places on the hard drive. This means it takes longer for each file to open as the computer has to find all the pieces of the file in the different places they are stored on the hard drive.

To tidy up the hard drive, Zara uses defragmentation software on her hard drive. All of the parts of the computer game file and the large project file are rearranged so that they are stored together again. This means it takes the computer less time to open each file.

PR	PR	PR	PR	PR	PR	PR	G	G	G
G	Y	Y	Y	Y	Y	Y	Y	Y	

Security software

Security software is software that helps keep data safe. Keeping data safe means stopping people who should not be able to see the data from getting access to it, and it means preventing data getting corrupted or damaged. Most security software that you use on your computer is an example of utility software.

There are several examples of security software that you might use on your computer. These include:

- encryption
- a firewall
- usernames and passwords (user accounts)
- antivirus software.

Stay safe!

We cannot rely completely on software to keep our data safe. We are responsible for using the available security software wisely. We must also be sensible about how we use computers so that we do not put our data in danger of being stolen or damaged. You can do this by:

- using passwords that are very difficult to guess
- never sharing your login details with anyone or writing them down
- always locking your computer if you move away from it while logged in (ask an adult how to do this if you're not sure)
- ensuring every file you download is scanned with antivirus software (this is often done automatically, but check if you're not sure).

Activity 4.7

You will need: a desktop computer, laptop or tablet with internet access and word-processing software

Get into pairs. Use the internet to research how one kind of security software works (choose from encryption, firewall, user accounts or antivirus). Each of you should choose a different kind of security software to research.

Then use word-processing software to create a short worksheet for your partner to complete, which will help them learn about the kind of software you researched. You could write activities such as:

- filling gaps in a paragraph
- true or false statements
- multiple-choice questions.

When your worksheets are done, swap worksheets with your partner and complete them. Then swap back and mark them.

Continued

Peer assessment

After completing your partner's worksheet and receiving your score, give them a star rating for the quality of their worksheet. Give them:

★★★   3 stars if you found the worksheet challenging, easy to understand and you learnt something from it

★★   2 stars if you mostly understood the worksheet and you learnt something from it, but it could be improved

★   1 star if you found the worksheet difficult to understand and complete.

Then suggest at least one improvement your partner could make the next time they write a worksheet.

All the different examples of software in this section were examples of utility software, which is a type of system software. Another type of system software is a translator.

Translators

Humans write programs in **source code**. Source code is a program that is often written in a **high-level programming language** such as Python or JavaScript. You have previously learnt that high-level languages are programming languages that are easy for humans to use and understand because they use English-like statements, such as IF and WHILE. But computer processors cannot understand high-level language – they only understand **machine code**.

Can you remember what all data needs to be converted to so that a computer can understand it? That's it: binary. Those little 1s and 0s (or high/low electrical states) represent all computer data. Machine code is made up of patterns of bits (binary digits) and each pattern corresponds to a specific command. A **low-level programming language** is closer to the language that a processor understands. One type of low-level language is Machine code, a processor directly understands this type of low-level language.

A **translator** is a piece of software that translates source code into binary code that the CPU can understand and execute. This is a very important piece of software for a computer, as without it, the computer would not be able to understand or follow any of the instructions from programs.

There are two types of translator that can convert a program written in a high-level language to binary: **compilers** and **interpreters**. These translators have different features. A compiler is a translator that deals with a whole program at once, whereas an interpreter deals with one line of code at a time. You can use either kind of translator with any programming language, but some languages tend to use compilers more often and others tend to use interpreters.

Table 4.2 compares the features of compilers and interpreters.

	Compiler	Interpreter
Translating and executing	It translates and executes the whole program's code at once.	It translates and executes code line by line.
Syntax errors	If there are any syntax errors, the code won't execute at all.	Code will execute until there is a syntax error. Translating and executing stops until the error is corrected.
Output	It produces an executable file – a special type of file that can be run in future without using a translator.	No executable file is created, so the interpreter needs to translate the code each time it is run.
Languages	Java, C, C++	Python, JavaScript, PHP, Ruby

Table 4.2: Features of compilers and interpreters

Activity 4.8

You will need: a desktop computer, laptop or tablet with internet access and word-processing software

Think what the benefits might be of using an interpreter rather than a compiler. Now think what the benefits might be of using a compiler rather than an interpreter. Use the internet if you need help. Find at least two benefits of each type of translator and create a table of your findings.

Questions 4.3

1   What kind of software are operating systems, utilities and translators?

2   Give three tasks an operating system does.

3   Name two kinds of utility software and state briefly what each one does.

4   What is a translator and why are they needed?

5   Give two differences between a compiler and an interpreter.

Summary checklist

☐   I understand which tasks the operating system does.

☐   I can describe examples of utility programs including device drivers, defragmentation software and security software.

☐   I understand the purpose of a translator and that there are different types of translator.

☐   I understand the main characteristics of compilers and interpreters, the differences between them and the advantages of using each one.

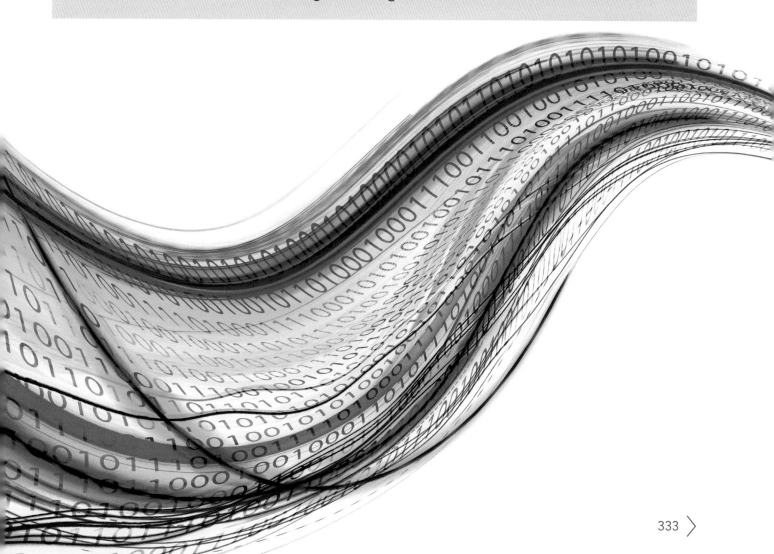

> 4.4 Data representation

In this topic you will:

- learn how analogue sound is converted to digital data
- learn how to convert file sizes from one data storage unit to another.

Key words

analogue

capacity

digital

sample

Getting started

What do you already know?

- Digital data is data stored using binary digits (0s and 1s).
- Analogue data is data that is made up of many different values.
- Humans understand analogue data, but computers can only understand digital data. All analogue data needs to be converted to digital data for a computer to be able to process it.
- You know how images and text are converted to binary.
- A bit is a unit of data storage that is the size of one binary digit. There are 8 bits in a byte and 1000 bytes in a kilobyte.

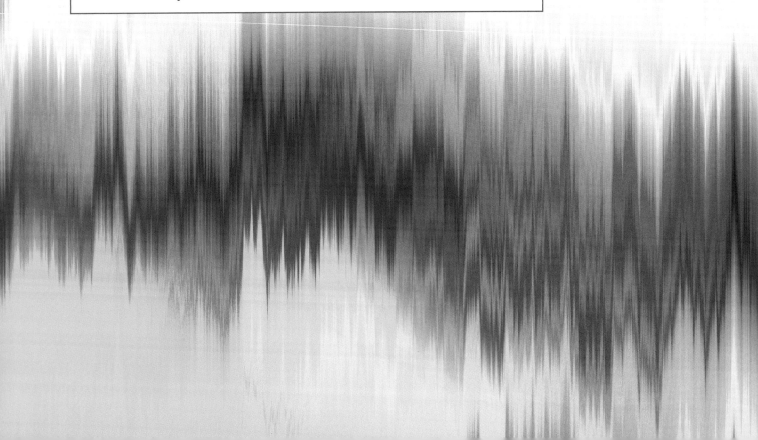

Continued

Now try this!

Look at the following images with a partner. Decide which images show analogue signals and which show digital signals.

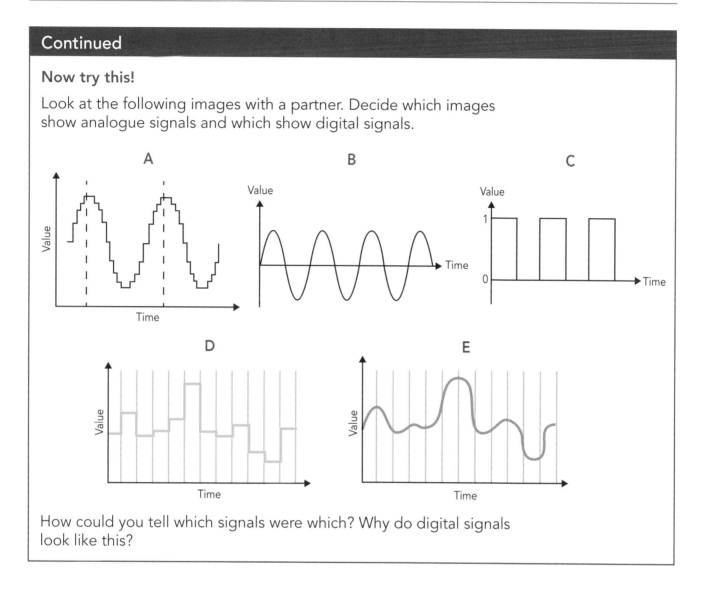

How could you tell which signals were which? Why do digital signals look like this?

Converting analogue sound to digital

You have previously learnt that for a computer to process it, all data needs to be converted to **digital** data. Digital data is data that uses binary digits to represent individual, separate values. Sound is one kind of data that needs converting to digital form in order for a computer to process it. When a musical instrument plays a sound, it creates a sound wave. This sound wave is **analogue** data. Analogue data is continuous data represented by a physical signal that can have any value in a range. In the case of sound, the physical signal is air pressure.

We can record sound using a microphone and computer. The microphone captures the sound from the analogue sound wave. The sound wave is then converted to digital data so that the computer can process and play it.

Figure 4.16 shows an example of an analogue sound wave.

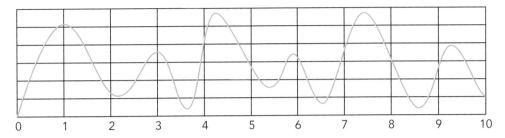

Figure 4.16: Analogue sound wave showing ten sample points

Each of the numbers across the sound wave represents a **sample**. A sample is a measurement of the sound wave at a certain point in time. The sound wave is sampled so that it can be converted to digital data. Each recording of a sound wave has a sample rate. This is the number of samples of the sound wave that are taken each second. A sample rate of 1 would mean that the sound wave is sampled once every second. Most recordings of sound have a sample rate of 44,100. That's a lot of samples taken every second!

To convert the example soundwave to digital data, the wave is measured at each of the sample points. Figure 4.17 shows what the points of measurement would be.

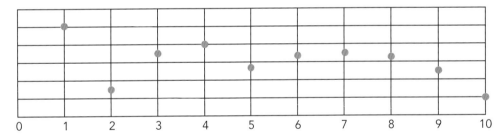

Figure 4.17: The ten samples taken from the analogue sound wave

Each of the dots is a measurement of the sound wave at each sample point. Each of the samples is converted to a binary value so that a computer can process it. After each sample, the binary value stays the same until the next sample. The idea is that when the samples are played one after the other, this recreates the sound wave. Figure 4.18 shows the sound wave that the computer would create if it took ten samples from the analogue wave.

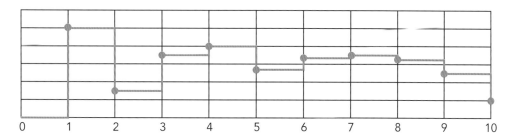

Figure 4.18: Digital sound wave created using ten samples

In Figure 4.19 this is compared to the original sound wave. You should be able to see that they are quite different.

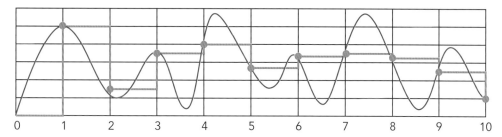

Figure 4.19: Digital sound wave compared with original analogue sound wave

This is because the sound wave changes quite a lot between the samples that are taken. As the sound wave is not measured at these points, the computer does not know the sound wave is like this. This is why the higher the sample rate of a sound wave, the more accurate the recording of the sound.

Activity 4.9

> **You will need:** a desktop computer, laptop or tablet with word-processing, spreadsheet or drawing software

Draw a new digital sound wave of the recording shown in Figure 4.19, but this time, take 20 samples of the analogue wave. You could do this using spreadsheet software, word-processing software or drawing software – decide which one would work best for you.

1 Does the digital wave with 20 samples look more accurate than the one with 10 samples?
2 How similar to the original recording would the digital recording sound?
3 What do you think the digital wave would look like if you took 100 samples?

How did you work out where the additional samples should go? How did you decide on the best way to draw the new digital sound wave? How would you do this kind of activity differently in future?

Data storage units

We measure storage **capacity** using different data storage units. Capacity means the amount of space there is available to contain something. The data storage units are:

- bit
- nibble
- byte
- kilobyte
- megabyte
- gigabyte
- terabyte.

A bit is the smallest unit of measurement for data. A terabyte is a large unit of measurement for data storage. There are larger units of storage than a terabyte – you could try to find out what they are!

Each unit of data storage is equal to a certain amount of the next smallest data storage size. For example, a nibble is equal to 4 bits. Table 4.3 shows the data storage units, their names, abbreviations (short form) and capacity.

Storage unit	Abbreviation	Capacity
Bit	b	1 binary digit
Nibble	(no abbreviation)	4 bits
Byte	B	2 nibbles or 8 bits
Kilobyte	KB	1000 bytes
Megabyte	MB	1000 kilobytes
Gigabyte	GB	1000 megabytes
Terabyte	TB	1000 terabytes

Table 4.3: Data storage units

Did you know?

Half a byte was named a 'nibble' because the English word 'bite' (a mouthful of food) sounds the same as 'byte'. A very small bite of food is called a nibble!

Unplugged activity 4.5

You will need: a pen and paper

Without looking at Table 4.3, copy out the table below but with the units in the correct order from smallest at the top to the largest at the bottom. Then in the second column, write how many of each unit above each one equals.

Storage unit	Abbreviation	Capacity
Kilobyte		
Gigabyte		
Megabyte		
Bit		
Terabyte		
Byte		
Nibble		

It is possible to convert between the different units of measurement. For example, a file that is 1.4 gigabytes would be 1400 megabytes.

Questions 4.4

1   How many bytes are there in 1 gigabyte?

2   A file takes up 2.5 megabytes of storage space. How many kilobytes is this?

3   The file for Unit 4 of this book was 1877 kilobytes before this sentence was written. How many bits were used to represent this file?

4   A photo is 5.67 MB. What is this in terabytes?

Summary checklist

☐   I know the differences between analogue sound and digital sound recordings.
☐   I know how analogue sound is converted to digital data.
☐   I know the main units of data storage and their capacity.
☐   I can convert file sizes from one data storage unit to another.

> 4.5 Logic circuits

In this topic you will:

- learn what logic circuits are and how they relate to logic gates

- learn how to draw logic circuits for different Boolean expressions.

Getting started

What do you already know?

- The circuits in a computer contain lots of logic gates. A logic gate is a tiny piece of hardware that uses Boolean operators to control the flow of electricity in a computer, like a switch.

- Boolean data can only have two possible values: True or False.

- You understand the role of the NOT, AND and OR logic gates. You also know the symbol for each of these logic gates.

- You know how to complete a truth table for each logic gate.

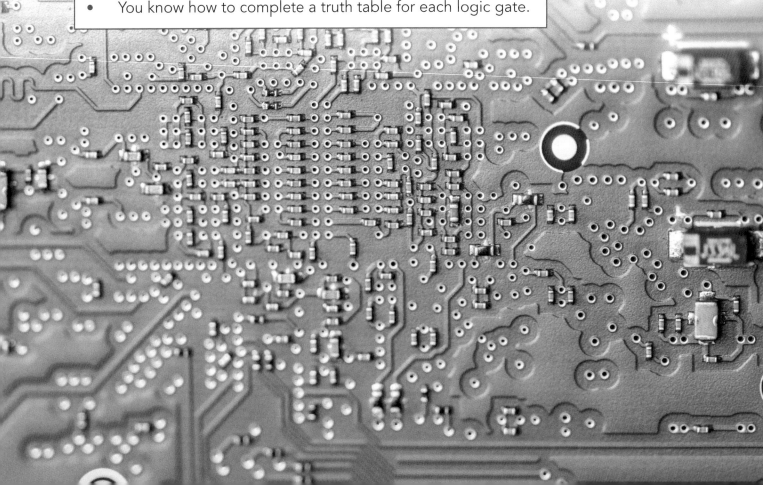

Getting started

Now try this!

Match each truth table with its Boolean operator.

a

Input 1	Input 2	Output
0	0	0
0	1	1
1	0	1
1	1	1

A **AND**

b

Input 1	Output
0	1
1	0

B **NOT**

c

Input 1	Input 2	Output
0	0	0
0	1	0
1	0	0
1	1	1

C **OR**

Logic gates

A computer is able to do lots of different operations and calculations because it contains logic gates. Combinations of tiny electric switches called **transistors** make up each logic gate. A transistor is a device that can partially conduct electricity and can switch or increase electrical signals. A computer's CPU contains millions of logic gates made up of billions of transistors.

You have previously learnt about three different logic gates: AND, OR and NOT. Look at Figures 4.20, 4.21 and 4.22 to remind yourself what the diagrams for these three logic gates look like.

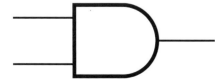

Figure 4.20: AND gate

Figure 4.21: OR gate

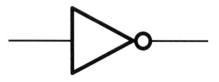

Figure 4.22: NOT gate

In a computer, logic gates are put together to create logic circuits. A circuit is a system of electrical components connected together. Creating logic circuits allows us to apply different logic combinations to the inputs of the circuit and get different outputs. Together, all of these logical operations enable computers to do all the things they do.

We can draw logic circuit diagrams to find out what the output of different logic circuits would be. A real logic circuit can contain hundreds of gates. You are going to learn how to draw much simpler ones that have two or three gates. One hundred gates would take a lot of drawing!

Two-gate logic circuits

First, you are going to learn how to draw a logic circuit that has two gates. We create a logic circuit from a logic statement, also known as a Boolean expression. A logic statement or Boolean expression is a statement that takes inputs, applies Boolean operators (such as AND, OR and NOT) and produces an output. Boolean expressions are statements of Boolean algebra. Algebra is an area of mathematics that uses letters to represent numbers, and Boolean means values are always either True or False.

A simple logic statement is:

$$X = A \text{ AND } B$$

Figure 4.23: Logic gate diagram for X = A AND B

This logic statement is for the AND logic gate, which has two inputs (A and B) and one output (X). If we drew this logic statement as a logic gate diagram, it would look like Figure 4.23.

Another logic statement is:

$$X = (A \text{ AND } B) \text{ OR } C$$

1   What do you notice about this logic statement?
2   How many inputs does it have?
3   How many logic gates does it have?
4   What are the brackets for?

You should have noticed that the logic statement has three inputs: A, B and C. You should have noticed that the logic statement has two logic gates: AND and OR. You may already know that the brackets show that this part of the logic statement is drawn first. To draw this logic statement, you first draw the section in the brackets, as shown in Figure 4.24.

Figure 4.24: Logic gate diagram for A AND B

Next, you need to add the second gate and the third input. The OR gate is placed after the AND gate. The first input into the OR gate is the output of the AND gate. The second input into the OR gate is the input C. The logic circuit is shown in Figure 4.25.

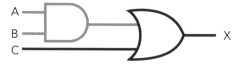

Figure 4.25: Logic gate diagram for X = (A AND B) OR C

Unplugged activity 4.6

You will need: a pen and paper

Draw the circuit for the logic statement X = (A OR B) AND C.

Peer assessment

Compare your logic circuit with a partner's.

- Are they the same?
- If there are differences, what are they?
- Do the differences change how the logic works?

A different logic statement is:

$$X = (NOT\ A)\ OR\ B$$

To draw this logic circuit, as before, you draw the section in brackets first. Next, you need to add the second gate and input. The OR gate is placed after the NOT gate. The first input into the OR gate is the output of the NOT gate. The second input into the OR gate is the input B. Figure 4.27 shows what the logic circuit looks like.

Figure 4.26: Logic gate diagram for NOT A

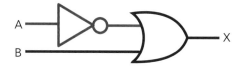

Figure 4.27: Logic gate diagram for X = (NOT A) OR B

Three-gate logic circuits

Now, you are going to learn how to create a logic circuit that has three logic gates. A logic statement with three gates is:

$$X = (NOT\ A\ OR\ B)\ AND\ C$$

To draw this circuit, you need to draw the section in brackets first. You already know how to draw this section as it was demonstrated previously.

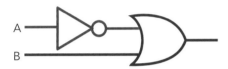

Figure 4.28: Logic gate diagram for NOT A OR B

Next, you need to add the third logic gate and input. The AND gate is placed after the OR gate. The first input into the AND gate is the output of the OR gate. The second input into the OR gate is from the input C.

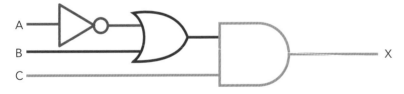

Figure 4.29: Logic gate diagram for X = (NOT A OR B) AND C

Sometimes, the logic statement may have two sections in brackets, for example:

$$X = (A\ AND\ B)\ OR\ (B\ AND\ C)$$

To draw this logic circuit, you first need to draw the sections in the brackets.

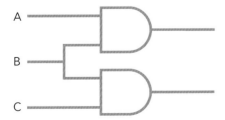

Figure 4.30: Logic gate diagram for A AND B, B AND C

These two sections are then combined by the logic gate that is not in the brackets, the OR gate.

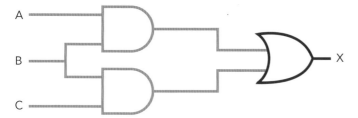

Figure 4.31: Logic gate diagram for X = (A AND B) OR (B AND C)

Activity 4.10

> **You will need:** a desktop computer, laptop or tablet with internet access and drawing or presentation software

Create circuit diagrams for the following logic statements. You could find images of each logic gate online or draw them yourself using drawing or presentation software. Alternatively, use an online logic circuit simulator.

1   X = (NOT A AND B) OR C
2   X = (A OR NOT B) AND C
3   X = (A OR B) NOT C
4   X = (A OR B) OR (B AND C)
5   X = (B OR C) AND (A OR C)

Activity 4.11

> **You will need:** a desktop computer, laptop or tablet with internet access and drawing or presentation software

Write a logic statement that contains three logic gates. Give it to a partner for them to draw the logic circuit in presentation or drawing software or using an online logic circuit simulator. Then mark their logic circuit diagram for your statement.

Give:

* 1 mark for each correct logic gate
* 1 mark for each logic gate that is in the correct position
* 1 mark for each correctly labelled input or output.

Next time you draw a logic circuit, what will you do differently? Is there anything that would help you remember the symbols for each different kind of logic gate?

Questions 4.5

1 What is a logic gate and what is it made of?
2 What is a logic circuit?
3 What do logic circuits enable computers to do?
4 What do brackets mean in Boolean expressions?

Summary checklist

☐ I understand how logic gates are combined to create logic circuits.
☐ I understand how logic circuits enable a computer to work.
☐ I can draw logic circuits for different Boolean expressions.

> 4.6 AI and computerisation

In this topic you will:

- discover different uses of machine learning
- understand the benefits and drawbacks of computerisation and automation in manufacturing and industry.

Key words

automated system

Industry 4.0 (Fourth Industrial Revolution)

machine learning

virtual assistant

Getting started

What do you already know?

- Some artificial intelligence (AI) systems have the ability to learn from their experiences – this is called machine learning.
- AI robots can work autonomously, capturing data from their surroundings, making decisions and adapting their actions without human input.
- Automation and AI robots are used in industries such as health, manufacturing and advertising.

Continued

Now try this!

You learnt about machine learning, robotics and automation in previous stages. Get into a group of three or four and discuss the answers to these questions:

1 What is the difference between AI and AI with machine learning?

2 Do you know of any examples of machine learning?

3 How are automated systems different from AI?

Machine learning

You have previously learnt that machine learning is a form of artificial intelligence (AI). **Machine learning** is a system's ability to learn by analysing data. It can then adapt its own data and rules, improving its ability to do its job in future. Machine learning can be used in lots of interesting ways.

Image recognition

Imagine you are on a nice walk with your friends and you see an interesting plant. You've never seen it before and you don't know what it is. You ask one of your friends if they know what it is – they don't know either. You then remember an app called PlantNet. PlantNet is a plant identification application. A user can take a photo of a plant and use the app to find out what it is. The app will analyse the photo and compare the features of the plant against a large database of plants. The app will then tell you what type of plant it thinks you've found.

When the app analyses the photo, it looks at all the features of the plant. When doing this, it might find a new feature that it didn't know about. For example, it knew that a daffodil can be yellow and cream, but it did not know that a daffodil could also be orange. It takes this new data that it has learnt and adapts its own rule base to now know that a daffodil can be yellow, cream or orange. It can do this because it has machine learning capabilities. Many image recognition systems are examples of machine learning.

Figure 4.32: Using a phone to analyse the features of a plant

Activity 4.12

You will need: a tablet or smartphone with internet access and image recognition software

You are going to use an image recognition app. On your mobile device, open the app your teacher will tell you to use. Then see if you can use the app to identify an object in the classroom such as an electronic device, an item of clothing or a book. See if the app can tell you information about the object, such as:

* what it is
* which company made it
* where you can buy it
* how much it would cost to buy.

Virtual assistants

Imagine you are lying on your bed at home and you want to relax to some music. You can't decide what you want to listen to, and you think it would be good if someone knew what music you liked and would play it for you.

A **virtual assistant** can do this. A virtual assistant is software that performs tasks for users based on the user's voice commands. You can command it to do lots of tasks such as play music, read audiobooks and answer questions. Examples of virtual assistants include Apple's Siri, Google Assistant and Amazon's Alexa. The assistant analyses each voice command's tone and accent. It can learn which voice is yours by repeatedly hearing it and adapting its data and rules about what your voice sounds like. It can do this because it has machine learning capabilities. It could learn the voice of each person that lives in your house. This way, one of you could say 'play my favourite music'. The virtual assistant will know your voice and will play your favourite music. Many voice recognition systems are examples of machine learning.

Figure 4.33: A smart speaker with virtual assistant software

Did you know?

Amazon's Alexa is one popular virtual assistant. Here are some facts about Alexa.

- Alexa started life in 2013 as a speech synthesiser developed in Poland, which Amazon bought and developed further.
- The word or phrase used to 'wake up' your virtual assistant so that it listens to your instructions is known as a wake word. With Alexa, you can choose from several different wake words including 'Amazon', 'Echo' and 'Ziggy'.
- In November 2018, Amazon employed 10 000 people to work on developing products and technologies to do with Alexa!

TV and film recommendations

Imagine you have a friend over at your house for dinner. You decide that after dinner you want to watch a movie. You can't decide exactly what movie you would like to watch so you look for inspiration. Netflix is an online streaming platform that learns which movies and TV shows you like from what you watch and rate. It will then make recommendations for new movies and TV shows for you to watch, based on those you have already watched and rated.

Each time you watch a movie or rate a movie, Netflix adapts its data and rules about you, so that it can make better recommendations. It can do this as it has machine learning capabilities. Many online streaming platforms are examples of machine learning.

Activity 4.13

You will need: a desktop computer, laptop or tablet with word-processing software

Write a blog post or an article for a website about an example of machine learning. You could use an example from this book or research your own. Include the following details.

- How is the machine learning used?
- What are the benefits of using the machine learning?
- Could there be any problems with using machine learning in this way?

Automated systems in industry and manufacturing

An **automated system** is a combination of software and hardware that operates without much human interaction. Automated systems are usually robotic systems that are programmed to automatically do specific actions again and again the same way every time. They capture data from their surrounding environment and, based on this data, make decisions and produce a particular output.

Automated systems are used a lot in industry and manufacturing. For example, in a factory that makes cars, automated robots are used to build the largest and heaviest parts of the car. Also, in a bakery that mass-produces bread, an automated climate control system is used to make sure the temperature in the bakery remains constant.

Developments in technology and increasing interconnectivity and use of AI are transforming the way modern society works, and this includes manufacturing. The whole process of product manufacturing is becoming more computerised and automated. This transition to a more automated and interconnected world is called **Industry 4.0**, or the **Fourth Industrial Revolution**. At the foundation of Industry 4.0 is data and machine learning.

Benefits and drawbacks of automated systems

Automated systems are becoming increasingly popular in industry and manufacturing as they bring several benefits. However, there are also drawbacks. Table 4.4 shows some of the main benefits and drawbacks.

Benefits	Drawbacks
Automation can save costs in several different areas. The company no longer needs to employ workers to complete the tasks that the automated systems can do. There may be lower wastage costs as the automated system is less likely to make mistakes.	The cost to set up the automated systems and to maintain them can be very high.
It can create new jobs for people as there will be new job roles for maintaining and updating the automated systems.	It can take away jobs from people who used to perform the tasks that the automated systems now perform.
Automated systems can work 24 hours a day, 7 days a week if required. They do not need to take a break. Therefore, they can be a lot more productive and efficient than a human worker completing the same task.	As there is no human input to each product, the end product will only be as good as the program that is written for the automated system.
There can be safety benefits, as robots can do work that would be too dangerous for a human to do. For example, they can work with poisonous chemicals or in very high or low temperatures.	

Table 4.4: Benefits and drawbacks of automation in manufacturing

Unplugged activity 4.8

You will need: a pen and paper

Look at the tasks below. With a partner, choose two or three of the tasks and discuss whether a human or an automated system would perform the task better, giving reasons why. You might disagree, or decide that it depends on the specific situation. You might decide that some parts of the task would need a human to do them but other parts could use an automated system. Write down your decisions and your reasoning.

Continued

1. Inventing a new kind of chocolate bar and designing and producing all aspects of it.
2. Writing the next bestselling children's book.
3. Measuring the temperature of a recently erupted volcano's summit every four hours.
4. Making sure that only a specific cat can eat from a certain food bowl, and feeding the cat twice a day.
5. Adding windows to luxury dolls' houses and checking that they open and shut correctly.
6. Creating a fun, imaginative and complex new board game.
7. Taking a sample of water from a river every day and testing it for pollutants.
8. Cutting planks of wood that are exactly the same size and thickness and stacking them in boxes.

Self-assessment

How easy or difficult did you find this task? Did you rely on your partner to suggest ideas, or did you contribute the most? What have you learnt from this activity?

Questions 4.6

1. Name three examples of machine learning that we can use in everyday life.

2. Suggest a benefit of each of the examples of machine learning you named in question 1.

3. What is Industry 4.0?

4. Which of these would you expect to improve if a bike factory automated its production process?

   A   production speed   B   amount of waste   C   cost of production

   D   local employment rates   E   safety for workers.

Summary checklist

☐ I can describe some different uses of machine learning.

☐ I understand the main benefits and drawbacks of computerisation in manufacturing and industry.

Project: Wearable technology

A big technology company called Emiko has opened a competition for 11 to 16 year olds to design a new type of wearable technology. Have you ever wished that your bike helmet could help you avoid accidents, your contact lenses could show you directions to the nearest park or your grandmother's necklace could call your parents if she has a fall? Well now's your chance to make that a reality! The winner will get the chance to visit the company headquarters in Japan and will have their invention made into a real product.

The company is asking young people to submit their ideas for their design as either a presentation, a video or an animation. Competitors will also need to supply a written guide for the manufacturer, containing information about how the product should be made to work.

The new product must:

- have a great user experience
- have excellent accessibility features and ergonomics
- use at least one emerging technology
- use machine learning to tailor the user experience to each user.

Task 1: Video or presentation

Produce a video, animation or presentation telling Emiko about your design. You could style it like an advert for the product if you like. Include:

- a diagram or model of your design
- an explanation of what the product's main features will be
- details about what the user experience will be like (you could act out someone using it!)
- details about the accessibility features
- information about what emerging technology the device will use
- how the device will use machine learning to customise the device for each user
- the reasons behind your design choices.

Continued

Task 2: Production guide

Using word-processing software, write a production guide for the company to tell them:

- how the device's operating system will manage:
  - memory
  - power
  - user accounts and security
- what utility software the device will have
- how to translate the program code for the device into machine code
- how the device will access and follow the instructions it is given
- how much data storage capacity the device should have, and why it needs this amount
- what automated systems could be used to produce the device.

Check your progress 4

1 What are the missing words in this passage? **[3]**

The design of a computer device is important. The design should ensure that the device gives a positive ____a____ (the user feels happy when they use the device). The device should include ____b____ features so that people with different needs and abilities can all use the device. The device should also be ____c____ so that it does not cause the user injury or discomfort.

2 Name each emerging technology described. **[4]**

   a This technology involves manipulating individual atoms and molecules to create useful structures and substances.

   b This technology uses the measurements of human features for security and personalisation, for example facial recognition, fingerprint scanning and voice recognition.

   c This wireless communication technology has very fast data transmission speeds.

   d This is a simulation of human intelligence within a computer system.

3 Is each of these statements true or false? Correct the false statements. **[4]**

   a A computer stores lists of instructions that are executed one by one.

   b The exact order of the instructions is important as computers can only perform one instruction at a time.

   c The fetch-decode-execute cycle only involves the CPU.

   d The CPU fetches each instruction one by one until they are all fetched, then decodes each one, then executes each one.

4 Someone once said 'A prototype is worth a thousand meetings.' Explain why this might be true. **[3]**

5 Match these functions of an operating system with their descriptions. [5]

Power management		storing data in an appropriate place in secondary storage, keeping track of the data and moving or copying it when required
Device management		preventing unauthorised access to data, allocating storage space and keeping track of different access levels
User accounts and security		moving data between the RAM and the CPU while making sure that all the necessary processes are able to run
File management		conserving electricity by making sure that only the parts of the device that need to be using electricity are using it
Memory management		being aware of the status of each hardware component and moving the right data to the right components

6 What are the missing words in this passage? [6]

Defragmentation software and security software are kinds of ____a____.
Security software helps keep data ____b____ by preventing unauthorised
____c____ and preventing data getting ____d____. Examples of security
software include ____e____, which scrambles data so that unauthorised users
cannot access it, and ____f____, which finds and removes harmful files.

7 Explain:
   a what defragmentation does [2]
   b what main benefit you would expect to see after defragmenting a hard drive. [1]

8 Copy this table and put a tick (✓) in the correct column(s) to show if each statement is true for that kind of translator. [4]

	Compiler	Interpreter
The translator translates and executes the program code all at once.		
If there is a syntax error in line 15, code will execute up to line 14.		
You can use it with any programming language.		
As well as executing the code, the translator outputs an executable file so that the code can be run again without a translator.		

9 In analogue to digital audio conversion, what is a sample? [1]

10 CD-quality audio recordings usually have a sample rate of at least 44 100 samples per second. Why are so many samples taken? [1]

11 If a laptop has 256 GB of storage, how many laptops would you need to store 1 TB of data? [1]

12 Explain everything you possibly can about this diagram, what it represents and what it means. [6]

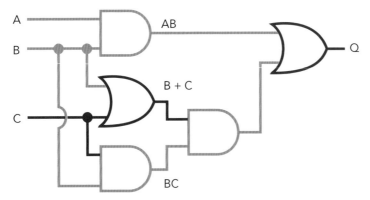

13 Imagine a virtual assistant had AI but not machine learning abilities. Describe what the limitations would be of this system. [3]

14 What is the main reason why manufacturing companies are increasing their use of automation and computerisation? [1]

⟩ Glossary

Accessibility: designing a system or technology in a way that allows people with disabilities to access, use and interact with it effectively and independently   301

Acknowledgement (ACK): an indication that a computer has received the server's response and will wait or start transmission   276

Algorithm: a series of steps that solve a problem   13

Analogue: represented by a physical signal that can have any value in a continuous range   335

append(): a Python function that stores the data in the brackets at the end of a list; for example, `myList.append(1)` will store 1 in the next space in the list `myList`   110

Array: a data structure that allows multiple data values of the same data type to be stored under one identifier   105

Ascending: going up, for example 1 to 10 or A to Z   129

Attribute: a field name in a database   218

Automated system: a combination of software and hardware (often a robotic system) that is programmed to automatically do specific actions again and again the same way every time without needing much human input   351

Backbone: the long cable devices connect to in a bus topology   262

Bandwidth: the amount of data a communication channel can carry per second   280

Big data: the huge volumes of complex data generated from different sources – the volume of this data is so huge that, by themselves, traditional methods of processing data are inadequate   248

Binary search: a search algorithm that is run on ordered data – it uses greater than (>) or less than (<) to search   129

Biometrics: measurements of human features and/or technology like facial recognition and fingerprint scanning, which use these measurements for security and personalisation   305

Boolean: data type that is either True or False   90

Boolean algebra: an area of mathematics and logic that uses letters to represent numbers and only deals with values that are True or False   342

Boolean expression: a statement that takes inputs, applies Boolean operators (such as AND, OR and NOT) and produces an output that is always either True or False   342

Bridge: a network device that joins two segments in a local area network   269

⟩ Acknowledgements

The authors and publishers acknowledge the following sources of copyright material and are grateful for the permissions granted. While every effort has been made, it has not always been possible to identify the sources of all the material used, or to trace all copyright holders. If any omissions are brought to our notice, we will be happy to include the appropriate acknowledgements on reprinting.

Thanks to the following for permission to reproduce images:

Cover image: *Cover* StudioM1/GI

***Inside* Unit 1** Yuichiro Chino/GI; Universal History Archive/GI(x2); Bubaone/GI; Porcorex/GI; Paul Taylor/GI; Kelvin Murray/GI; Howard Kingsnorth/GI; Daniel Dani/GI; Patty Lagera/GI; AleksandarNakic/GI; Baona/GI; Pattadis Walarput/GI; Sean Gladwell/GI; Sunchan/GI; Huizeng Hu/GI; Blue Planet Studio/GI; Ullstein Bild/GI; Enot-Poloskun/GI; Traffic_analyzer/GI; Adventtr/GI; Phil Scroggs/GI; Andrzej Wojcicki/GI; Flavio Coelho/GI; ThomasVogel/GI; Kali9/GI; Begin Again/GI; Chadchai Ra-ngubpai/GI; Mike Brinson/GI; Jamesjames2541/GI; Peter Dazeley/GI; Damircudic/GI; Tanja Ivanova/GI; We Are/GI; Martin Barraud/GI; AndrewRafalsky/GI; Iana Kunitsa/GI; Capuski/GI; Mikroman6/GI; Ilyast/GI; Joe McBride/GI; Евгения Матвеец/GI; EyetoeyePIX/GI; Debra Roets/GI; Yuichiro Chino/GI; Ray Bradshaw/GI; Filo/GI; Maskot/GI; **Unit 2** Manuel Breva Colmeiro/GI; Svetikd/GI; Tanja Ivanova/GI; Kali9/GI; Peter Cade/GI; Vlatko Gasparic/GI; Hill Street Studios/GI; Wikimedia; Casarsa/GI; George Pachantouris/GI; Moncherie/GI; Enot-poloskun/GI; Steven Puetzer/GI; Scanrail/GI; Edwin Remsberg/GI; Jose Luis Pelaez Inc/GI; Solskin/GI; Cundra/GI; Hocus-focus/GI; Andriy Onufriyenko/GI; John M Lund Photography Inc/GI; Ktsdesign/GI; Yuichiro Chino/GI; JohnnyGreig/GI; **Unit 3** Tetra Images/GI; Morsa Images/GI; Nariman Safarov/GI; Artpartner-images/GI; Kameleon007/GI; SDI Productions/GI; Ranah Pixel Studio/GI; Busakorn Pongparnit/GI; Mint Images/GI; Nenov/GI; Henrik5000/GI; Adam Gault/GI; GCShutter/GI; Fotograzia/GI; Baranozdemir/GI; Kim Steele/GI; MR.Cole_Photographer/GI; Krisanapong detraphiphat/GI; **Unit 4** We Are/GI; Recep-bg/GI; Sarah Mason/GI; SaevichMikalaiGI; Erikona/GI; Ktsdesign/GI; Da-Kuk/GI; Lightspruch/GI; Teera Konakan/GI; Glowimages/GI; Shulz/GI; NicolasMcComber/GI; AtomicCupcake/GI; Bsd studio/GI; Teera Konakan/GI; Eternity in an Instant/GI; Prykhodov/GI; D3sign/GI; Javier Zayas Photography/GI; MoMo Productions/GI; John M Lund Photography Inc/GI; Oxygen/GI; Mrs/GI; Kryssia Campos/GI; Annie Japaud/GI; Imaginima/GI; Hundreddays/GI; Lupengyu/GI; Rosemary Calvert/GI; Gabort71/GI; Westend61/GI; Jasmin Merdan/GI; Witthaya Prasongsin/GI

Key GI = Getty Images

Scratch is a project of the Scratch Foundation, in collaboration with the Lifelong Kindergarten Group at the MIT Media Lab. It is available for free at https://scratch.mit.edu

Illustrations and photos showing the BBC Micro:bit are created and used with permission from the Micro:bit Educational Foundation

Screenshots from Microsoft Excel are used with permission from Microsoft